Isabel Flick's life story is co-authored with Heather Goodall, a friend and historian who has researched widely into Aboriginal and general history in NSW and whose first book, *Invasion to Embassy*, was awarded the NSW Premier's Prize for Australian History in 1997. Isabel asked Heather to assist her in 1998 to research and write her life story by recording her memories and editing the transcripts. By the time Isabel suddenly became seriously ill late in 1999, she had recorded many hours about her early life and the little-understood tensions in rural townships in the 1950s and 1960s. When it became clear her illness was terminal, she passed the work of completing the book over to Heather, who has since this time worked closely with Isabel's family to take up the story of Isabel's later life and her search for understanding of her community's history.

As it has taken shape, Isabel's life story is told largely in her own words, but now incorporates insights from her family and close friends and colleagues, many of whom were those who knew her best throughout her turbulent life. One of Isabel's many strengths was her ability to form deep and productive relationships with non-Aboriginal as well as Aboriginal people. The contributions to the book, as well as those segments about Isabel's later years which have been authored by Heather, reflect those relationships with white Australians and others as well as Isabel's complex and dynamic engagements within the Aboriginal community.

'This is a wonderful book—moving, intelligent, and informative. It combines the genres of autobiography, oral history, and biography to tell the story of the life of a clearly remarkable woman, Isabel Flick. It made me laugh, cry, and think afresh.'

Professor Ann Curthoys
Author of Freedom Ride

Heather Goodall is a Sydney-based historian and activist. She has worked in collaboration with Aboriginal people on many projects since 1972, when she first met Isabel Flick. In New South Wales and central Australia, Heather has recorded oral history and memories with Aboriginal people for many projects, such as the documentation of community sites, including the Collarenebri cemetery; research in Land Rights and Native Title; the investigations into Black Deaths in Custody and research into women's history and community history. Her book, *Invasion to Embassy: land in Aboriginal politics in New South Wales*, was awarded the NSW Premier's Prize for Australian History in 1997. Heather teaches at the University of Technology, Sydney, where she is an Associate Professor in Social Inquiry and a member of the Centre for Trans/forming Cultures, and is also continuing her research and writing in Aboriginal history, environmental history and inter-cultural relations in Australia. She lives with her husband, Paul Torzillo, and her two daughters, Emma and Judith, in Glebe.

To Jean to a lady who
has the same family value
as my mum.

Any FER

Isabel Flick

The many lives of an extraordinary Aboriginal woman

Isabel Flick *and*
Heather Goodall

ALLEN&UNWIN

Published with the assistance of the
Australian Academy of the Humanities

All photographs were found in Isabel's collections of
papers and albums, unless their source is otherwise stated.

First published in 2004

Allen & Unwin
83 Alexander Street
Crows Nest NSW 2065
Australia
Phone: (61 2) 8425 0100
Fax: (61 2) 9906 2218
Email: info@allenandunwin.com
Web: www.allenandunwin.com

National Library of Australia
Cataloguing-in-Publication entry:

Flick, Isabel.
Isabel Flick: the many lives of an
extraordinary Aboriginal woman

Includes index.
ISBN 1 74114 123 0.

1. Flick, Isabel. 2 Aboriginal Australians – Women –
Biography. I. Goodall, Heather. II. Title.

994.0049915

Set in 10/13 pt Goudy by Midland Typesetters, Victoria
Printed by Ligare Pty Ltd, Sydney

10 9 8 7 6 5 4 3 2 1

Contents

I dedicate this book to my six children: Ben, Larry, Brenda, Tony, Amy and Aubrey, who were denied full commitment from me as a mother as I was always working, trying to provide just a little something extra for them.—*Isabel*

My writing for this book was in memory of Isabel, but is dedicated to the wider Flick family, to Isabel's brothers and sisters and their families as well as her own, those warm, brave and extraordinary people who have changed the way we see the world.—*Heather*

Foreword

The art of story telling—and the value of personal narratives—is beautifully captured by this wonderful book about an amazing woman who lived through tough times. The life of Isabel Flick is the story of an Australian hero. A hero who fought injustice with her every breath, every minute of her life. Isabel Flick did not just take up the battles of her own people; she took up the battles of decency and fairness for all.

Isabel's story is also a reflection of the treatment, policies and life experiences of the indigenous people in north-western New South Wales. It captures experiences of shocking racism, injustice and incredible pain, and also the important bond of family and community. It shows Isabel's wonderful humour, her love of life and her great humility, all mixed with an iron will. The collaborative effort of Heather Goodall and the Flick family in putting this book together strengthens *our* collective narrative.

There is one story that, for me, captures Isabel Flick the person. One of her dreams was to get a tarred road from the township of Collarenebri to the Aboriginal cemetery, which is located on private property about six kilometres out of town. For over twenty years the dream was passionately pursued. In November 2002, the road was finally completed, eighteen months after Izzie's death.

I attended the opening of Bell's Way. There were people, both Aboriginal and non-Aboriginal, from all over. The northwest towns were represented by the elders and senior people from those communities, and the Flick family were dignified and present in great force.

What that road symbolises is a tribute to the life of Isabel Flick. Bell's Way and the battle to have it constructed is a very important stitching in of an additional beautiful piece of fabric to the mosaic of our Australian story. I am forever grateful to Isabel Flick and I know her spirit flew high that day—every speaker invoked her memory.

Aunty Izzie rests in that cemetery in the knowledge that her many visitors these days will be able to come no matter how much rain falls. The coloured glass that defines the family graves sparkle just that little bit more.

It is a great honour to provide a very inadequate foreword to pay tribute to a true battler—and a giant in the collective memory of the thousands of people touched by Isabel Flick. She truly did touch many lives, had many of her own and was an extraordinary Aboriginal woman.

Linda Burney
MP, Member for Canterbury

Acknowledgements

There are many people whom Isabel would have liked to have thanked for supporting her throughout her life and in the process of making this book happen. I can record at least some of them here.

First there are Isabel's family. Her eldest son, Ben, became tragically ill and passed away just before Isabel's own final illness, but his interest in her wide political experiences was an important spur to her decision to begin the book. Her surviving children, Larry, Brenda, Tony, Amy and Aubrey, have all contributed in different ways. They talked over the themes, encouraged her to find the time to do the recordings, suggested what might go in and what should come out, found photos and papers, laughed and cried over drafts and encouraged me in the final writing. Isabel's partner, Ted Thorne, patiently listened to and talked over every word of the draft. Isabel's brothers and sisters have all been encouraging, and Joe and Rose particularly have been central in researching and in contributing memories. Isabel's sisters-in-law, Isobelle Flick, Rosie Flick and Doreen Hynch, were each generous with their contributing stories and deeply involved with Isabel's research into her family and Collarenebri's history. Isabel's nieces, Barbara and Karen, and her nephew, Joey, have been tireless in offering words, images and memories. There has been a wider circle of friends, from Collarenebri, Toomelah, Gunnedah and many other towns of the region, who supported Isabel as she gathered the threads of her life together. Finally, Isabel could not have begun and I could not have continued with the work of this book without Isabel's close friends, Kevin Cook and Judy Chester, who supported Isabel and me with encouragement, careful reading of drafts and sustained confidence over many years.

The research for the book involved country travel, photography and audio recording, and this was resourced by a generous grant from the Union of Australian Women, an enduring and important organising body of women who wanted to support an Aboriginal woman to tell her story. The Rona-Tranby Foundation assisted the UAW to administer the funds and together they allowed Isabel to accomplish research for this project which otherwise would not have been possible.

Isabel's family wish to thank Ted Fernando of the Collarenebri Local Land Council, for assisting to fulfil Isabel's dream of sealing the cemetery road.

Many people were consulted in the research for this book and those with close links to Collarenebri who were most generous in their assistance were Harry Denyer, Dawn Stallworthy and Archie Kalokerinos. Nadia Wheatley showed me ways to make the collaborative writing approach work well and her confidence in the project helped to keep it going. Peter Thompson, Judy Torzillo, Paul Torzillo, Meredith Burgmann and Brian Doolan have all read sections of drafts and offered perspectives, comments and memories. I am grateful to the readers of the manuscript, Ann Curthoys and Bain Attwood, whose valuable responses and suggestions have strengthened the work.

Elizabeth Weiss of Allen & Unwin has been a clear-sighted and encouraging publisher and we have been fortunate in having the valuable editorial judgement of Colette Vella and Belinda Lee. This book would not have been created, however, without John Iremonger, whose persistent encouragement nurtured a chaotic dream towards reality. John's insight, generosity and warmth continue to be deeply missed.

And because all writing grabs every spare minute and every last shred of concentration, I want to thank my daughters, Judith and Emma, and my husband, Paul, for their extraordinary patience, love and warm encouragement.

Heather Goodall
January 2004

Isabel's Family

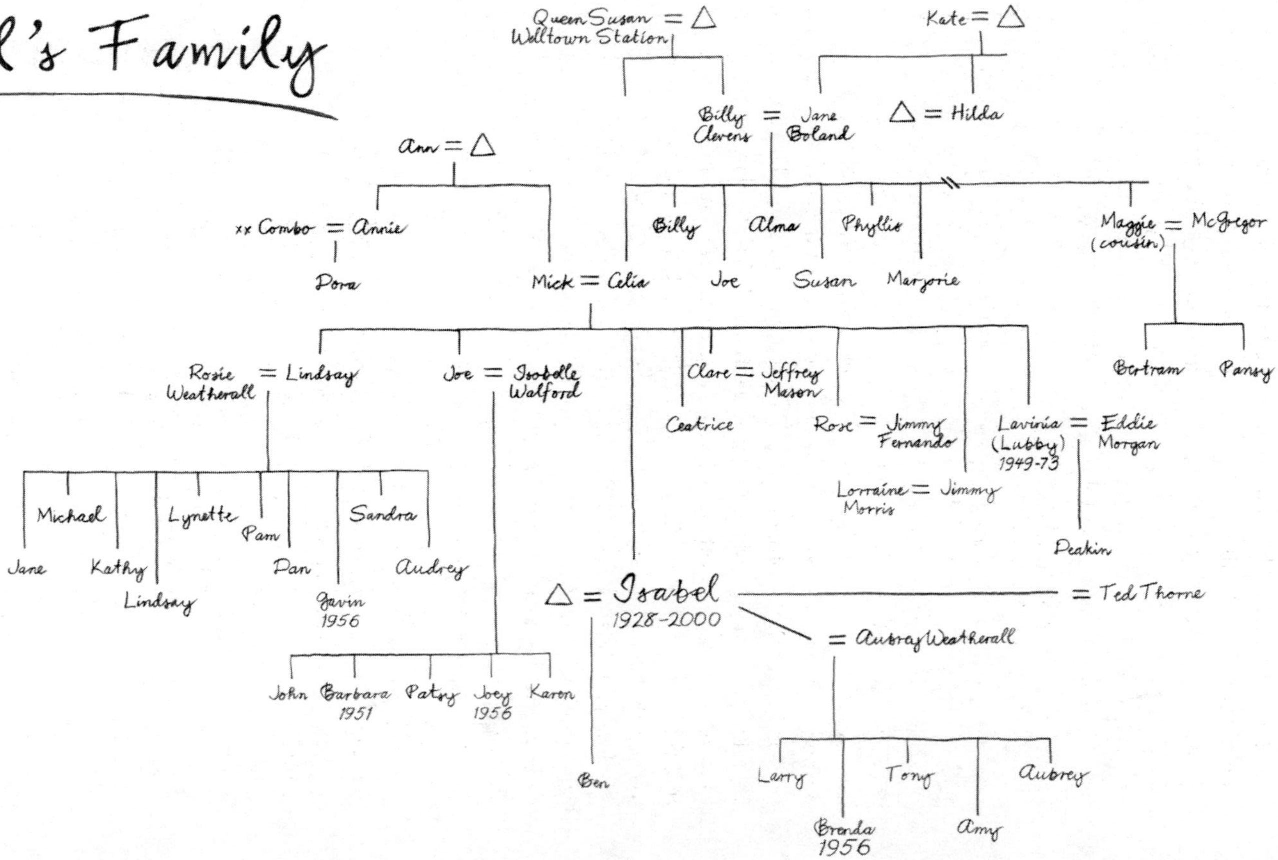

Queen Susan = Welltown Station

Kate = △

△ = Hilda

Ann = △

Billy Clarke = Jane Boland

Billy   Alma   Joe   Susan   Margrie

Phyllis

Maggie = McGregor (cousin)

Bertram   Pansy

xx Combo = Annie

Dora

Mick = Celia

Clare = Jeffrey Mason

Beatrice

Rose = Jimmy Fernando

Lavinia (Libby) 1949-73 = Eddie Morgan

Lorraine = Jimmy Morris

Deakin

Joe = Isabella Walford

Rosie = Lindsay Weatherall

△ = Isabel 1928-2000

= Audrey Weatherall

= Ted Thorne

Ben

Michael   Kathy   Lindsay   Pam   Lynette   Pam   Sandra   Audrey

Jane

Gavin 1956

John   Barbara   Patsy 1951   Joey   Karen 1956

Larry   Brenda 1956   Tony   Amy   Aubrey

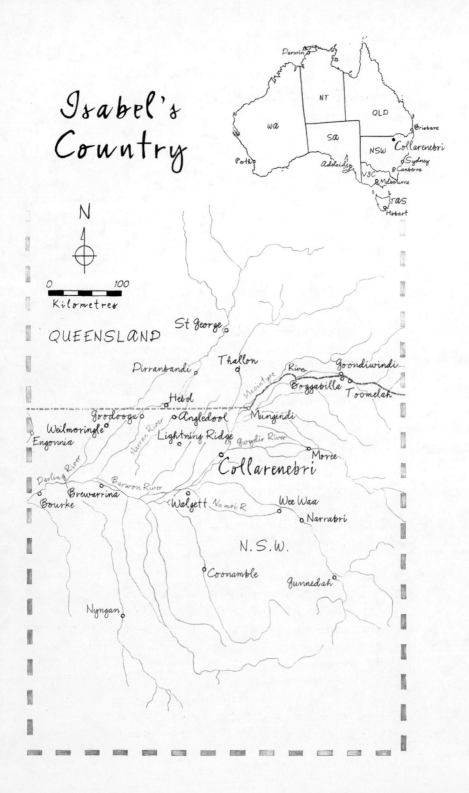

Introduction: Making Trouble

'And I said that to this old fella at the ticket box: "I want you to come and fix this. Take these ropes off! What do you think we are? Our money is as good as anyone else's and we want to sit where we want to sit". I kept standing there in front of the ticket office, and by then my sister-in-law was there too. The two of us, making trouble! And my poor little heart, I don't know how it stayed in my chest, but it did. Even though I said it as calmly as I could, I was so sick within myself. I heard my own mob saying: "Oh God, she's making us shame!" But they were afraid of the confrontation too. And then someone said: "Good on you Isabel. It's about time that happened". And then old Mark Cutler could see I was just going to stand there and keep standing there. Sometimes I think if he'd waited just a little bit longer I'd have gone away. But then he said: "Oh, all right, you can sit anywhere then!" And that's what happened.' *Isabel*

When Isabel Flick stood her ground under the big 'Liberty Picture Show' sign in Collarenebri in 1961, she was challenging more than a single businessman in a small dusty town in western New South Wales. She didn't just want an end to the colour bar which saw Aborigines roped off in a narrow space under the screen. She was confronting a century-and-a-half of discrimination and segregation.

Picture shows were only the most recent places to rope off and shut out Aborigines from the daily life of country towns. Long before the picture shows, there had been the shops and the pubs, the streets and the schools, all closed to Aborigines on racial lines no matter how hard they had demanded their rights of access to public places as citizens. The petty humiliation of being forced to sit, roped off, right under the screen every Friday was only the easy end of this system. The daily police patrols, policemen pushing their way into houses, welfare officers hauling kids away and constant arrests for being uptown after dark, were each more frightening and even harder to stand up to. But they all made up part of the same thing.

This was the system which had choked down rural Australia, robbing it of talent, breeding fear and suspicion, dividing towns on colour lines and destroying lives. This was the fossilised structure that the 1965 Freedom Ride was to bring to national attention. But the reason the Freedom Riders' bus went to the towns that it did was that the fires of change had already been lit. Courageous people like Isabel Flick had begun standing up and 'making trouble', forcing the ropes to come down and the doors to be opened, one by one, town by town. Their sparks were a beacon to the student activists as they planned the trip. The Freedom Ride stirred the conscience of the nation by making these local fires visible. The people who broke the system on the ground, who were there before the Freedom Riders came and who remained after the bus drove out of town, these were the people who actually changed the way rural society worked.

'Troublemaker' was the insult that was frequently hurled at Isabel and people like her who gathered their courage to stand up to the restrictions of their towns. When they challenged the injustice of discrimination, when they refused to accept it, when they pointed out its waste and what was often just plain silliness, they were trying to change the way things had 'always been done'. That *was* a trouble to the people who had used the status quo to benefit themselves. But making trouble turned out to be the only way that this system could be dismantled. Isabel *was* one of the troublemakers, those ordinary people whose courage and persistence challenged petty and major racism and made the bush a better place for everyone to live.

Isabel was awarded a Medal of the Order of Australia in 1986, was honoured by her communities and by Tranby Aboriginal Co-operative College in 1993 and at her death, in 2000, her family received condolences from the Premier of New South Wales and the Deputy Prime Minister of Australia. She became a leader not only of the Aboriginal community, but a spokesperson for the whole town on vital issues such as environmental protection. In her mature years she was a powerful speaker, who could express her ideas lucidly and inspirationally, or convey a damning picture of an opponent with a subtle gesture, a shift in intonation and a dash of wicked humour.

Yet Isabel had not been born to be a leader and a spokesperson. She grew up on riverbanks and in camps. She was denied any education in a schooling system which pretended to be public but was in fact racially segregated. Isabel's first hesitant steps in politics didn't occur till she was in her thirties.

Confrontations like the one at the Liberty Picture Show made her ill with tension and she suffered periods of deep depression as she battled doubts and family crises. To reach her mature assurance, or even to stand her ground outside the Liberty, meant a long journey for Isabel. She steered herself from her shy childhood to her first embarrassed steps onto the political stage, through to the confidence with which she could speak to Federal politicians and mediate in acrimonious meetings between local government and contractors so she could get her community's building projects underway.

The unfolding of her life from a hesitant child into a mature and confident activist is one of the stories in this book. Isabel was always puzzled about how she had taken the first steps along this path. She returned to that question over and over in her recordings. She had decided to tell her life story with encouragement from her old friend Kevin Cook of Tranby College and with funding from the Union of Australian Women and the Rona-Tranby Foundation. She asked me, as a historian who was an old friend as well, to help with recording her memories and finding the contextual material she might need. We all thought she would tell a story about her later achievements but instead she wanted to pursue her own recurring question: Why did my life take the road it did? Why did I stop drawing back from conflict and begin to stand up and challenge the things I saw around me that were wrong? This cluster of questions led her persistently back to her childhood and to Collarenebri, even though the actions of her later life were played out on a far wider stage.

So the other story in this book is about the town of Collarenebri on the western bank of the Barwon River. In many ways, Collarenebri is on a border. Not only is it close to the border between New South Wales and Queensland, which played such a major role in Isabel's life. And not only near the border of the Gamilaraay and Yuwalaraay language groups among Murris,[1] or on the border between the pastoral land to the west and the cropping lands to the east. But this town, being smaller than its neighbours of Moree or Walgett, allows us a better glimpse of the border between black and white in rural Australia. In some ways that border is very harsh and the gulf between the two communities unbridgeable. Collarenebri still seemed like a frontier town when I first went there in 1975, with no sign of communication between Aborigines and whites. A palpable tension hovered in the main street. The intensity of hostility which saw white men running the Freedom Riders' bus off the road just a few miles to the west of Collarenebri, had been poisoning those western river towns for decades. It was no surprise to Isabel and her family when it erupted in the ugly conflicts in Walgett and Moree in 1965.

But what Isabel's story shows is that such polarisation is only part of the story. The colour lines were actually—sometimes—elastic and flexible. They could be stretched and lifted, even if they often did snap back into rigid tension under some sorts of pressure. The Freedom Ride recordings of the street abuse traded in 1965 show very clearly the exploitative sexual contact between whites and blacks of these towns. But Isabel's story opens up many different types of relationship: from casual courtesy to casual cruelty; from thoughtlessness which wounded children for life through to respect and affection, shared in both directions. Relationships in the everyday politics of the town ranged from cautious, temporary alliances to distant respect through, just sometimes, to staunch, warm comradeships that endured over many decades. One of Isabel's extraordinary skills was her ability to keep talking to all sides, within and across the colour lines. Her frank and thoughtful memories about the white residents of Collarenebri, as well as of the Murris, open up a new way to see into the complicated relationships which underlie bush Australia to this day.

And her portrait of the town itself is important in suggesting the powerful hold which places and communities have over the people who inhabit them. Collarenebri was a hard town embedded with problems of economy and environment which pressured all of the relationships there to breaking point much of the time. It was a town from which people, black and white, escaped and vowed never to return. And yet they often came back, even though they might leave again and return once more. The security of community closeness vied with the suffocating grip of repression, poverty and isolation to keep many people in a state where Collarenebri always had a claim on their thoughts if not their hearts.

Isabel had known me a long time before she decided I could help her with her book. She had advised me in my earlier work in researching the history of Aboriginal people and their relations to land across New South Wales. She had also called me in to work on the documentation of the Aboriginal cemetery in Collarenebri, which involved recording people's memories about the burials and family histories, as well as searching the archives. For her book, she asked me to record her as she retold her memories and to research the historical context she needed to give her story its background. We began this work with the recording sessions, taping hours of Isabel's reflections on her early life, as well as fragments on some of the later issues I asked her to talk about. We went to Collarenebri a few times, and had really just plunged into this exciting process of visiting places and people when Isabel was suddenly diagnosed with inoperable cancer. She knew she was not going to finish the book herself. Before she died Isabel handed that job over to me and her family, passing on to us the job of making her book tell the stories she had wanted to tell.

This book was always going to have many voices in it. Isabel had loved talking over her memories with the family and friends she had grown up and lived with all her life—all of them checking, discussing and comparing their versions of the events they had shared. But her sudden death meant that her voice had been interrupted far earlier than it should have been. There were gaps in her recorded memories; on deeply important issues, perhaps those silences were deliberate. But there were other events which Isabel hadn't covered yet simply because they weren't the priority areas for her at the time. And anyway, as she told me dismissively, she expected me to check up the details.

On her death, her family gathered her papers as she had asked, and passed them to me to look after while I worked on the book. In the end her family will decide where they go. Another of the ways in which Isabel was extraordinary was in the care she took to keep her papers and letters together, even though she had moved around so much over the years. Many Aboriginal families in the west have treasured their family keepsakes—photos, cards, children's reports and trophies, baby images and toys—and kept them safe against the odds in lives full of movement but with few other possessions. Isabel was not too different, but her collection had, alongside all those things, the minutes of meetings in her own hand, eviction notices, notes for speeches, drafts of letters she had written to politicians and public servants, cards from funerals, meetings, diaries and the re-read, deeply worn letters to her from those she loved, as well as some of her own many letters to others which had found their way back to her. Some were handled so much they were held together with sticky tape. Others had been torn to pieces and then carefully gathered together and placed in envelopes to be saved. Together, all these photos and minutes and toys and letters form pieces in the jigsaw of a woman's activist life.

So Isabel's family and I looked over these things after her death and began to talk about how we could put them together in a way which would do justice to her ideas about what her book could be. Although her papers were a rich archive of Isabel's later life, a strong balance to the recordings about her early life, what was still missing was something of the dynamism of Isabel's relationships, her mercurial humour and the energy of her presence. In the end, we needed to hear from other people about how Isabel had been in their lives, some perspectives outside Isabel's, from blacks and whites, to understand some of the many layers of her life.

The book has taken its shape from these discussions. The early chapters, one to five, have Isabel as the principal author. I have drawn on the recordings she made for the book, but also on some interviews from the 1980s with myself and with other people, and on tapes recorded at formal speeches or at informal, but highly charged, occasions like the Western Women's Council meeting at Winbar in 1985. The transcripts from these recordings have been lightly edited, but then reordered to make up a chronological account of Isabel's early life, from the early 1930s until she left Collarenebri in 1972. There were not many differences in the ways in which Isabel told stories about the same events, but there were some where her views changed over time or in different circumstances of retelling, and I've drawn attention to those differences. The context Isabel wanted me to provide is there in these chapters in the form of italicised sections which offer background to the stories she is telling. There are also, importantly, the voices of the other people whom Isabel called on to tell about key events, particularly the school segregation issues in Collarenebri and the Liberty Picture Show confrontation. Their words are indicated by a single vertical line. Her sisters-in-law Rosie Flick and Doreen Hynch, her sister Rose Fernando and her niece Barbara are important story tellers in this part of the book.

In the second part, chapters 6 to 10, which cover the years from 1972 until her death in 2000, we have far fewer of Isabel's recordings. These chapters are written by me as the principal author, with Isabel's voice heard wherever possible. The chapters are based on Isabel's papers, on her general conversations with me over the years and on the research I have done into this period of her life. But they also draw very importantly on the memories of people who knew and worked closely with Isabel. In this section, it is Isabel's words as well as those of others that are indicated by the vertical line. Her sister Rose, her brother Joe, her son Tony and her close friend Paul Torzillo have all contributed their reflections, as I have, on the complex person who was Isabel Flick.

In writing and editing this book, it has been important for me that it remains Isabel's book, with an autobiography at its core which explores the questions she wanted to ask about her life. In many ways the book is the story of all of us who have contributed, because Isabel shaped so much of each of our lives in dramatic and unmistakable ways. But, ultimately, this is Isabel's story, the story of a strongly unique individual who was always deeply embedded within her family and community, even when she felt most isolated and alone. She reached out to people across the lines of colour, class and education, speaking their own language fluently to each of them, whether it was the language of the riverbank or of the courtroom, building a network of people linked by the extraordinary experience of her friendship. Her commitment to her community never wavered, but she had the honesty and courage to challenge her own mob as much as she challenged those who oppressed them.

Her own most frequent reflection on her life was: 'Oh, yes, but I've had many lives . . .'

Heather Goodall
January 2004

1

'Owning the World': The Old Camp at Collarenebri, 1930s

I was born in Goondiwindi in 1928, near where my mother Celia came from. But my story really begins with my Dad, Mick Flick, and his people. He was born sometime in the 1890s at Miambla, just up the Moree road from Collarenebri. He was a Gamilaraay man and that tribe is a very big one, from up in Queensland down to the Barwon River around our way in Collarenebri. Between Goodabluie and Mogil Mogil stations and Collarenebri was where Dad's people came from and they wandered from one place to another around there. But Dad's mother Ann died when he was about nine. She's buried in the traditional way in a tree at Moonlight Point, north of Collarenebri, and Dad showed my brothers Joe and Lindsay that tree when they were working up that way in later years.

When Dad's mother died, he and his sister Ann were looked after by their relations around Collarenebri, by the Croaker family and particularly by Granny Fanny Combo, who used to be a Mundy. Granny Fanny adopted Dad and reared him up. His sister Ann stayed at Collarenebri, but as Dad got a bit older he went out to work on some property. A few boys his age went through The Rules[1] sometime then, but Dad didn't, and I think maybe he was trying to keep out of the way so he wouldn't have to go through it.

Then when the First World War came in 1914, Dad was working for a Chinaman, and he decided he would run away to join up. He and Harry Mason, a mate of his who had gone through The Rules, headed off at night. They walked from Pokataroo to Narrabri in three nights, and that was where this big conscription buggy was going around. They were too young to join up then,

1

Mick Flick, Isabel's father, a
hand-coloured photograph taken
around the 1940s.

maybe 15 or so, but they put their ages up. And because they were Aboriginal,
there was no birth certificate to cover them and so they were accepted into the
army. And from there they just had six weeks' training and they went overseas
to the Western Front. They weren't the only Murris who enlisted. There were
four or five Aboriginal servicemen from Collarenebri alone in the First
World War.

Dad fought in the Somme Valley, and was wounded more than once. He
was hit by a bullet in the stomach, but went back to the front to help in the
Ambulance Corps. But then he was wounded again and sent to England to
hospital there. And then he was sent back to France and before you know it
he was in the firing line again. When we looked up his records (number
4292), it turned out he was in the Lighthorse, he was trained as a machine
gunner, and he also served with the Ambulance Corps. And he volunteered
to stay over there! But he never talked much about it when we were kids, so
we never found all this out till later on! But the thing he used to say, when
he did talk about the war, was to say: 'Only the poor man suffered, where the
rich man never suffered . . . only the poor men suffer'.

Now when he came back, he was working up over the border in Queensland, and that's where he ran into Mum's mob, the Clevens family. Mum was
about 16 at the time, around about 1920. The Clevens were from Bungunyah,

Celia Flick (née Clevens) taken around the 1940s.

not too far from Toomelah, but on the northern side of the river. Their language was Bigambul, close to Gamilaraay, and when I was little some of the family lived on the Yarrawanna Creek at Welltown station. I've only just got fleeting memories of them there, but I remember being with my mother, Celia, and some of her brothers and sisters there. And I remember my great-grandmother, Granny Susan—she was the Queen of Welltown station—which was a big stud station. Apparently the boss of the Welltown station used to say to her every year: 'You take your people in there and you get whatever they want. Now, whatever you want to get for them, you get anything you want. You just go into the shop'.

So she goes in to the station store. I remember I was there, and I must have been only four or five and we were going along in this old sulky and a dray. Granny Susan was the focus, everyone was making sure Granny Susan was all right. That day everybody was so happy. My uncle was working on another station and he'd come in specially. And when we got there, the only thing she wanted was two plugs of tobacco!

And the shopkeeper is saying: 'Now do you want to buy anything for the kids? Do you want to buy . . .?'

And everybody is saying: 'Do you want to get a pair of slippers or . . .?' Trying to get her to buy something.

Celia's relations: Bigambul men, working on Welltown Station c. 1910, dressed ready for ceremonies. Isabel had cut out and enlarged the photo of the fourth man from the left. She then circled and highlighted him in her album, indicating he was her direct relation. (AIATSIS N3591.2 Photo reproduced with permission of AIATSIS.)

And she said: 'No'. That's all she wanted. She couldn't speak English, but she knew how to say 'biaka'. And that's all she wanted was two plugs of 'biaka'.

And I remember everyone going back out to the sulky and the old dray. And we had a great laugh afterwards, you know. My uncle bought a big bag of lollies for us kids, 'cause he thought the kids would be disappointed. But everyone else was saying: 'Look here, I was planning on getting this'. And 'I was planning . . .' Everybody was planning on getting something, because the boss had come out and told them what was happening: 'Go in with her and tell her . . . tell the shopkeeper what you want'. But she had the okay, you see. And I thought what a wonderful thing to happen to us, and especially the way the people handled it, you know. Because they went home laughing like hell!

It had been from the Yarrawanna that they took a lot of Mum's people. There was a problem where there was a fight, and a terrible accident where my mother's father was shot dead by one of his sons, my uncle Billy. Then the cops came in and they used that as an excuse to be able to send them away and apprentice them out. Most of Mum's family were sent to Cherbourg,[2] and Mum married Dad then and that's how Mum escaped the send-away part. But that's where her life was just completely broken with their family, I think.

Alma, one of my aunties, told me not long ago that after she got sent to Cherbourg, she got sent away to work and ended up spending most of her life on Palm Island which was the penal settlement. She used to try and get back to Bungunya. Sometimes she'd dress up as a bloke and nearly get away with it, until she got to Goondiwindi and then she'd be questioned about where she come from: 'Never see you around . . . So, where did you come from?' So 'bang', she goes back to Palm Island again. And she'd dye her hair and stuff . . . you know, do anything. She got away with two or three different disguises and things like that, and then she'd go back to Palm Island. When I said to her: 'Oh, what was Cherbourg really like?' she said: 'Well, I don't know, Bell, because I spent most of my time on Palm Island'. But that's all Aunty wanted to do really—was to be back with her people.

Dad and Mum moved back over the border, towards where Dad's people were. While he had been away, his people had finally moved to Collarenebri from Mogil Mogil station, to where our tribal cemetery is now on that lagoon.

Mostly, although we were around Collarenebri, I just remember that we kept moving all the time. I think this was Dad's idea of keeping us away from the system. It wasn't just in Queensland, because in New South Wales the welfare was starting to come in then and pick up kids and shift blokes from one place to another and . . . *interfering* with our lives.[3] So as I see it now, everywhere he worked as a shearer or fencer or whatever, we were camped in the scrub close by. I think one of the reasons why we was always on the move was because of the fear of us kids being taken. And we moved like that until Dad felt that all the re-settlement things were over. I remember coming to the camps in Colle then after that.

Now when we moved in, about 1934, the Murris were living on what I call the 'Old Camp', but the lagoon camp had been an even earlier one. This is a particular piece of land, 160 acres around the lagoon, that was set aside in 1899 for the use for Aboriginal people. I can imagine, first of all, Aboriginals roaming in their own style and for their own reasons. And then all of a sudden, authorities started to herd them into different areas. We freely went from one place to another up to around the turn of the century, but I think our people were pushed into different situations and different areas by . . . station owners, I suppose, settlers, and maybe government officials. So the lagoon land got reserved.

Granny Fanny Combo had actually lived out here at the lagoon. A lot of Aboriginals lived there and she was the main person in the community. I remember being told that she used to walk three or four miles from the lagoon camp to town, do a day's work for food and then bring the food right back— she'd walk in and walk out.

When I was about nine, I remember Granny Fanny going up pretty often from where we were camped to work up at the cemetery near the lagoon. She used to be telling me about the really old cemetery that's further away still, a mile or two beyond the lagoon. But we grew up associating the really old cemetery with this one near the lagoon. And as I grew older I started to realise just how important this lagoon site was, because Granny Fanny had been a young girl herself there. And Fanny Combo was one of the oldest people I grew up knowing. She died in the forties, I'd say, in the late forties. And she was well over the hundreds then. No one could really say exactly how old. My father was a part of that family, because you don't really have to be born into the family to belong to it. In our particular group of Aboriginal people here, my Dad became a part of this scene after his mother died. And so I in turn became a part of it.

That lagoon reserve was revoked in 1924. Some kind of epidemic broke out because the only water they had there was lagoon water. There was three huts there, so I think the authorities, the police and perhaps landowners around, burnt those places down and shifted the blacks in about a mile or two closer to town. The people were displaced once again to a police paddock that we call the 'Old Camp'.

And that's where I remember we came to settle down about 1934. Dad built a camp there but still when he went to work he always took us with him, until after Angledool and those missions were all broken up and separated, in 1936. I think he felt the security then, 'All right, that part is over'—it's just like saying, 'The war's over, we can settle down now'. And that's how he sort of settled into our camp and we could say we were going to camp there for months and months.

There wasn't many people living at the Old Camp on the river at that time. It was like other people was just settling too. I don't know whether they'd been like we were, always camped in the scrub. But there was only about six or seven families when we came in 1934, each family camped in clusters close together, you know? Then each of the family camps were spread along a high bank of the river, a long way back from the water. A path came from each end of the camp down the steep bank to a big grassy flat about 200 metres wide then down to the edge of the river.

There was always a difference between the top end of the camp and the bottom end and the middle of the camp. But there was no feeling of factions I can remember then. The Thornes were in the top camp, where the road came in, furthest from town. That was Ida and Colin Thorne's place, and they had a big camp there. Ida was a Murphy before she was married, and their kids were Ted and Roy, Linda and Jessie, Margie, Dulcie and all that mob. Then us Flicks in the middle, then the Combos and the Mundys. The Mundys have always been there as far as I can remember. And Granny Fanny was there with them. And that was the three main families.[4] And up at the top end as well

The Old Camp
1930s & 40s

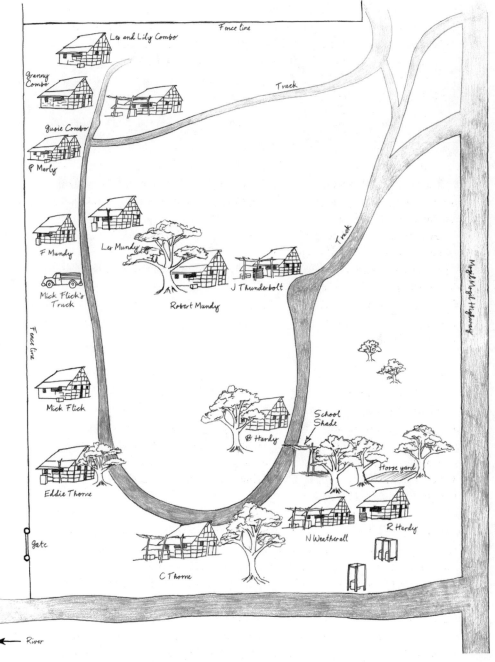

This illustration is based on a sketch that was hand drawn by Isabel and other members of the Old Camp community when Isabel began work on her story in 1998.

Granny Fanny Combo's camp at the Old Camp, Collarenebri, 13 March 1930. These large houses were constructed with timber frames and walls and the roofing from kerosene tins. Water was boiled in the tins to burst the seams, after which they were beaten flat. Bough shades were built and replenished as required for outdoor shaded living areas. (Photograph by D.H. Way, Department of Health, State Records 12/5572.1, Special Bundles 1911–1939. Reproduced from the original photograph with permission from State Records Authority of NSW.)

Colin Thorne's camp, Old Camp, Collarenebri, 13 March 1930. The boys standing under the bough shade are probably Roy and Ted Thorne. (Photograph by D.H. Way, Department of Health, State Records 12/5572.1, Special Bundles 1911–1939. Reproduced from the original photograph with permission from SRNSW.)

was two old fellas who used to live on their own, they had their own one-bedroom little camps up there—Hector Murphy and old Billy Hardy.[5]

Their houses were made in the same way, but everyone could do it a bit different from the others. They'd build a bush timber frame and put flattened tins over it. The tins were kerosine tins or some square tins. You'd fill them with water and put them on the fire. As they boiled, the seams would burst and then you could hammer them out flat. The roofs were tin and some houses had breezeways, the windows were small and the rooms were dark inside. The floors were dirt, but they were swept so much they were smooth and hard. Outside was swept too. And people usually built a bough shade up against the side of the house and we used to live out there a lot of the time—in summer 'specially.

We were what you'd call a middle-camp mob, close to but not right on the fence. There was only two camps there, ours and Old Maudy Thunderbolt, an old woman who had three little camps: one for the boys and one for her and one for her brother. The Thunderbolts were part of the Murray group. And then later on people like the Weatheralls came in from Angledool.[6] And then the main Murray group from Bre came in, Old George Murray and his family (during the 1940s). But they came when those missions broke up. So it was only a little camp when I was a kid there.

Dad always encouraged us to be involved with the three main groups in the Old Camp—the top end, the middle camp and the bottom camp. He'd say to us: 'Now don't just go to the one mob all the time. You've got to go to the other mob too'. And if he'd be going in to town from our bush camp, he'd drop us off at the bottom end, and then the next time he'd go in to town he'd drop us off at the top camp, and we very seldom strayed away from there, unless those kids came with us down to the bottom camp. And then I noticed if he'd got a porcupine[7] or something and brought it in, he'd try to share it around. If he'd got two he'd be right, he'd be able to share it with the whole lot—bring a little bit for this group and a little bit for the other. So he was very careful . . . I suppose he must've seen the faction before I saw it, but I can't remember them being factions then.

I remember Granny Fanny Combo so clearly. She was very old then, she was over 100 when I was about 15 or 16. She always used to wear those big long dresses. Granny Fanny got an award from the Red Cross for her involvement with them: she used to do a lot of stuff for them. Even though she wasn't one to tell us much about a thing like that.

And Nanna Pearly Mason was a midwife who used to help with all the births out at Angledool before her family moved to Collarenebri.[8] She told me that she was nine the first time she had to help her sister because the matron wasn't there at Angledool. And I said: 'Oh Nanna!' And she said:

'Oh, I was nearly cryin!' But I couldn't be because my sister was in charge of the whole operation and that was that!'

And Aunty Bea was another one I remember so well . . .

The stories Isabel knew about people at the Old Camp reflect the relationships among the people there, so they are collective stories, rather than individual ones. Many of the details they remembered were talked over and compared when Isabel and her relations and friends were visiting the places where they had lived, as they did during 1998 and 1999. Isabel was often with her sisters-in-law, Doreen Weatherall Hynch and Rosie Weatherall Flick, and her younger sisters, Clara Flick Mason and Rose Flick Fernando. On one of these trips out to the Old Camp, Aunty Bessie Khan [Aunty Bea], by then very elderly and frail, was able to come too, and this is how some of the conversation went:

> *Doreen:* Aunty Bea used to wear a lot of jewellery.
>
> *Isabel:* . . . and she used to wear these big high heeled shoes, eh Aunty Bea? [Laughs] She used to wear those big stilts, stilletos, big stilts there . . .
>
> *Bea:* . . . [laughs and giggles]
>
> *Isabel:* I'll just tell you a bit about Aunty Bea. Aunty Bea was always a very stylish lady, and she used to wear lovely long dresses with flared skirts and she always had shoes to match, handbags to match. Yeah, she used to wear the makeup and all, eh Aunt? . . . and all the scarves . . . Everybody used to say: 'Oh, don't know how she walks in them shoes'. No worries. Aunty Bea used to walk along with 'em . . . I'd swear they'd be that high . . .
>
> *Doreen:* Five inches?
>
> *Isabel:* Oh, she was a real stylish lady. I can tell you that.
>
> *Rose Fernando:* What's the name of that horse you used to ride?
>
> *Bea:* It was Creamy . . .
>
> *Isabel:* I never heard about that. 'Creamy'.
>
> *Rose Fernando:* Yeah, that's it, Aunty Bea. And you used to ride in from out there, eh, to go into the movies . . .
>
> *Bea:* Oh yeah . . .

My first memories of becoming settled, I guess I was six or seven years old. Dad built a tin hut out of scrap iron; that was how I came to discover our 'wonder world', the *rubbish tip*. All along on the other side of where the road is now, that was the tip for the town. The other kids who lived at the Old Camp already knew about this special place before we came. Oh, we used to love that!

Old Aunty Maude used to say to us: 'You want to ask your mother now, this afternoon I'm going out to the rubbish tip'. Oh, away we'd go. Everybody would take off home and everybody would get their shoes, or whatever they had. I never ever had shoes. I had a hat though. And we used to jump around there waiting for her. And we're hop-scotching and everything waiting for her to be ready to go. Because that was just like we were going to a big circus or something. And as soon as she started moving off, we'd all start moving. And we'd bring back all this stuff for a cubby house . . . dragging it back. 'What did you bring this back for?' 'That's for my cubby house.' 'That's for my room.' Everybody would have something from the tip. You wouldn't think how it meant so much to us. That was one of the real exercises that excited us, I reckon, we all went together. One lot would be climbing into old motor cars and around . . . and . . . 'I got this'. 'Look, what I got!'

It was always a treat. Sometimes we'd find high heeled shoes, handbags, broken dolls. I remember we'd show off with our stuff. I used to imitate Bessie Khan, she was Bessie Mundy then, because she always had nice clothes and shoes, lipstick and face powder.

We played a lot of outdoor games: cubbie house, hop scotch, hide and seek, prisoners' base, sheep shed come home. Our parents played their own games. Men played marbles, Mumbler Peg,[9] cricket and rounders. Our life-style was pretty simple, we went fishing a lot.

And then there was Kenny Mundy and Granny Fanny, they used to get out there on Sundays, every Sunday, and they'd have a game of rounders going. It's probably taken off baseball, because it was run similar . . . One week it'd be the kids playing the grown-ups, then it might be married versus singles, and the next week it'd be the boys playing the girls, little girls right up to the oldest—and the oldest person had to bat, always had to bat, and they had to bat first. Those games mostly used to be held down at old Granny Fanny's place. And we played rounders for hours, you know.

There was always that person in the society, you know, always someone that motivated people to have dances and sing songs and sometimes just sit around and have a yarn, you know? And I remember when we were kids, this was George Combo—he went overseas with Dad—and he was always the one to organise the dances up at the camp. We used to have Black dances. And he'd just go around and tell everybody and then he'd come around before they started and they'd got the big fire going, and he'd come around and say: 'Oh come on, come down. Just come down for a while' and he'd coax every-body that way.

And I know that some people, like Ted Thorne's old mother Ida, used to say: 'Well, I don't dance but I'll go down for a little while'. And there were other people like that, that didn't dance, but who'd go. And sometimes they'd just have someone playing the mouth organ, sometimes there'd be the wind-up gramophone. And sometimes they'd get someone to play the accordion. There was a family from Mungindi—the Troutmans—they were very musical, they played the accordion and the guitar. And if we got them to come down it was a real special time, so nearly everyone would turn up just to listen to them. And then there'd always be someone that got out and sang a song; somewhere along they'd say: 'Come on so-and-so, you can sing to me'. And it wouldn't take long and three or four of them would be singing a song in the break.

Then in summer, there'd be these water fights. It'd start off with someone just walking past and if someone was just sitting around doing nothing, they'd just hit them with a bit of water. Then someone would do the payback thing, and then everybody would get splashed and everyone would get into it. It was only the ones that were sick or really old that would miss out. But I used to see everyone drawn in to that. And it's a wonder people didn't get cranky, you know, sometimes they'd be all done up, like at Christmas time. 'Cause it'd especially happen on Christmas Day.

But then, after a while everybody started to realise they'd have to change straight after dinner, because they used to get done up really . . . Those were the times Old Aunty Bea'd really get done up. She used to have a hat to match every dress she had. Shoes . . . bloody heels three or four inches high. And she always wore rouge and lipstick and she'd always be done up and she always used to look nice.

And Dad used to say we weren't allowed to wear it, and we used to say: 'But Aunty Bea has got that lipstick thing on again'. And he'd say: 'Yeah, don't let me see you wearing that'. And we'd say: 'Why?' 'Oh well, you're not supposed to. If you were supposed to have red lips you'd be born with red lips.'

He'd go through all that. He really didn't like it. And so we never questioned him and I don't think many of the other girls did. I can't remember any of the girls doing it until Rana. Rana started copying Aunty Bea and then it was all right!

And on moonlit nights, we'd have great games, you know. But everyone was home at a certain time. No question about it. The older ones could stay a little bit longer. But Dad used to have three whistles for us. That was the only time we could go out, when he was in camp. You couldn't go and have a game when Dad wasn't home and sometimes he'd be out working on the stations for months. And Dad used to have one whistle for me, two whistles for Joe and three for Lindsay. The first whistle would go and everbody would stop! All the girls would be saying: 'Come on, come on, that'll be for the boys . . .' And just at odd times he *would* want the boys to go home first, and sometimes he wanted to give me a little bit longer. And then all the girls would take me home later on.

But these two old single fellas that used to live up at the top end, no one ever went near their camps. Until one night, some boys thought they were going to be smart and they were pelting on the place or running sticks along the tins of the camp. And they thought they got away with it, see, because the first time the old fellas let them go. A couple of times they did that until at last Hector Murphy come out, and didn't he go for these kids! And every-body knew they were in trouble. See, soon as he made it public, we knew they were going to cop it. If they didn't cop it from him they were going to cop it from their mothers. Now my brother, Joe, and Ted Thorne was in that this one night that it happened. I can remember I was being questioned by Mum about it. And I said: 'Oh I don't know. I don't know'. I didn't know whether to put Joe in or not, because he'd stand on me. And another one of the other kids walked up and they said: 'Yeah, you know, you was there because of such and such . . .' Bang! Didn't I get a whack! Mum was the real hiding person. Dad never hit us. But it had to happen. And then they took Joe straight back up to Hector and said: 'There he is. You do what you have to do'. He gave him a biff under the ears and said: 'Don't you come back here no more'.

I enjoyed wash days at the river. On Mondays was when all the women went to the river to wash, swim, fish, cook and I guess enjoy their kids. We sometimes went at sunrise and came home at sundown. Everyone used to help each other carry things like pots and pans, billy cans, mugs, plates and bags to sit on. I remember lots of women and children helping to carry the wood and water, then make the fires. These tasks all seemed to be fun . . . Two or three different lots would be making the fire and set their boilers up so they can boil the clothes.

The river always seemed to be clear and the beach was really sandy and clean, you could see the bottom then. It was lovely. One section in this area of about 100 yards was rocks, where us kids swam. Our mothers or aunts or someone would teach us to swim. The kids' part was right up where the rocks were, where it's shallow. That's where a lot of us learnt to swim. They'd take us out and give us a push back towards that shallow part, and we all learnt pretty soon, you know. Except Mum. She never learnt, she was in a different time really. But all of us, we had to learn. They'd say 'Come on. Get in here', you know, so we were more or less ordered to do it. This was always a very special place. You could swim right along some parts of the bank, or fish, whatever you wanted to do. And the grown-ups never interfered with the kids' part of the 'swimming pool' as they called it.

But on one side of the rocks was what we called the 'dipping place'. This place was not to be just for anything, it was only for taking the water up home, for our cooking and drinking. You couldn't do nothing else there. We were not to swim there. In trouble if we dared. Oh, you wouldn't dare swim around where the dipping place was. Not even *fish* there. A bit past there was where we fish—and if someone was fishing there, then don't make a noise.

We used to play skids across the river there: we'd get mussel shells and little stones and we used to just skid them across the river. Sometimes you'd get them right across there, you know. But one of the things was, the river was so clear. You could nearly see right across. There was reeds all along the edges in some places, except round where we dipped a lot for drinking water. There was never any there because we used to just rake it away.

We were all encouraged to have a go at catching a fish, bait a hook with worms or shrimps. One part of fishing none of us really liked however: if we caught a fish we had to learn how to gut and clean it, that was one part we didn't quite take to. However to 'big-note' ourselves and cook our catch was something else. That was the first time I big-noted myself. I don't know if I embarrassed my mum or not, because I remember she kept saying, 'All right, anyone can catch a fish. Pull your dress down. Sit down and eat your fish!'

We were living in the middle camp there, camped right near the fence. And I remember my dad made a little cart—just had two wheels and a 44-gallon drum. And my brothers had to make sure that they took that down to the river and filled it and brought it back. And that would happen nearly every Saturday morning. I never realised what a load of water that must have been to push back up the bank and over that old rough-looking country. Sometimes that'd be our drinking water for the week. And I think we were the only ones that had that carted water supply. But other people, they'd have the yokes, you know, the two kerosene-tin buckets and have a yoke like the Chinese have. Anybody'd carry water, but mainly it was the women did it because most of the time the men were out working.

I never used to hear people whingeing about it, or talking about someone being just too lazy to go and get water or something. It was just something that was done. And weekends, Dad would cut so much wood up. They'd be all carting wood. And sometimes they'd have to walk across the flat to get wood and bring it back. And then, after dinner, I remember the men used to play marbles.

Every Monday people would go down there and do their washing. And that'd be special. You had get-together day and muck-up day and washing day. And then, you know, even on Fridays. Nearly all the men was out working, and Fridays you'd see everyone going down the river about two o'clock and they're all having a swim, a bath and getting ready for the pictures. So as they'd have plenty of time to get home and have tea before they go to the pictures. That happened nearly every week. I have fond memories of those times, the Mondays and Fridays with the full community . . . together. So it was certainly a different lifestyle to what we've got today.

And when I think of the services we had! There was the Chinamen's garden with two old chinamen—one fella had a white horse and one fella had a black horse, and they used to come around the reserve. One would come on Wednesday and another one would come on Friday. Kong Hing was the one we called 'the black-horse Chinaman' and he and his family later moved to Sydney. He came around and never talked very much to us, but I know that the Aboriginal men used to sort of get around and make him talk to them. The women didn't bother so much.

And the other old fella had a white horse, and he used to come around, and the same thing used to happen there. We used to get excited when we saw them coming up the road, because sometimes they'd give us a little bit of extra grapes or melons and stuff like that, and it was just exciting for us to see the horse coming and the little carts, and so they became a part of that service delivery to us.

There were funerals I remember from this time, but we were sheltered from a lot of grief when I was a young kid. I don't think I actually attended a burial till I was about 16. But I remember when we were kids, as soon as anyone passed away, they were brought straight home to the camp. The body would be placed in the casket and either kept inside or outside under a bough shade. It was a terrifying thing for me, because I didn't understand what it was about, and everyone was sad and there was a lot of crying. And next morning everyone'd be getting ready to take them up and they walked up, with the black casket on an open dray, from where we were camped, right up to the cemetery by the lagoon. There wasn't a lot of involvement by ministers or white people at all. The community men conducted and took care of the fact that they were buried properly, so it was very much *our* business. And of course us kids weren't allowed. I had a terrible fear of it and we knew it was a sorry time. I didn't go to the cemetery much, but I remember the older women when I was a kid, worrying about 'no one's going to look after it'—and maybe that was implanted in my mind, but it wasn't until the years went on that I realised how important it was.

Nearly all of the men had work on stations and shearing sheds. Remembering these things about my childhood, I don't recall my two older brothers Lindsay and Joe being with us a lot. They were nearly always out in the bush with our Dad, learning to work.

Some men stayed at their jobs for months. I don't remember seeing our people really drunk, shouting, argumentative or any out of order conduct. Of course Aborigines were excluded from pubs and alcohol. However, if their boss appreciated their work, they 'supplied'. I know that this happened with our dad. Plenty of times, Dad would skite up a bit and the next thing you'd know he'd be asleep.

But it's good how when I look back at the laws that they had in our little society. I suppose everyone was careful not to attract too much attention as well as wanting a fairly okay little community, our own world if you like. Our security was each other because we were always monitored, assessed, oppressed by the police. Regular morning and afternoon patrols. I always felt really afraid when I saw the cops coming. I'd always take off home or if I was with other kids I'd make sure I was close to the adult there, or all of us kids would stay inside, whatever we were instructed to do!

See, there was two laws, eh, there was community control . . . the Aboriginal Law still was enforced, you know. But not with the approval of the police, because the police had their own law and they were pretty heavy and we had to live by them. But then the community had to live by that community law as well. And if there was a bloke messing around with somebody's wife, and I remember that, and I remember asking: 'Oh, why they don't talk to "so and so"?' and they'd say: 'Oh, he done a bad thing, you see, and you'll know about it one day . . . you mustn't mess around with somebody else's wife'. And he was so colded out he ended up leaving here and that was a part of the law.

And just like there was always someone to organise things, like rounders, there was always someone to settle an argument too. And if they had a fight they'd have to get out there and fight, you know. We never ever saw any blues. If some started a fight, the older blokes'd take them right away from the community and they'd go somewhere else and fight—down the river or wherever. And you'd hear of the fights going on after. They must've used to knock it out of them and have it finished and that was it. The fathers would take those boys away and they had a referee to watch it and they had to fight it out. And I reckon, when I look back on it, there was lots of times where the punishment had to go both ways because they'd have that fight out, but no one back at the camp knew who won the fight. And I remember the oldest brother a couple of times he was in those blues, but no one ever knew who won the fights, so there was still a lot of clean parts of the law still being practised.

When Isabel was at the river bank near the Old Camp during 1999, she felt peaceful and relaxed. Again and again she said to all of us who were there with her:

Isn't this a lovely area? When you're here, you can't help feeling that you own the world, eh? You listen to the birds. Especially up at the cemetery, you can hear a lot of birds' sounds. And, there's always a lot of birds here at the Old Camp, in these trees across the river. Why wouldn't you feel as if you owned the world living here?

And I think that's what we did feel . . . we had a feeling of safety. See, to live in a society like that was a wonderful time. It was only later on that I realised how segregated we were. All that wasn't in my life then. That's why I say I've had many lives . . . different lives.[10]

When we settled down at Colle, Dad always wanted us to learn to read and write because he thought it was the greatest thing for us to learn. But of course, we didn't even know what the big building in town was for—the school . . . because that's where we just . . . There was certainly no chance of black kids then getting educated in that school. We didn't have nothing to do with the white kids in town at all. And when we went to the pictures we always knew that we lined up and we got in the certain little section. All the blacks were herded down the front and all the whites at the back. We were right under the screen, screwing our necks up.

Now those two old Chinamen who used to come around the reserve— the one fella with the white horse and one had a black one—we realised

This photo appeared on the front page of Abo Call: The Voice of the Aborigines *(an Aboriginal-edited newspaper) in August 1938, in a story about racial segregation at Collarenebri school. Back row from left: Dougie Mills, Edna Thorne, Aubrey Weatherall, Shirley Cunningham, John Thorne. Middle row from left: Joe Flick (partially out of picture), Cecil Croaker, Isabel Flick (being held by Aub), Gracie Thorne, Dulcie Thorne (one of last two girls in this row). Front row from left: Rene Thorne, Rene Weatherall, unidentified girl.*

that their kids were going to school, but we couldn't go because we were Aboriginals.

The school was straight across the road from the old Presbyterian church, and I think the Presbyterian minister's wife, Mrs Peakes, must've decided . . . 'Oh, we'll try and give these black kids up at the camp some kind of education'. So twice a week for a half a day we used to skip along down. The other kids used to go down more often than me, so they were concentrating on the older ones.

But I learnt to count to ten the second time I was there and I remember this. The minister said: 'Come on now, children' and gave us a little tin and said: 'Come on, we'll go out and get some pebbles'. And we all went out there into the yard, but nobody knows what 'the pebbles' are, see? Well, Ted and Lindsay and the older boys, Robert Mundy and all those blokes, they're all starting to go towards the gate because they didn't know what 'the pebbles' are. And I'm thinking: 'Now, if these blokes go, I'm going too'. And everybody is sort of edging towards the front gate . . . you can imagine that scene, can't you?

And I remember I had no shoes on and this minister came over and he said: 'Come on, Isabel, come on, you bring your little tin here and we'll show the others . . . How many pebbles do you want to pick up, dear?' And he starts picking up some stones. Well, then everybody goes . . . 'Oohh!' and so everyone is picking up their 'pebbles' then! And he said: 'How many do you want to go to, Isabel?' and I said: 'Oh, ten'. And he said: 'Oh, you do want to learn something don't you?'

And I remember putting these little pebbles in a row and I counted up to ten with him and then Mrs Peakes came out and she said: 'Now, Isabel, they tell me you can count to ten. Well, come on, let me hear you'. And I counted right to ten. Oh, everybody thought that was great. And of course, I thought it was too, you know . . . I'm counting to ten. And when we went home that afternoon then, I said: 'Oh Mum, guess what? We counted a lot today', and she said: 'Oh, did you? What did you count?' . . . 'We counted pebbles, guess what "pebbles" are?' Mum didn't know. She said: 'What?' 'Little stones, that's what they are'. So . . . I'll never forget that!

I never questioned why we didn't go to school, you know, we just didn't question it because the minister at the church used to take hold of the kids, half a day, twice a week.

But people started to make a noise about the fact that we weren't entitled to an education, and the big scene came up then about Aboriginal kids going to school. I remember when old Eva Kennedy and old Olive Shepherd started to go along to P&C meetings and talk up and push for getting Aboriginal kids in school. They started to kick up all the fuss in the world, you know, and then something like a fear started to come out among the black people—people were frightened to talk about it and didn't want to know about it. They'd say: 'Let them talk about it, we don't know what they were talking about'. Nobody knew. . . . they knew but they didn't want to know!

When you look at the way those Kennedys had to grow up, eh. And people would say: 'Oh, they're uptown niggers,' and all this and that, you know. And I think, well they were people with white skin. They couldn't be black. To get into the school they had to act like whites. And then they had to live up to that. It must have been a terrible strain. When you think about the way they had to cope with the whole society. We're coming clean early today. When some of our kids have a white parent now, we say: 'Oh, your mother's black', and things like that. But in those days you dare not mention that you were related to a black, you know?

Well, those two old women must have decided, then, they'd catch them white fellas down the street. And one of them was a minister too. And old Granny Eva said: 'Oh look, you just the bloke I want to see'. I remember her saying that one day, there were a lot of people in the Post Office. 'Oh, he's a big minister . . . the big church man', she said. 'You're the fella standing up there, and you talk about this God. You say, "Oh, suffer the little children to come unto me", and all this bullshit. Then you, then you go up there and you say, "No, we don't want these little black kids in the school. Because they might marry our white kids."'

And he said: 'Oh no, I'm not . . . I haven't said that Mrs Kennedy'.

And she said: 'Well I'm telling you. I wouldn't let one of my kids marry your kids. If I could stop it, I wouldn't let one of my kids marry one of your kids'.

So that was one day, then the next day both of them was together, the two old women. And this minister and the secretary at the hospital, they were standing together and she said: 'Oh, here they are. Here are the two big white gods got their head together again. Come on let's us old black girls have a go at these white gods now'. And everybody in the street, you could see all these blacks saying . . . 'Oh, they make us shamed, gee they make us shamed'.

Yes it's always been a bloody fight. Well, round about that time, I remember we used to have Sunday School under the bough shade on the camp here. I remember going to the Sunday School there, around middle camp. I'd like to get Rosie's story on that, because she got involved as the teacher in the correspondence school that started to happen in that bough shade.

When Isabel and her sister-in-law, Rosie (Weatherall) Flick, were at the Old Camp in 1999, they talked a lot about this bough shade school, and Isabel asked Rosie to tell her memories of it:

Rosie: That bough shade school was across the road from old Billy Hardy's. He lived near to that belah tree and the shade was straight across from him, and that's where the ministers used to come for Sunday School. Old Edgar Mason was the first fella who suggested it for a school. Then Molly Murray's husband jumped in. It never took them long to build the shade up. And I used to put all the reading books and all that in a box and put them on old Billy Hardy's table. He used to look after all the pencils and everything for us . . . [11]

I didn't have any schooling at Colle. I think I must've finished my school at Angledool, you know before we shifted down in 1936. Old Mr Peakes, he was a Presbyterian minister in the manse down there at Colle and he was a fella fighting for . . . the fight was on to get the kids into the school, see. That was in 1938, and it was big. Now everybody like Old Aunty Amy's family, when they was on living on Moongulla station, the kids done their own schooling by correspondence, you know? And they had to bring the kids to school in Colle then. So they had to fight for this correspondence to get sent to Colle and that's how this old minister found out that there was a school they could get if they could get somebody to sit with the kids. And I already used to help Aunty Amy then. So Mr Peakes got the correspondence and he had it on the side of the manse there, on the sunrise side of the verandah.

Well it was nothing to do with the Education Department or the Colle school, you know. The white fellas used to kick up a stink about the Murri kids. Some of the little fellas used to be cheeky enough to go and have a look. All the kids would be playing at the school there and the Murri kids would come across the road from the manse and have a sticky-beak at the white kids. They weren't allowed in the gate, they'd look over the fence. And the white parents kicked up about that and the teacher started to write letters home to the parents to keep the kids away.

And so the old minister said: 'Then the only thing to do is take them up and school them in their own environment'. So he took me down to Armidale, him and his wife, and I had to go to school down there. Well, that's what they were saying; but I think myself, what they took me down for was to see if I could handle that correspondence work.

And so I was the one helping the kids: I'd just watch them, anything they couldn't do I'd help them do it. The old minister used to come up every day for a while to see if the kids was behaving themselves. But they thought it was hilarious. Only Freddy Mason used to bail up on me for a bit. Then this old minister would come up after school closed and he'd take this big box with him. Because we had no place to put it or anything, and in the morning about eight-thirty he'd bring it back up. Open for business again!

But then old Uncle Billy Hardy said he could leave his trunk over there, so we used to just put it in on his kitchen table. And then in the morning the old fella used to cart it across then and Mr Peakes just posted all their work, and then he'd bring the new stuff back when it was all corrected. I had to hand the postage to him. The parents was paying 15 pennies to the minister, and with that money he was getting he used to give me a wage, see.

And it all had to be worked by clockwork, because I think by then the Education Department started to poke their beak in. They was waiting for something to stop it, you know. The school inspector come, he came up there twice . . . I had to go around and tell them. I told old Una Thorne, she was a good old fallback, and I said: 'They bringing the inspector up, this might get our kids into the school . . . ' Old Mr Peake used to write letters and get me to sign it and everything, for the kids to go into the public school. So I used to tell old Una then: 'They're sending the bloke up to inspect . . .'

And every second day or third day it seemed like a white policeman and somebody would come up to inspect them for sores and everything, you know. That was the shameful part, I thought. But any rate, everybody took it in their stride. The little fellas would be sitting there cleaning their nails in the morning. Clean fingernails, that was a must, you know . . . clean skin. Old Una used to tell them then: 'Do them kids' heads for *muni*,[12] the policeman is coming up to look again'. Because the parents had the sole idea that any kid that was dirty would be taken, and so the kids was always shining and plaits in their hair and everything. And when the inspector come, he was fascinated how clean they was. And they was working under a bough shade! So any rate, they got a teacher then— a white man. But the Murris didn't want him there in our camp. They wanted anybody except for a white man, you know. I think they was all happy with me teaching the kids because they'd smile and tell me things about the kids too.

The kids was good, they all done their work. Even the older ones. If one couldn't do anything, the older ones would help. One girl, Una's daughter, if a kid was saying 'I can't do this', she'd be the first one to get up and have a look. She used to break a stick off the bough shade and break it up into, say, twenty twigs and she'd say: 'Put that eight away and count how many you've got left and put that down'. And they used to rub a slice of bread into a little ball for a rubber. So you made use of whatever you had around.

The parents'd come up to me and say: 'There's 15 pence for so-and-so', if they was up that area, and put all the money there and I'd give it to this old minister. He had an exercise book and he used to write the names down and who was paying all this money and he had to keep a record of it for their correspondence Education Department, see. The parents wanted their kids to get educated, see. They was finding that 15 pence, yeah, finding the money and giving it to this old minister. The kids used to take their books home and show their parents what work they was doing, you know. Because a lot of their mothers and fathers couldn't read and write too, and that's what they were saying: 'That's a good thing to think he's going to learn to read and write, because I can't'.

So that's how Rosie came to be the black teacher at the school on the Old Camp, but I didn't see that correspondence school straight away.

The Colle camp was the first one where we'd started to feel settled. But Mum had bad eyes and all of a sudden she was going to have to go away to Tamworth for operations. And I remember the coppers talking to her one day on the camp there . . . I always remember the way the dust sort of settled on these leggings. They used to have these big leggings and big shiny shoes and one thing I used to always remember was the way the dust was on those shoes . . . 'Cause we was always looking down, I suppose . . .

And I remember him saying something about '. . . because the kids would be better off', and then something about these 'homes' and '. . . Oh, they'd be a lot better off'. They thought Mum wasn't a proper person to look after us. And when they started to talk about Cootamundra and Kinchela I started to get real sick in the tummy.

And a couple of times they'd come back, and we . . . well, we got away then. It must have just been the next few days or so. I remember we was all taken to Toomelah mission. Dad took us up and me and Joe stayed there with our Granny Jane, Mum's mother. And at the same time Toomelah itself was just being settled. Coming from Old Toomelah at Euraba [because the water supply had failed]. So after I learnt to count to ten, I graduated to Toomelah, you see . . .

A lot of people can't understand that the bitterness—about the picture show colour bar and the other segregation in Collarenebri—didn't stay with me. But I think the bitterness about us not being allowed to go to school stayed a long time, because I was eager to learn a lot and I was getting frustrated and hurt because I missed out on that education. But I think things like that helped me make the changes in my life. And so they were the people that directed me to where . . . I guess, where I am today.

2
Toomelah Mission: A Place of Learning, 1938–1942

'I look back now and say that at Toomelah I was introduced to school—
a place of learning or one could say a whole world of yearning . . . '
Isabel's notes for a talk she gave in 1999

When I look back I think even though we had a hard life in lots of cases,
like going through being sent to Toomelah, I can't remember us crying or
being sad about being sent there. It was like we expected that as something
that we had to do. I think Mum and Dad handled that very well, there
was no tears, we weren't upset. 'You'll only be there for a little while', they
said, 'so the main thing is to do what you're told and Granny Jane will look
after you'.

And sure enough, she did. When we got there she was so matter-of-fact
about everything, and she'd just arrived herself. We got there just when
everybody else was being moved from Old Toomelah, to Toomelah just out of
Boggabilla. We had no house there. We just had to get on there and make our
little camp, a little bush break. Joe stayed with another family and there was
three of us there with Gran—me and my cousin Florrie and the other cousin
Bob. Florrie Boland was one of Mum's cousins. It was Gran's brother's
daughter, and he'd died when she was only little so she was with her. And
from time to time my aunties came and went.

Because they'd all just arrived, they only had little makeshift camps, just
old pieces of tins and some had little bark huts. It was like they were all
refugees. And I don't remember anyone being nasty or upset about being

there. They just accepted that we must make it good for ourselves. This was when the Protection Board was really in.

And it was cold, or we used to think it would be cold when they were talking about it. But she showed us how to help her build her little *mia mia* out of leaves, by putting three sticks up like a ti-pi, then putting leaves all around. Then she helped us to build one for each of us. Then she said: 'Oh, we'll show you how to make a little bed', so you'd dig a little place to lie in and she showed us how to put all the leaves in there to make it soft. Then you'd get the hot water in the saucepan from off the fire, and you'd place the saucepan in the hole there and warm it up. I remember we had a couple of coats that we had to lie on, military coats, and a couple more to cover over with. And we had the snuggest little bed. And I had my own, Florrie and Bobby had theirs and Gran had hers. So we had the three little *mia mias* circled around hers. This was the first couple of nights we were there. And then they started building little tin camps, you know, everybody finding what they could and building camps from just about everything—bags, bark, tin . . . Granny Jane used to get in and start nailing the tins up, and then somebody else would come along and nail a few more tins, until we finally got our own camp.

Granny was such a lovely person to us. She was real caring and she'd tell us yarns and then all of a sudden she'd say: 'But you don't want to worry, everything will be right now. You'll be right. We're going to get youse out

Mia Mia like those Isabel remembered at Toomelah in 1938. This was constructed by Isabel and the other women during the making of the film about Toomelah, Inard Oongali: Women's Journey, NPWS, 2000.

soon, they going to build a house for us'. And then when they built the houses, we were watching the houses being built you know, and she'd say: 'Oh that's our house over there . . . '—a little two-room house.

Then there was these builders coming in and old Fred Reece—a Murri from round Lightning Ridge—was one of them. The people started to say: 'Oh there's a black fella up there, he's a builder. And he's building these camps and . . . ' As one house would go up, one family would go into it. And they turned out to be nice houses, you know, they built nice houses.

Old Ronnie MacIntosh used to be the handyman and he used to come around and be talking to everybody all the time. He'd be saying to Gran: 'Now don't worry about nothing. You don't have to worry about anything'. And he'd go right around saying: 'You leave it to us Murris now and we'll talk to the managers. Don't you worry because we don't want you fellas to row with them. We'll fix things up if anything goes wrong'.

And then old Aunty Kate—the old woman next door to us and Gran— they were talking and laughing about this one day and Gran said: 'You know that Ronnie, he's a real two-face, eh? He's telling the old boss this, and the poor old boss believing it too. But he's telling us different eh? We know its different! He's a real two-face, eh?' And they were both laughin'! Old Aunty Kate would say: 'Yeah, that boss don't want to find out!'

And I was really hurt, because everybody loved Uncle Ronnie because he used to teach people to dance or garden or anything. He was real good at everything. And I went round to my cousin and said, 'You know what I heard Granny saying about Uncle Ron? She's trying to say that he's got two faces! But I don't think he has! Because I only seen the one face. She's trying to make out he's got two heads or something!'

Now she was older than me, you see, 'Oh you're silly', she said, 'They're only saying he's trying to make everything right for us. It's nothing to do with his face'. And she busted out laughing! I could hear her telling Gran and Aunty Kate after and they thought it was a great joke because I was looking for the other face! I forgot about it straight away. It was funny . . . until later on, and you know, when you think about it, everything was so serious, every-body was so serious.

And then I remember something else about what I'd call a mass migra-tion of Aboriginals being brought from Tingha, there was some kind of fear about it but I didn't understand why, there was a feeling of fear among the people.[1] So it makes you wonder just what tactics these people might've experienced before they came to Toomelah to make them move. Perhaps it could've been talked around, but that's something that's always confused me. Why? Why did we all feel such fear when these people arrived? That was not long after we arrived at Toomelah, say 12 months after. There were no houses built for them, they sort of lived around with different people that was game enough or willing enough to take them in for a while until further houses got built.

I remember we used to try and avoid them, it didn't matter who they lived with, and they did the same with us. So, you know, they were torn away from their rightful place and rejected because of a feeling that they had somehow carried out an invasion on the people in Toomelah. Finally they were accepted, as the houses were built. But I don't think they stayed very long either, they stayed about another 12 months and then they returned to wherever they came from.

Now when we first went to Toomelah, when everybody was settling there, I had my first introduction to a blackboard and class. A young man called George Cubby was teaching us on an old log. That's a fabulous old log, the biggest fallen tree I've ever seen. That became our blackboard and we were learning how to write a–b–c and 1–2–3 on it with charcoal. This was before any of the buildings were finished, while we were still waiting for all those things to happen.

George Cubby was about 18 or 20, and I don't know how it was arranged that he was going to teach us, but he used to go up there first and then we'd all wander up there. They'd say: 'Your Uncle George has popped in'. And when we'd get there he'd start saying: 'Today . . . you probably want to learn how to write this. And you make your letters first. You've got to make your letters first'. And I'd hear him saying, 'Tomorrow youse bring your own charcoal. I've got some charcoal here, but tomorrow you bring your own charcoal', and every-body'd have their own charcoal. 'And you learn your numbers 1–2–3. And you learn your A–B–C', and that's how we learnt. I used to want to learn to make a 2 like he made the 2. And he'd say: 'Just do it like that. That'll do'. I said: 'No. I just want to make a 2 like you make it, with all the curls on it'.

He was such a patient fellow. And we'd go and play and some would come back and some wouldn't come back. But the ones that came back, well, they were learning something. And he was the only fella that all the people trusted with the kids. He could take them swimming and he could take them into town, anywhere. And he had a way with us, you know. He never shouted at anybody.

Joe didn't want to stay with Granny Jane and us, because he and gran didn't get on and that happened straight away. He wanted to stay with Ted Hynch, old Uncle Daduwin we used to call him. And I could hear the old woman, old Aunty Nora, she was saying, 'Well let him come and stay with us, we can all watch him. We're all going to try and watch him, you know, and look after him'. And Dad: 'Yeah, I think he likes going with the Old Fella'. And that was it, Joe lived with them, and I lived down here. We didn't meet a lot, you know, and we were all in the mission together. And then we'd go to school, of course, we'd meet up there. He had his mates, I had my mates.

It was a very controlled time in our lives when we lived at Toomelah. You had to get permission for everything. Everything was arranged and there was a lot of church services and Sunday school. (Of course, some of us *liked* going to Sunday School!) I think Granny protected us, kept us away as much as possible from the manager but it was very bewildering really, you could say it was frightening. You knew Mondays and Wednesdays the manager's wife was going to do a big inspection. Not only looking through the houses, but looking the kids over to see if they've got sores or headlice. And so, Monday morning everybody's up early and you're all cleaned up and the house was cleaned up and everybody was just standing around waiting for this visit. And then once she visits the house, everybody relaxes.

We could look through the cracks in the door and see, 'Oh here comes Matron Clarke'. And Granny would herd us all into one place and we'd be watching to see what's going on. And if she decides she wants to go in and see the whole house, well, she would walk in on us—all peeping through the crack! It was incredible the way people relaxed after she went. When you remember it back and see how uptight everybody was before the visit and then how they relaxed after it, it definitely was fear they were feeling.

New Toomelah Sunday School, c. 1940. (Photograph from Aborigines Protection Board files, AIATSIS N3719.1 Reproduced with permission of AIATSIS and the NSW Welfare Board.)

Any little thing being wrong at that house, might be just something to affect the families personally, the Matron had the right to correct it all or have it done the way she wanted it done. And if it wasn't done, it was reported to the manager and the manager would send for them. The handyman would come and say, 'The manager wants to see you in the office', and if you didn't go to the office, you had to be prepared for another visit from the manager. So mainly they'd go to the manager to save this further intrusion like that.

Once they got the buildings up, the manager and his wife taught us at the school for a long time, about six or eight months and then they got an additional teacher. We were there all day, different from Collarenebri. But we did a lot of marching and raising the flag . . . a terrible lot of that, and assemblies. If we didn't march properly first, I remember, it was 'Halt!' and pull the offenders out, put them back in a line again and off we'd go again. I remember myself and Lizzy Ellis—we were two returned servicemen's daughters—and we'd always be out of step. Lizzy would mainly try to be really erect, but I couldn't seem to get into it anyhow, even though I remember I was trying because I thought, well, it was very important the flag flying and this big march. It's stupid when I look back on it now! And then a lot of time was spent with his wife learning us to knit.

But I did learn to read and write there. I don't think I learnt a lot from the manager himself. There were two classrooms and he used to be back and forwards and stand you in a corner if you didn't do this or that, and correct your book. I don't know what he was doing really, I don't think he did a great deal in actually teaching us anything. But when the new teacher came along . . . I don't know whether she concentrated on me a bit more but maybe she felt that all she could do was try and give some kids some ideas on how they can learn to read and write and leave it at that. This is what she did to me. She said, 'Now if you don't know a big word, sound it out'. First of all we were learning the sounds so you can put the words together and see what it sounds like and keep at it until you find out. And she said: 'Read and read as much as you can'.

And that's the only way I got what bit of education I got, because I can't attribute it to anything else. You know, history and all that was only Captain Cook and how brave he was. There wasn't anything at all about Aboriginal people. The only thing I can remember them saying was—in my last year there—'Oh, one day you will be working with white people and so you have to be able to dress well and speak well and so you should concentrate on your work'. I think that's all they taught us, that one day we were going to be . . . well, they didn't say 'assimilate' which was good I suppose, because we didn't anyhow, but they said, 'you'll go into the white society'.

See we'd had very little contact with white people at all. So as soon as we saw white people coming, well, maybe we were warned, 'Have nothing to do with them', in case we might've said something that indicated where we might be found or something, I think. Because I still feel this. But we had very little contact whatsoever with white people off the mission. If anyone wanted to go into town they were strictly on the manager's wish. We knew that the white manager and matron were there to control the blacks, to make sure they didn't leave the mission without permission, or come onto the mission without permission, or someone sneak in and be a bit drunk (it didn't have to be quarrelsome or abusive or anything)—that's the only way I could see it. They were there to keep law and order.

Not long ago, I was helping to make a film with other women about our early times at Toomelah. And we went out there and camped. And then the white farmer that owns the place, and some of the neighbours too, came in there and had tea and a barbecue and dampers. They sat around and talked straight out about how some parts of their family was nasty towards Aboriginal people. And another lot used to just have little run-ins with them over different groups of Aboriginals and things like that. I could see a lot of that stuff must've been happening to them. This one fella said: 'We couldn't even go outside when the Aboriginal people came to the homestead for something. We had to stay inside'. So, they were much like us. When the white people used to come we used to go under the bed!

There were a couple of kids taken away while I was there, because they thought the mother was mad, and that was my grandmother's brother's wife. Yeah, there was two—Henry and Susan, that's right. And years later Henry tried to make some kind of contact with his people. He joined the merchant navy in the Second World War and we read in some paper where he was trying to contact some of his people and by the time we tried to contact him he was out at sea and there was an accident or something and he was killed. We never, never heard about Susan. But they thought their mother was mad, which wasn't so. She just couldn't handle the situations she was in, you know, coming from different places. The manager's wife was closely in touch because I suppose she was summing her up to see whether she was mad or not. And then when the Matron decided she was mad, that was it.

There's one thing I remember clearly. There was a mass wedding once. It wasn't a double wedding, it was about six couples married at once.[2] I couldn't figure it out—you know, you couldn't all just fall in love and all decide to . . . [laughs] There had to be a reason, there had to be a reason for those kind of marriages because they weren't worrying about getting extra houses for these newlyweds, making them marry properly in their churches and things. They got married on the mission in a little hall there they had, got the minister out from Goondiwindi and just stood them all up there and they were all married there. And it makes you wonder about that, doesn't it? And those marriages didn't work out at all. You'd hear the old people say: 'Oh I don't think that one will work out' or 'I don't think that one will last'. I don't think any were a real long term partnership. As the managers kept changing, some of the girls were more favoured by certain managers and it always makes me think this could've been the reason, you know? I've heard it said that it's happened in other places where managers did have their little fling with the girls, and perhaps they got afraid that they might be pregnant and so set them all up with mates and married them off—so they're protected again. And the Protection Board was working well—you know, in their favour! And I think nearly all of these girls, with the exception of one or two, worked at the manager's house, and the others were apprenticed girls.

And of course, they were changing their system all the time, as they're doing today, they keep changing the system so the protection goes on in their favour, to keep us from ruling our own lives. It's so true that we won't rule our own lives under the present systems that they keep setting up. Because they set up blacks to fight blacks. You get blacks in the public service that go around and make it sound all rosy and it's not going to work—you know, people are going to have to rebel against it. And I'm one that's ready to. I am ready!

The treatment room was a big part of our lives as kids. All of us had sore eyes, and we'd have to get this stick of what they called bluestone.[3] They'd rub this little stick across our eyes—and it used to sting like hell! Then we used to have these brown drops put in our eyes, or sometimes it'd be pink. And if we had a sore, there'd be all this pink paint all over us. We had a lot of our own stuff too. If we had boils, Gran's main thing was a soap and sugar poultice, where you'd rub the sugar into the soap and make a paste out of it. Then there were other different plants they'd boil up for us and make a cough mixture out of it. So we had a lot of our own medicine, and we had a lot of our own food too, because the only thing we'd get on the rations was flour, sugar, tea, jam and condensed milk. And that would just be a small order. So in most cases we'd have a lot of fish. And that's where old Uncle Daduwin used to be the real bloke to teach the kids how to hunt, so we'd always have rabbit or goanna or emu, whatever they could get.

We used to watch these rations given out, and everybody's standing in line to get their rations. And this other girl—Jeannie Bathman—and myself, we thought: 'Well, we don't get enough condensed milk', and we loved condensed milk. So we were looking at ways and how we could nick a couple of tins, which we finally did one day. We saw the board was loose under the storeroom, got up there and got our tins of condensed milk. But of course, we were found out not long after, and so we got the hiding of our life. My Granny gave me a good hiding, Jeannie's mother gave me a good hiding. Because the manager went down and said:

'What a dreadful thing they've done. You wouldn't believe what these girls did? They took a board out of . . . '

—well, it was a loose board, all we had to do was shove it up and we were in . . . no, *she* was in, she was skinnier than me—

' . . . and these girls went up there and lifted the floorboards and pinched condensed milk.'

—Gees! we got a hiding for that!

See they set up blacks to fight blacks. And it was hard to trust people. Like old Granny Kate our next door neighbour used to say: 'You can't trust this Lizzie'—she was my older cousin . . . 'you can't trust this Lizzie, you know, she's got a big mouth this Lizzie'. 'No, not Lizzie', I said, because she was my mate, she was my best mate you see. And Granny Kate used to say: 'Don't you tell her now. Don't tell nobody'. And I said: 'I won't tell nobody'. 'No, but this Lizzie, you can't trust Lizzie'. We used to say to Lizzie, 'If you tell I'm going to tell on you!' We never ever caught her out or anything. But we knew we had to be very careful.

And when I look at Toomelah, I can't say that I had an unhappy time there. I had a very protected time. There was only one old woman that used to drink, and not too many women used to drink at all then. We used to think that she had some kind of sickness, and that's the way they let us think about her. And I said one day to Gran: 'Why is it that Old Mary has this bug in the head?' And Gran said: 'I suppose she has too. I don't know, that's how when she gets sick she don't know us anymore and she'll go to sleep or fall over and she could hurt herself'. And so she was telling us all the things like that, you know.

And of course, we got it in our heads then that she was a bit *wamba*[4] and that's how they let us leave it until we got older and then we started to know that she was drunk. But she was the only woman that was drunk. I didn't think much of it then, and later old Dad said: 'Oh, poor old Mary she'd had a few'. And I said: 'A few of what?' 'A few drinks', he said, 'you know she's a drunk?' And I said: 'Oh, so she was *drunk*'. And then a long time after I was telling her about it and she laughed: 'Oh yeah not many women drunks then!'

And isn't it marvellous when you think about that. A lot of men used to drink the grog, but not too many women. You can say that right up until the 1960s when I realised I was coming in contact with many more women who was drinking; before that there have been two Aboriginal women in my life that I knew were drinking. And I didn't think much about white women drinking either, because they said only men did it.

Mum and Dad used to come up and see us, but not always together. Mum kept coming up to Toomelah, she was back and forth to come and see us. And we had a little sister, Ceatrice, when Mum came up. And she stayed for a while—I don't know whether I was sick or Joe was sick—but it was then that we lost that little sister; she was only a couple of months old I think. She died when Mum came up to see us.

If Dad came to see us he had to ring up and get permission, and then he was only allowed to stay for an hour. So, he'd just come in there long enough to sort of promise us that it wouldn't be long, that Mum was coming out of the eye hospital and we were going to go out on a big station somewhere and live. They'd only let him come in sometimes. Other times he'd go there and think he was going to visit us and they'd tell him that he couldn't see us, or they'd tell him that we were fishing or something. But I don't know how they kept him away from there because he was forever trying to make things right for us.

Gran would've been the nicest little person I ever met. I think she showed me how strong you had to be and you could be. One day the manager caught her talking to us in the lingo . . . She did everything for us, she made sure there was hot water for our bath and she'd fill the little bath tub and everything. And this day, he'd come around the corner and stood by her: 'Jane I heard you. You were talking that lingo again to them girls. You can't do that you know. You know you're not supposed to that. I'm disgusted with you Jane!'

And I could see Gran standing there and she didn't know what to say, you know. And he kept going on about it . . . 'And you know you're not supposed to talk that stupid lingo now. We're finished with that. You've got to be like white people now'. And Gran would say: 'Yeah, I know I shouldn't have said that. I won't do that no more'. And when he went away then I felt really hurt about it. The funny thing was, I wanted to blame Gran. I said to Florrie: 'Gee Gran makes you mad, eh? She knows she's not supposed to talk that lingo to us. And yet she'll keep on talking it to us. Oh, and listen to her'. And Florrie said: 'Oh you don't take any notice of Gran, you know, they talk it all the time. I hear them talking, I don't take any notice. You want to shut your ears off'. I knew I couldn't talk to Gran about it, and she never ever spoke the lingo to us again. Years later I can remember that hurt, and I'm bitter that I was angry with Gran herself, although I didn't understand it then of course. But when I thought about it after, you know, I thought: 'Fancy me being angry with Gran, and Granny was such a lovely person to us'.

But being at Toomelah was a good learning thing for us. Joe must've learnt a lot about hunting; because I learnt a lot about getting baits for fishing, the best way to put a worm on the hook, what were the best berries and fruit to eat, what was dangerous. And Granny used to take us down one side of the river, around the bend, to go fishing. And it was real fun times, you know, we used to run along—no shoes on—I don't know how we did it, you know. Old Gran would say, 'I don't know what these kids are grizzling about?' . . . [laughs] Sometimes Gran would drag her little feet along in front of us to make a path for us, and then if Florrie was in a good mood she'd be next to Gran and she'd do the same and it was a bit better for me. And Bobby was the youngest. And of course, he'd be the bloke getting the piggyback. He was all right.

The boys were allowed to go hunting more often than the girls were allowed into the bush, the older people there in that community made that rule. Charlie Denison was the oldest one there. And then, some of the older women would take us fishing for miles. Sometimes we'd walk all those miles for nothing—they wouldn't catch a fish. Of course then it wasn't a real good trip back. We'd go hunting for fruits too, you know. But the boys would go out and hunt the animals when they were anything from nine up, and even younger than that, some of them could knock a rabbit in one hit with a *bundi*[5]—they were shown how to make them so they all had their own little *bundis* the same as what kids have got their little tennis bats and things today.

People used to fish with mainly cord lines and make up their own lines out of anything—especially the set lines, whatever they could find they'd fix up and make their own hooks out of wire. They very seldom used nets, but some of the older women got into the streams and actually caught fish in their dresses. Our Granny did, and Old Granny Kate—they'd do those kinds of things, you know. And we used to go and get craybobs in buckets, and sometimes we'd walk miles to get them—that was . . . oh, anywhere we went, like, even Toomelah or Colle—that was a real treat to go out for cray-bobbing. Sometimes we'd make our own little nets, and other times just sit there and fish them out one by one with our hands or with cotton lines or rag-lines or whatever we could find. We'd end up having a big meal out of it. We used to mainly put them in the ashes and of course, a lot of people liked to just put them in the big billy and boil them up and put plenty of salt on them . . .

Now one of the McGradys, Widdy McGrady, old Aunty Carrie's son, was a really talented artist. He made his own guitar out of a willow tree and won the prize at the Goondiwindi show and people offered a lot of money to buy it. Now he was always playing tricks on people. I suppose in our communities we always had a joker, like we always had an organiser. And this day, he drew a fish and cut it out from the thin, flat tin they used to line a fireplace. My old Granny and a couple of the old women would always go fishing in this one spot, and they'd have their lines set. So he went down and he hooked it to one of the old girls' lines. When she went down, she started pulling the line in and she's saying, 'Oh look out! I got a *big* fish!' And everyone's running up and saying 'Oh, somebody's gotta help her!' and she's pullin' this line in and the fish is swaying in the water, but it's really this tin! Well! When they got it out, they didn't know what to do . . . they just sat there lookin' at this tin fish! Then someone said: 'I know who did this!' So they got really cranky then. Old Aunty Carrie was a Christian and everybody's sayin', 'You can't go and tell her'. But the old girls said, 'We're gonna tell her all right! It don't matter how she takes it, we're still gonna go and tell her!' And I think the lad was getting a bit uneasy too because the word was getting around! Well Aunty Carrie went mad and called Widdy home and went really crook on him. And then after a while, the old girls was saying: 'I knew the next thing he'd do would be something silly like this!' And then they all started laughing! So that became a very special fish yarn!

They used to have a lot of dances at Toomelah, and very well controlled dances because they still had community leaders. Anyone that wanted to kick up a fuss, well they just made them leave. They had that kind of control. Some of the old people went along just for that purpose. Ronnie MacIntosh was a wonderful dancer. He and his wife had a lot of ballroom dancing skills. When they had dances he was always the MC and he'd take charge of it. And if anybody'd be playing up, which they very seldom did, he'd be the fella that'd have to put them out. I can't remember anyone having a real problem with the dances because there was no alcohol, but of course there was people sometimes who'd get jealous of their wives and he'd go around, wording people up . . . You know, 'Don't be dancin' too much with this one over here' and things like that. I suppose he had the real knowledge and control over what people were doing at the time, and he played a very valuable role with the boss, as they called the manager. And we learned later that Uncle Ronnie was able to make a lot of suggestions like building the tennis court for the kids and the hall. See the dances we used to have were all on the flat. Then we ended up getting our own hall and stage and we used to have concerts and dances there then. They had accordions and gum-leaf bands and spoons—that was mainly the music.

But there's one dance in the lingo I can remember, but it's a funny one. It tells the story of the black fellas looking out and they see this great big ship coming—and it's the landing of Captain Cook. That was the Salt Water one. And it was sung at nearly all the dances. This Teddy Trapman would come in and this was a highlight of the dance, he'd say:

> salt water
> nagurabi
> bandurabi
> wandingayii, salt water
> nagurabi, bandurabi
>   Yaiyii![6]

He'd go on with this—it was terrific. And that was telling the story, singing the song and moving back at the same time. He used to focus with his hands like he's got binoculars and this is how this little song used to go . . . saying that this ship was coming over the salt water. And there were movements, like choreography, that were part of the dance, but I suppose we just called it the Salt Water or the *Nagurabi* Corroboree. The music was mainly the people stamping out the song. Sometimes others joined in, but mainly Teddy Trapman took the floor because he could do it so well and graceful. And he'd get up to such a high pitch! I don't know what other people thought of it but I guess they thought like me that it meant that the Murris started to move back when they saw this big ship coming in and wondered what it was. And so it was the landing of Captain Cook. That dance was made up somewhere in that region—Mungindi or Boggabilla way, somewhere out there. And Ronnie MacIntosh was another one that could do it really well.

And that was the thing in those days. Today they've got this 'Porcupine and a Flagon of Wine' song they sing.[7] But I remember that in those times, *Nagurabi* was the little song. That was a very popular part of any dances that was held in the area at that time.

They used to have more corroborees on Toomelah when they first moved over there. I remember the Emu dance being done, and with such reverence, you know, everyone just sat around and there was no laughing or giggling or any of that allowed. There was one dance that they'd do that was the funny one, I used to laugh at that one. But with this other one, don't you dare laugh, it was so serious; so we were getting briefed on it, so we knew how to conduct ourselves. And I remember that Emu dance was done mainly by the women—old Granny Whiteman and all them. I remember one where these women got dressed up. But men were in that dance as well, that was before the Tingha people came down, must have been in late 1938 or 1939. I'd say that was one of the last corroborees that they'd held out that way.

The mission manager used to go to town and sometimes he'd be in there till late. The girls in the house would tell the handyman and he would get the word out that they were going to be in town all day. So the word would be out that everybody was going out to Granny Whiteman's for the corroboree. Someone was watching for the truck, and they were sneaking that corroboree.

They held it down a bit, on the side of the mission where old Granny Whiteman had her place. And I remember watching when the old couple would be walking around hitching themselves up and getting ready for the dance. And everyone else was all sitting around having a good old time, you know, with the boomerangs.

I thought how smart they were. They'd have the two boomerangs and they'd hit 'em together and somehow they'd make all these different sort of sounds. And now when I think back, they used to make different notes, I suppose you'd say. And then they'd have these clap sticks. Old Granny Whiteman, I was watching her doing that Emu dance.

And when they'd start the corroboree, this bloke would go up the tree—and he was about 16 or 17—he was the watcher. He used to watch for the truck. And I didn't think about it until later, you know, I started saying to some of the other women: 'Do you remember how Charlie used to be always running and then he'd swing onto something and he'd go up in the tree, and he was a real smart young man'. And they said: 'Yeah, he used to be the lookout'. And they'd do this Emu dance and a couple of other dances they used to do. I used to love old Granny Kate doing that—the Emu dance . . . oh, they'd be having a helluva time, you know. Everybody laughing.

And then all of a sudden this fellow would give out a loud whistle and be coo-eeing out! And then down he'd come. And they'd all be saying, 'We've got to go home now. Don't you go saying nothing about this'. I wasn't allowed to tell anybody. We had the message, we weren't allowed to talk about it again. 'Don't tell who [ever] asks you.' They'd know it would only be the boss that would ask us anyway. They'd say: 'Don't tell who asks you. 'You're not to say nothing'. So we made sure to say: 'We wasn't anywhere. We didn't go anywhere'. They see the manager's car coming—everybody'd just go back to their own business again, looking like they were visiting one another and things like that. [laughs] Oh, they were smart that way too, you know.

The way they started to build that place, it makes you think. They built the manager's house and, of course, that was a big house and it had a verandah all round and the teacher's house and the big treatment room. And where they used to give the tucker out. They had a bell. On dole days everybody would be ready and waiting for this dole. And for the old bell to go.[8]

Looking back on it, I can see everybody sort of waited to make sure they could do that corroboree safely—whatever it was they had to convince themselves that it would be okay, they wouldn't have any problems. So they were always on guard. And we were still doing some of the things they didn't want us to do. To me, they had this determination that they weren't going to let anything make them unhappy.

I was lucky I was able to have a bit of insight into mission life as well as flat life and then scrub life too, I suppose you can say. Because that's how we got a broader knowledge of what was happening, although we didn't realise that at the time. And then you can compare that mission lifestyle to the lifestyle on the Old Camp up at Colle, where you had the police patrol coming around anything up to three to four times a day. They'd probably be coming around in the morning about nine o'clock, sometimes earlier than that. You'd never know what time. You wouldn't get used to the time, because they'd do like swoop raids—or musters if you want to call it that, you know. So it wasn't so different from the mission.

It was while I was at Toomelah that I began to realise that we were people without rights. I remember the time that Bill Ferguson and Bertie Groves came. Even though they were Aboriginals, they weren't allowed on the mission (when I heard them later I understood why!) and so they were camped about half a mile across the road. Those two activists went all over New South Wales saying to Aboriginal people: 'You fellas have got to get up.

NEW SOUTH WALES GOVERNMENT
ABORIGINES PROTECTION ACT, 1909-1943, SECTION 18c.
[REGULATION 56]

CERTIFICATE OF EXEMPTION
From Provisions of the Act and Regulations

THIS·IS TO CERTIFY that CELIA FLICK

HALF Aborigine, aged 53 years, residing at RAILWAY SIDING, BOGGABILLA
(caste)
is a person who in the opinion of the Aborigines Welfare Board, ought no longer be subject to the provisions of the Aborigines Protection Act and Regulations, or any of such provisions, and he/she is accordingly exempted from such provisions:—

Issued in compliance with the Resolution of the Aborigines Welfare Board and dated the

FIFTEENTH day of NOVEMBER, 1960

Chairman.
Member.
of the Aborigines Welfare Board.

Countersigned by The Secretary.

Photograph of CELIA FLICK

Signature of Holder *Celia Flick*

35927 8.58 V. C. N. Blight, Government Printer

Celia Flick's exemption certificate.

We gotta be saying, "We want citizens' rights in our own country—We *own* this country!"' I remember my Gran saying to us, 'Now these men that's camped over there, they want to talk to us about what we should be doing. But we gotta wait till it's dark and we gonna sneak out so youse all got to be quiet! So no cryin' or anything when you get bindi-eyes in your foot or stuff like that'. I can just remember all of us going through the tall grass and sneaking out to that meeting. And everyone *was* really quiet and you could only hear those two men talking to us . . .

One of the things that always stuck in my mind was Billy Ferguson saying: 'We can't do it for you, you fellas gotta do it for us, we all have to do it together. And we have to make this government realise that we're citizens, we want rights in this country! And if we don't say it, nobody else is gonna say it for us!'

Another thing they said was that because we were not even citizens of our own country, that we had to have a 'licence', which I later got to know as 'dog licence'.[9] I heard a lot about these 'dog licences' from time to time after that, but never actually saw one until 1978 when I began to care for our mother when she became ill. She asked me to sort her personal papers for her and I opened a box and there it was, her dog licence! 'You can have that if you like', she said, 'your father didn't agree with these papers, but I got one because I had friends who had them. They went to hotels and clubs and to other places, where other Aboriginal people couldn't go, because they had these papers'.

That night at Toomelah was my very first meeting other than church. Although I didn't understand much about it at the time, I think I was prompted from there. Anyway, I can remember us all sneaking back home again, and those two old ladies who lived next door to us, they came over to Gran's and said, 'Well, we got away with it, eh? I don't think anybody gonna get in trouble over it'. Nothing ever happened over it, but they were still anxious.

I look back now and say that at Toomelah I was introduced to school— a place of learning or one could say a whole world of yearning . . . but I didn't learn so much in school. Most of my education came from the street!

3
Learning From the Street, 1940s

Isabel and Joe had remained at Toomelah for around three years, and Isabel remembers doing 'first and second grade' at school there. That was all the formal schooling she ever got. Her older brother, Lindsay, had remained with her father Mick, working on local stations. Joe later taught Lindsay how to read. The economy improved with the onset of the Second World War, making it easier for Aboriginal people to regain the jobs they had filled in the sheep and agricultural industries before the Depression. Many Aboriginal families felt confident enough in the improved economic climate to take their families away from the missions into which they'd been forced by the combination of economic depression, school segregations and Board pursuit.

Mick Flick gained a permanent job managing a property called Longswamp, 10 miles out of Collarenebri on the Mungindi Road, and brought his family away from Toomelah around 1942. The family spent a lot of time in Collarenebri and in 1946 Mick leased a block of land on the northern edge of town, at the beginning of the Mungindi Road which passed the 'Old Camp' a mile or so further along. Mick continued to work on Longswamp, coming in at weekends, while Celia and the family lived in town on what they called, from then on, 'the Block'.

Isabel returned to learn a new view of Collarenebri, as she negotiated adolescence, her first jobs and relationships and learnt 'from the street' how the town worked.

Once we could read and write, then it was time to come back to Mum and Dad and Collarenebri. Dad did a bit of everything. He was a shearer and a fencer and he managed properties like one at Longswamp. It used to be owned by a fellow called Arthur Brown, who had two properties, Wirrabilla and Longswamp, and Dad worked on both of them.

Lindsay had always been with Dad—because they worked, you see. The boys started working when they were 12. Mum was back at Longswamp with my father then at the station and we lived a while there in a house. And when we used to come into town, Dad used to bring extra sheep in and give a bit of meat here and there. And that was always the way with all of the workers, all the fellas that used to do work on properties, they always used to bring in extra meat and big tins of fat and stuff like that, and share it right around, it was a real sharing system that we had. And if one lot missed out, well, there'd be always someone to make sure that that sharing was happening evenly across the uptown—or the top camp and the middle camp and the bottom camp.

When we were in town, the cops would come round and notice us, then they'd be wanting to know who we were staying with . . . They'd ask: 'And where's your mother staying? Does she stop out in the bush or in the camp?' you know, and then Mum would always say: 'We've just come in for an hour or so'. But when they came back again, that would have been a long hour, you know? It might be in the afternoon or something like that, because Dad used to still get grog even though they weren't supposed to have grog. And sometimes we wouldn't go back until late to Longswamp. But one of them little army jeeps'd be coming to check us out, just like they checked everyone out.

Dad got the Block about 1945—just after the war. He was working on Longswamp and so he could get a pastoral lease on that piece of land. He put up his name into the ballot for a soldier resettlement block, but he didn't ever hear back. That's one of the ways he started to educate us. And I suppose it was a way of helping me to become politically aware of what was happening to Aboriginal people, because he said, 'You take me, for instance, every year I put my name up to be balloted for land. And I follow it up. I try to question: "Was my name submitted? Was my name put in, or not?" and I can never find out whether my name was ever put in to the draw'. He had very strong feelings that it never was. And he felt that it was very unlikely that any Aboriginal people's names were put in, anyhow.

I think it was local RSL officials who selected the names to go in and maybe go on to regional, but there wasn't much information. And he was a man that asked a lot of questions in that area. But there was very little indication that other Aboriginal people had been successful. So yeah, he had very strong feelings that they were never submitted anyhow.

'The Block' was an area of around two acres, situated on the northern town boundary, upstream and across the road from the hospital, and on the same side of the river as the 'old camp'. It had a narrow edge abutting the hospital grounds and

continued back and down to the river, with a gully running across it. Isabel's younger sisters Clare and Rosie and her brother Jimmy were now of school age. Mick built a tin house on the centre of the Block like those on the Old Camp. Flattened kerosine tins for walls and sheets of corrugated iron for roofing were nailed to a strong, large bush timber frame to build a flexible structure which could accommodate their growing family and occasional visitors. Mick's was the only tin house on the Block or on the camp which was built up on a platform, with a raised wooden floor covered in lino for the main sleeping rooms and a lower, dirt floor swept smooth for the kitchen. There was a rainwater tank built into an alcove in the side of the house, accessed through a little door, but often the family still needed to cart water from the river by bucket, windlass and pulley until the 1960s.

While Isabel was away in Toomelah, the struggle to have Aboriginal children admitted to the public school in Collarenebri had continued. Sustained pressure from Aboriginal people and supporters led to a decision to allow Aboriginal children into the school in February 1941. This was to be the first trial of the new State Government policy of assimilation. But white parents immediately objected, 'striking' by removing their own children from the school. Within a fortnight, the Education Department had backed down, offering Aboriginal children only an 'Annex' school, a makeshift classroom up on the stage of the School of Arts next door. The children and teacher were not allowed to use the piano and had no access to the tea room, and had to haul the long, heavy form seating up onto the stage each morning to be their seats and desks and then put them away again every afternoon. After continued demands, and in the face of the obvious silliness of the situation, the Aboriginal children were finally allowed, family by family, into the public school in the mid-1940s and it was formally declared integrated in 1947.[1]

Rosie (Weatherall) Flick, who had taught the correspondence lessons under the bough shade, related the sequence of events, and to her those brief days in the 'real' school in 1941 were so fleeting that she didn't even mention them:

Rosie: So we were petitioning the public school for a while, at the same time as we were under the bough shed. Even going down to Armidale, that was their head office for Education, you know, we went down for two or three meetings in 1939 and 1940 to see if we could get into the school—that's what they was fighting for . . . And any rate, they decided then to teach them in the Town Hall,[2] they could go into the Town Hall then, you see. So we'd had to petition even to get that Annex, me and this old minister and the policeman. There was never any meetings in Collarenebri itself, they used to take it all to Armidale, see, that was the Education Department's head office, and that's where it all had to go down there. The policeman was always sort of on our side, even when we'd go to the meeting; but there was a lot of white families would go down and the things they used to say about the Murris! Used to make me sick! And there was white people going down to these meetings in Armidale all the time.

Isabel and her younger sister Rose (Flick) Fernando talked in 1994 about their memories of the Annex and public school in the 1940s:

Isabel: When we came back onto the Block at the end of the war, Mum started to say: 'Oh, Clare can go to school now . . . and Jimmy and Rose', and someone said: 'Oh, Isabel should have gone back to school', and I said: 'Oh, no, I'm too old for that'. I was feeling really cocky then, I was out of that. I didn't want any part of it.

So Doreen [Weatherall] and Clare went into the Annex, and then Rose and Jimmy. Oh, yes. Oh, they were the third family to get in, we weren't so fair, you see? So, they took the fairest kids in and then the second fairest lot. And when it was our turn, these poor kids, once they got them into the school the terrible fear of going every day. Jimmy and Clare was so miserable. They cried about how they didn't want to go to school and . . . 'They call me black . . .' and all this. Jimmy came home every day bashed up because somebody called him black.

Dad used to say: 'Hey, listen, you are black, you know, you're a black fella. What do you want to be a white fella? How are you going to do that?' And he'd say: 'You've got to be proud you're black. I don't care. Look, I go out and I earn my living and nobody else buys my tucker, I buy my own . . . So, get it in your head, you are black and you are entitled to go to that school. And they're not going to stop you, just keep going'. He was starting to really get it into us that we've got to be working towards being proud of ourselves, you know.

Rose: And he used to say too: 'You won't beat a white man by fighting . . . You've got to be just as good or you've got to be a bit better'.

Isabel: If somebody said: 'He's good that white fella'. You've got to be a bit better than him. You've got to make sure you . . . you can't step out of line but he can, see.

Rose: And that used to frighten me that, because I didn't know what 'a bit better' meant. I do now . . . 'a bit better'!!!

Isabel: 'Look, as long as you don't get into trouble, Jimmy', Dad would say. 'Look, Rosie don't get into trouble, Jimmy, Clare don't get into trouble . . .' But our little Clare used to be hiding down the side of the house, she wouldn't talk to Mum and Dad . . . When she and Rose and Jimmy used to get me on my own they'd tell me what was happening at school, you know, especially when they went into the white school. They was all right while they were in the little Annex but when they shifted them over to the other school . . .

Rose: The Annex used to be the old Town Hall, and then there was a big fence and that was the school next door, see.

Isabel: That's when the colour of the skin counted then. Because if your skin was fair you was over there in the real school, and they used to look at our hands to see if they were clean underneath the nails and clean hands and behind your ears, and check with a ruler for *munis*. Every one of the kids would be standing up to attention so stiffly . . . it was just a ritual . . .

Rose: . . . yes they'd have to scrub up before they go to school and they had tight little curls and everything.

Isabel: Yes, but I won't ever forget that show of hands . . .

And when Jimmy went into big school, the headmaster used to be up there looking for Dad all the time and Mum would always say: 'I don't know nothing. I don't have nothing to do with that'—that's how Mum used to handle it. Dad was out on Longswamp, but she said he was the only one that had something to do with it. And so he said: 'Oh, I can never catch him'.

But anyway, when he did catch up with Dad one weekend, he said: 'Look, I don't know what you're going to do with this boy. But he's got to stop taking knives to school. Where does he get the money from?' . . . And Dad said: 'I give him money. He carts the wood and does things for me and I give him money. That's his own money'. And he said: 'Well, look every time you give him money he buys a knife. Every Monday morning I have to take the knife off him because he's going to stab someone because they call him black'. And Dad says: 'Oh, well, I'll have a talk to him' . . . And he'd say: 'Now, you're not going to solve it, you're not going to fix these fellas up by putting a knife in them; you're going to make it worse . . . make it worse on all of us'. But I don't think it ever sunk in with Jimmy. He fought . . . whole time he was in school he fought his way all the time.

Rose: He used to hide. He'd go to school through the gate with me and then hide and he'd still be at the gate coming home. Anyway, this letter came in the mail and Dad said: 'Read this to me', and I read it to him . . . '14–15 days absent from school'. Old Dad said to me: 'What's that mean?' and I said: 'Well, he hasn't been going to school'. And he said: 'But you were telling me he is' . . . 'Yes, Dad he is going to school.' So he said: 'Well, watch him'.

Now every time this fella used to go to school we'd go through the gate together, so this day I went through the gate and I went and hid underneath the big school . . . My little brother took off around to the pepper tree. That's where he used to hide, in the pepper tree. And he'd sit there all day and then at three o'clock . . . three-thirty he was standing at the gate waiting.

Isabel: But, I used to feel so cocky, you know, when they used to talk about how bad it was . . . Clare used to say, 'Oh, I hate it. I hate that school'. I don't see how they could've possibly learnt anything when they're sitting there and all they're thinking about, you know, they're going to fight this bloke when they get out of the class and . . . I think that was always in their mind. So they didn't learn that much. But Rose is the one to tell you about the milk . . . the lumpy milk. It was a cheaper sort of milk that the black kids used to get.

Rose: Yeah, when we'd go to the Annex we used to make powdered milk—mix it up with cold water into a thick paste, see. Two little kids used to have to go with a bit of water, and we never had no glasses . . . the tin with a little handle and that's how they used to make the milk for us kids over there. The milk for the white kids was fresh milk and it used to come in the big silver canisters, but we used to have the powdered milk. And as little kids we were licking our lips, and the big girls used to give us a lick of the spoon. Sometimes the kids used to say: 'I like my milk lumpy', so whoever was making that milk that day would make it lumpy because his little sister or his little brother liked it lumpy. Those are the things we had control over, they were just . . . just the making of the milk, you know.

There was a man with some kids who used to come over for a dance and they were trying to get the white kids to look at us when we were in the Annex. So they'd march all them little white kids in for a dancing lesson. And before all the white kids came in all the class was the stage, see, so we used to push our desks out of sight, because the music was there . . . the piano had to be pulled out . . . and the white kids were lined up there, and they used to say to them: 'Okay, now, they won't bite, they won't bite, pick a partner now. Come on they're just . . . come on now . . . ', and I remember one kid saying: 'But they smell . . . they might smell', and the teacher said: 'Oh, come on then, here, you can dance with so and so', so she gave him a white partner so as not to upset him.

In the end all us little Murris turned around and we danced with each other . . . we wouldn't dance with the others. But those little things used to happen quite a lot. Like we used to get the pastels and mainly they used to bring over the boxes that were broken in half. Then one day, I remember, the first time I was using the full pastel . . . because I was used to the stubs . . . All of a sudden these white boys brought over these big cartons . . . they were full!

Isabel: Yeah, you know . . . and it still goes on.

Rose: Then there was things like this Freddy with those drawings . . . They said to the class—this was in the Annex times, eh—they said: 'Now, boys and girls, I want you to draw what you've got in your kitchen . . . your tables and chairs and cupboards and things like that', and, anyway, Freddy draws these four little round things and this little square thing, and near the square things there's two more little round things . . . and then he drew another little cupboard and . . . the teacher said: 'Oh, what's all these circles, Fred?'

And he said: 'That's our tables and chairs. That's our chairs, Sir . . . All these fellas haven't got chairs, they only just drew them like chairs. They haven't got chairs', he said, 'they've only got drums for their chairs . . . like us, that's all we've got. And see them . . . these round things here, we've just got one of them and we've got the big board across it like that for a table, and Mum puts a tablecloth on it . . . and all these folks, they're only telling you that, Sir'.

And these kids are all saying, 'Freddy, shut up . . . Freddy . . . ' I always remember that. They all waited on him after school, see, and oh they bashed him up then, and then the parents said: 'I wonder why them kids all got into Freddy for?' and . . . 'Oh, Freddy must've got cheeky or something', everybody is trying to figure it out, you know. And then he had to say why, and he said: 'Well, I only just told the teacher the truth, they only had old drums for their chairs . . . '

Isabel might have been cocky at escaping the distress her younger sisters and brother were feeling at the school, but she hadn't forgotten her own intense desire to learn. And she hadn't forgotten the humiliations she had been forced to go through to get her little bit of schooling. She recognised in her sister Rose the same fierce desires. When Rose started at the 'big' school on the other side of the fence, Isabel gave her a present which meant more to Rose than any other. Rose remembered in 2002:

Rose: When Isabel came back from a job, she always used to buy me gifts, her and Clara. When Clara had her first job, she bought me a little cup and saucer, I never seen porcelain so fine, you know we'd always had tin pints. And then Clara opens this little box for me. She was working at Kerrigans, and she'd bought me this beautiful little china piece.

Then when Isabel bought her parcel over, it was a big parcel wrapped up in brown paper and tied up with string. I couldn't get the paper and string off this thing, and I remember getting the butcher's knife and Dad saying, 'Not that knife, that's my good knife!' So I had to go and get another knife to undo this string. And I opened it, eh. And it was what I always wanted. 'Cause I was *ngarragaa*.[3] Only had sandshoes, and Dad used to put the Vulcanised patching on them to keep them going. I had sandshoes, no socks, and Dad used to get the ribbons from the cemetery for our hair. And I always wanted a navy tunic and black shoes and white socks.

And in this brown paper packet was my first serge uniform . . . for school . . . my snow white blouse, my white socks, and my black shoes. And she bought that out of her pay. And when I opened that parcel, oh mate! I lifted my uniform up, 'cause it was a little bit long, and I looked at it, and it was just what I wanted! 'Cause Nancy Lawlor had one!! All the *waajiins*[4] had one! And now I had my first uniform!

And I remember I wanted to go and put it on right now. And Isabel said, 'No you *bandu*[5] yet! You gotta clean yourself up!' So I went out, and I said, 'Oh I gotta have a wash, I'm gonna put my uniform on, gonna put my uniform on!' She said, 'Oh Charlie it's hot!' I said, 'No, no no . . .' Anyway they poured the water on me, I had a wash, come back then, eh? My uniform was long, but I had white socks, black shoes. And she standing at the door and she said, 'Oh, that fit you lovely Sis! Now remember the buckle of the belt'. It was a metal one. I thought it was the best buckle out! She said, 'You like it?' 'Oh mate', I said, 'I love it, I love it!' And then I said, 'Don't forget my birthday!' 'Don't worry, I got that picked out', she said.

'Cause I was just learning to read when I went from the black school over to the white school. And I'll *never* forget it. When my birthday come it was the book, *The Cruel Sea*, Nicholas Monserrat. That's my first book. And to *read* it!

When I got it, I was so proud of it I took it to school, and the teacher said, 'You can't read this, little girl, you can't read this. You not up to them words. You black kids just come over'. But I made a *point* of reading it. And I'll never forget who wrote it, 'cause in those days, when you read something, you read every line, see. So *The Cruel Sea*, by Nicholas Monserrat.

My first book. When I read that one to Isabel, I read a couple of pages and I said, 'Look, I can read this now!'

She said, 'You always mucking around with books and reading . . . I'll get you another one!'

And I was about 11, 10 and 11 when I got those books, they were about that thick you know, and I *read* them! Those were the gifts I remember most . . . That was my sister!

Dad's and Mum's relationship must have been pretty rocky all the way, I reckon. Because she'd take off. She wouldn't necessarily go to Gran's because she had groups of friends everywhere and she would go to some of them in Dirranbandi and Lightning Ridge. Or she'd go into Boggabilla where she had friends who used to work on the railway and so she'd spend a lot of time with them. The first time she really went away and left us, I thought he was going to go after her and shoot her. He was really raging. And then apparently she wanted to take the kids, Jimmy, Rosie and Clare. And that's when he used to drink a bit, he used to really get out to it.

Anyway, this welfare officer came up and said: 'Well, looks like your wife wants to take the kids'. That really put a spark into him. He said: 'Well what can I do?' The welfare officer wasn't real happy about it. He said: 'You've got to be careful they don't get sent away'. Then one of these old JP's Dad used to work for come up one day and said: 'Do you know, when you go to court, if you can say that you don't drink, that you've given it up . . . Then, you know, you've got a bit of a case . . . And that I'm working with you and all that . . . But if you're drinking', he said, 'we can't help you at all'. 'Oh, right', Dad said. You know what? He never drank from there on.

We were all a bit older then, nearly grown up. And we were saying: 'Oh gee, this won't last', because we'd be there to pick up the kids and everything. But he wanted to be independent and have the kids in the place with him. So he didn't drink again. And then none of the younger kids wanted to go with Mum when she would take off and go. As they got older he'd say: 'Oh well, they're big enough to know what they want to do now'. But they'd never want to go, you know.

And after he got over the anger part of it, he started to say to us: 'Well, look, I've made up my mind about everything, you know. The Old Girl's going to come back. She'll come back. And she'll come and go for the rest of the time. Because I want her to come back and be with the kids when she wants to be. It's no good her being here if she wants to row and fight and kick up. So the best way to do that . . . because you've only got one mother, you must realise, when she walks in the door, we're all out of it, she's the boss'.

And that's the way it went. Soon as she'd come home, he'd pack up and go. And we got to the stage where we could joke with him about it, you know. He'd say: 'Oh well, I'd better be packing my swag tonight'. And we'd say: 'Why do you have to go out for, Dad? You don't have to run away when Mum comes home'. 'I think it's better that way'. But he never did stay . . . very seldom, if he came in and she was home, you know he'd put his bed out on the flat and he'd just have a night there or something, with the kids, because he wanted to be with the kids all the time. And then, after a while everybody got pretty used to it, you know, because she still used to go crook on him, as if she owned him and everything.

She was a funny old woman. But I think about her now, you know. I used to think she was very nasty to me because she couldn't understand that me and Dad got on really well. I think she was jealous of that fact. But when I think about it, she must have had a hard time after that tragedy up in Bungunya when her father got shot and then most of her family got sent right away. And then she wasn't allowed to visit them. My mother lost her family and she had very little contact with the rest of her sisters and their children. So that was a whole lifetime wiped out. We've got one aunty that's living now in Cherbourg, which is where she was sent to. And she's got a big family. And there's big families on our mother's side that we don't even know, you know, and we'll probably never get to meet because of our financial set-up.

They wanted her to go up a couple of times, but she wasn't allowed to go onto the mission at Cherbourg. So, only time she met up with them was if there was a funeral and there was only two occasions that I can remember, where they went home for a funeral. So she must indeed have had a hard time coping with all that. When she married Dad she was only 16, but they had to put her age up. I think it saved her from getting sent away as well. And, of course, Dad was older, he'd gone over to the war and come back. So she must have had a hard time. Then the tragedy of losing our young sister [Ceatrice] up at Toomelah really took its toll on Mum after that. So I've pieced all these things together in my mind, you know, years after.

And one of the things I remember Dad saying to me one day was: 'Anybody's made up of all kinds of things—blood and bones and muscle and feelings. You get all kinds of feelings'. He was trying to tell me about boys . . . but he didn't know how to get around it.

Mum had gone then and he was starting to worry about dealing with the girls. And he said: 'It's like, when you're going to a funeral, it's just a sad feeling. You're sad, so you don't bust out laughing. If you have to you get out somewhere where everybody is happy. You're like an old wet bag if you're sitting around being sad. It's the same thing, he said, with a man and a woman. That's a different feeling altogether. And if you're around with your mob, well that's okay, you're safe, you're right. But when you're only two that's different altogether, you're not safe then. So you've got to watch what you're doing. You're right if there's a mob of people—somebody there can help you, see. And you can swap places with them or something like that, you can get them to take you home or whatever. But if there's only two of you, you've got to watch your feelings'.

And I never thought much about it, because it was a very awkward moment for me. I wanted to get out of that to do something else and talk about something else. Because I *was* thinking about blokes at that time. And sure enough, I'd think: 'You're right, you have to control it. And when you're out there on your own, it is a totally different feeling'.

Oh, I remember I used to go and do something else—put the washing out or something, which I wasn't really interested in either. But what a wonderful way for him to have a go at it. And I think that's one of the reasons why I did my best to tell my kids early. Because I guess I remember those moments, and even when I first got my periods. And I said to Mum: 'Why didn't you tell us?' A lot of it is terrible I reckon. I thought I was going to bleed to death. She said: 'Oh well, I didn't know what to say. You probably wouldn't have taken any notice of me if I told you what you had to do'.

We were lucky we could live on the Block together like that. There's another time I remember Dad could see we were having more fights with one of the brothers as we were growing up, and I suppose we were in our teens then. And oh, we'd have a lot of rows. Dad told us: 'One of the things you've got to learn is that you've got to live together first. If you can't live with each other you've got no chance of living with other people'.

And there was one day when my brother and I had a fight and I took off and I stayed with Granny Fanny up at the reserve. Dad didn't worry because I was with her, and he knew when I decided to come home I'd come home. But he said: 'Oh you can't just run away. You've got to live with him. Take no notice of him. He's not easy to live with. But none of us are . . . look at us, we're all different people. You've got to get to understand him'.

I've often said to Clare, you know, Dad was very wise in making us get used to each other, learning how to live with each other. And I think I try to do that with my grandkids too, you know. But I haven't been able to have that kind of relationship again because we're all separated and living in different places.

We weren't allowed to hang around the older people much when they were talking before we went to Toomelah. So, there we missed out on learning a lot of things, if we wasn't such cheeky little kids as to be listening and things like that, and we didn't even as to be dare do that! But you could see the system in the black groups—the older men making sure that a fight was settled once and for all the following day. There was control among the community and if those old men rejected someone, that community had to reject that person, it was really there.

But it was hard to learn about your meat[6] and things. When I was later in my teens I started to think, 'Oh, we're going to lose everything if we don't start to find out some of it'. So I asked a very learned old man at Collarenebri, I said, 'Why? Why the different meats?' And he said, 'Well, it's always sup-posed to be one animal that can't hurt the other animal', and so in most cases these marriages worked out right. And he gave me three examples where he said people I knew were the wrong meat for each other; and he said, 'It'll become violent', and it did, in the three marriages. And one was his daughter—his daughter was married to the wrong meat—and he said, 'You look at . . . so and so, they're the right meat'. And they were such a close couple, the rela-tionship was so close and it seemed like so much understanding in it.

I was about 20 when I started to try to learn about all this, and I'm not really clear on it, but I think I'm a sand goanna. That's called a *mangankali*. I asked this older fellow because I wanted to try and learn the language and he could speak 12 different tongues. And when he started to learn me, he said, 'Well, the only way we can start is . . . I can see that I have to mix the two closest languages which is Gamilaraay and Yuwalaraay'. I never got to speak it all, but he taught me a lot of words and I picked up more as I went along.

Mum and Dad expected us to get work when we were old enough. And one of the conditions for us girls—well, you could say one of the luxuries that we had—was the wireless at home. We could—if we were working—just turn the wireless on whenever we liked. But if we weren't working after the three weeks, then we had to get permission to use that wireless. But the brothers were different. They had three weeks to find a job or get out. And that was it. And they knew that Dad didn't say things and then not carry it out.

Wages at that time for me were about ten bob a week. But I didn't have to buy my own clothes, my Dad did that. They were just learning me to become independent and know what it felt like to really work for my own living.

So my first job I was about 15 and Dad's boss had made arrangements with this other station owner down near Rowena. And so—they were nice people—but after I was out there a while I used to get really lonely at night and want to come back home.

It was hard, but it was funny too in those first jobs. Sometimes I think of the flutter in my chest when she said: 'Put the shirt on the horse, Isabel'. And

I thought: 'No, she didn't say that'. But the most important thing was that Dad had said 'Whatever that woman tells you, you do it. You've got to keep that job, you know, if you're going to be independent you've got to put up with a lot'. And that's the thing that went through my mind straight away. And that shirt was real nice and white and you know . . . oh God, and she said again: 'Would you put this shirt on the horse, Isabel'.

And I said: 'Yes. Yes, Mrs Y . . . ' And then I thought: 'Oh, so she *did* say put it on the horse'. And then I looked out and I could see this biggest draught horse you ever saw grazing along outside the verandah. So I'm walking towards this big horse and she must've woke up just as I was about to kick the door open. I had the shirt held up in front of me and she must've realised what I was going to do. And when she said: 'Oh Isabel, I'll take that . . . I'll put that on the horse and you watch the milk. I've put some milk on the stove and just make sure it don't boil over, dear'. Oh I was glad to get rid of the shirt because my heart was pumping! And I thought 'No I don't care what happens to the milk. I want to watch you put this on the horse!' She walked over and put it on this frame . . . oh God, and I was feeling so sick. You wouldn't realise how you can feel so sick over something like that, eh?

But I'll never forget that, when Dad said: 'No matter what that woman tells you to do, you've got to do it because she's a good woman, she's a nice woman. And she wouldn't tell you to do something that you shouldn't or that's going to be too hard for you'. And when she pointed at that bloody shirt and 'put it on the horse', I was thinking: 'That's the first and foremost thing: I must do whatever she says!'

A lot of people had those same sort of experiences in their first jobs. There was an old friend of mine in Dubbo who had her boss ask her: 'We'll have potatoes in their jackets tonight. You can do the potatoes can you? And we'll just have that corned meat'. And she said: 'Oh righto'. And the boss said: 'You'll find everything out on the verandah there, dear'. So little dear walks out there and here's the sewing machine and all the cotton and materials and scissors and right near it is the little frame with the little potatoes in it. So she's thinking: 'Oh gee, I suppose I can . . .' All the style was little bolero things then, and she told me: 'So I started cutting these little boleros out, and I saw all the pins there and I thought: "I'll pin them on like that" and so they didn't look too bad'. So she had about six or eight done and the boss comes back after a while and she says: 'Oh you didn't put the potatoes on then?'

And she said: 'Oh Missus, I've only got a few of these jackets finished, you know'. And she said: 'What do you mean?' And she said: 'Well, I only just got . . . look, you have a look'. And when this woman came and had a look she started laughing. And she told me years later: 'I'm feeling so sick inside, I'm thinking I don't know whether to laugh or cry'. She didn't know what to do. And she said this woman kept laughing. And she said: 'I ended up crying'. And she said: 'Oh look, I'm sorry I shouldn't have laughed dear, I should know that you don't know what I'm talking about, eh?' 'Oh, I know what you're talking about'. She said: 'No, when you cook the potatoes you should . . .' she started explaining it.

And old Ellen Draper from Moree was telling me about the horse too, when I was telling her about what happened to me. She said she had the same sort of thing, but she wanted to ask questions. Her boss said. 'Just put this on the horse in the kitchen, dear'. And Ellen said: 'No, you wouldn't have a horse in the kitchen'. She said: 'Yes, we have got our horse in the kitchen'. *Nobody* ever had a horse in the kitchen! And she said it took this woman a while to wake up when she said: 'But I'm talking about the clothes horse now'. And Ellen said: 'Well, look you've got me beat. I don't know what a clothes horse is!' You know, she was going to stick up there for herself. What a way to learn things, eh?

I must've been about 14 or 15 then, this was just after Dad was able to go and get us from Toomelah. And this is the same place where Clare, my sister and her brother-in-law, Freddy, were working there later on. He was learning to be a stockman and she was the housemaid. He said: 'Hey Sis, quick! Old Boss said bring the gun from behind the Kelvinator; what's the Kelvinator?' She said: 'I don't know, don't ask me Freddy'. He said: 'Oh you must know. Go and ask the *waajiin*'. She said: 'No, I'm not going to ask the *waajin*'. And they looked at the refrigerator door and it said K-e-l . . . He said: 'K-e-l . . . this might be it, eh'. He looked behind the fridge and there's the gun.

And there's lots of other stories about girls my age who had these sorts of things happen. This other girl, she was from Bre—she was one of the good niggers—she said she was working at the hotel and she said this bloke came in while she was cleaning the room out or putting new towels in or something. He had the big dish, but he didn't have the big jug, see. He said: 'Where's the pitcher?' And she said: 'Oh the pictures were last night, we only have it every Wednesday'. And she said: 'And when he looked at me he said: "Oh no, I don't mean the picture show, I mean the jug, you know the big jug that . . . ?" 'Oh yeah', she said . . . Well, she told me, 'When I went outside I was thinking to myself I don't really want to take this back up. I feel so bad'. But oh dear all the wonderful ways you learn . . . I suppose when you think of it, we just imagine how our other old people before us got to know . . . anything really. And they became good stockmen and everything, eh?

But some of the experiences weren't funny. There's a real sad one that's what happened to my aunty. And she was only 13. She had to go out to a station, and the boss where she went out to said to her: 'Now you're going down to the stockmen's quarters tonight, you have to clean up down there'. She didn't say nothing, because she was a bit frightened. But when she gets down there the stockman was eyeing her off, see. And he's saying: 'They said you was 18'. 'I'm only 13', she said. And he said: 'Well, they told me you was 18'.

See, they must've made arrangements for her to sleep with him. And . . . 'Oh no, I'm not 18, I'm only 13. And I'm just turning 13'. And the poor old thing, she was telling me you know, that went on for a long time. And every now and again he'd walk in and he'd say: 'You say you're 13?' 'Yes, I'm only 13. I won't be 13 till . . .' she was trying to tell him when she was going to be 13. And he said: 'Oh all right'. So, as the night went on, he just said: 'Well, you'll just have to sleep there. We'll tell them a story in the morning'. And she was terrified. She said she was terrified all night.

And then next morning he said: 'Just don't say nothing when you go back up there. You just don't say nothing'. When I think back, at least he did care enough not to touch her. But that's the kind of thing that did happen. You'd see a lot of those women . . . we used to see them at Toomelah . . . every time they'd come back they'd have a baby . . . a white baby, it was terrible, eh? One poor woman, they used to send her back to the same place all the time.

As Isabel moved between a series of jobs and her home in Collarenebri, she sustained close and enduring relationships with the young people she had grown up with, particularly with Ted Thorne. Work and circumstances separated them, however, and Isabel was involved for some time with a young man from just over the Queensland border. She became pregnant to him when she was 20. Her son Ben was born in 1949, into a supportive extended family in which his grandfather Mick played a strong role as carer and mentor.

Isabel's supported position within her family and the wider Murri community was very different from her sense of isolation from the surrounding white population. In her late adolescence and early adulthood, Isabel became increasingly aware of the hostility directed both at herself as an Aboriginal woman and single mother and at her community. Her father became more open about his frustrations with the town and Isabel began to experience personally the persistent, demoralising stings of everyday racism.

Dad was very careful about the fact that he was going to tell us about the war in his own time. And we grew up thinking what a great thing it was that he was a returned serviceman. Most Aboriginal people did think that way. But I remember I was about 18 when he finally said, 'Oh I think we'll talk about that now. It wasn't a great thing that I went to the war. When we look at our situation today, you say what rights did I have, really, to go to the war. It's not really my country. Politicians were the ones that should have been the ones fighting those wars'. And then he said 'War is all about people killing each other. I can tell you, it's not . . . it's not a good feeling to know that you can just move and be stone dead, you know. Or you could be wounded and . . .' You know, he's witnessed people lying and dying at his feet. But it was at that age we were told, we weren't told when we were younger. Then we started to think more about the fact that he was a returned serviceman.

He was a good worker, and he was never a man to half-do a job. And so Dad was never short of work and he was respected in that area. But I think he was looked upon as a bit of a militant, because he asked a lot of questions and in that time, you didn't need to ask too many questions before you'd be branded as someone with a militant attitude. I started to get the feeling that white people just thought he was one of those 'know-all niggers'. And I started to become aware of some of the things he'd been saying. When I was 18, I started to become quite conscious of what was happening around us. And I think it was through some of the things he'd point out to me.

I remember when the first RSL club was built in Collarenebri in 1947. Dad was very keen to become a member. I think he thought, 'Once I become a member, I'll be able to have my say and be involved more, and . . .' And then one of the officials of the club said to him, 'Look, we don't want to sound as if we don't, you know, go for you blacks, but we can't serve you in the bar. It'd be best if we passed it out the window to you'.

And Dad said, 'Well you know what you can do with your club. And your membership. 'Cause I won't pay to be treated like that'. He tried to get his money back, and there was a few that tried to convince him that that was only for a little while, until people got used to Aboriginal people being around the club. He thought they were thinking to themselves, 'Well, we'll see how you blokes go on, before we can let you come inside the club'.

At times we felt embarrassed by some of the things Dad'd say. You know, 'Oh they don't treat me like a bloody nigger *al*together', or something like this, and we'd say, 'Oh dear, here he goes again'. But it was all in the process of learning. I gained a lot by those kind of remarks that Dad used to come out with. He'd say, 'You take a look at how they treat us Aboriginals then. They'll go around to your door and make sure you're down there for the march, and make a big thing out of it. But the next day, you know, those same people wouldn't even bid you the time of day'.

We had a different understanding of him after that, about why he was always so close to us kids. And he'd always say, 'If anyone tried to take my kids away, I'd rather die fighting for them, fighting to keep my kids, than just letting them go'. But even then we didn't have a real understanding of what he was talking about, until later in life, when we started to learn how they were just looking for any excuse to pick up these kids and take them away, just to groom them up and send them back into servant duties.

I was really finding it harder to ignore the rudeness we used to meet in the street. We were going to a Slim Dusty show once when I was about 16 and everybody turned up for that. And I had to walk down this row of people who were already sitting, my seat was right at the end of the row so I had to walk all the way down there. I was with two other Aboriginal girls in front of me. I noticed the same thing was happening to the other girls as to me—this group of white people were holding their nose as we were walking past. I didn't want to be thinking that was happening. I thought 'Well, we can't do anything about it'. I just don't know how I was feeling about that at the time, but I was feeling pretty bad. I went back and I stood in front of those people and just looked at them and then I walked on again.

When I go home now I talk to those people and I never think of it. Very seldom that comes into my mind. But at the time I felt really hurt about it. I never even mentioned it to the other girls who walked in front of me. I don't know why I didn't, but I was always careful not to start any blues and I knew that that kind of stuff could start it. I don't know, maybe I was destined to do it that way, as I find out now.

I remember, one day I went into the post office, I was probably in my twenties then, and there were five or six other people who'd just been served and they were standing around talking, and I walked in just before the doctor did, and the woman behind the counter said: 'Oh doctor, yes, what can I do for you?' And he said: 'Oh no. I've got plenty of time. Isabel was here before me . . . ' 'Oh yes, Isabel . . .' and she came back to me then. But that was the only time I ever heard someone do something about it.

That's the same thing that happened when we were in segregation in the hospital—you heard people whispering about us, the nurses and the sisters whispering about us. Saying it wasn't good to have babies without being legally married and all that. Even if they were talking about one of the other blacks it still hurt you. And you thought: they talk about all of us in the same way. I suffered a lot of snide remarks from the sisters and nurses going through those things. I can still say, you know, 'Hello . . . '; they still talk to me now and I can feel no hurt. But at the time it used to hurt like hell, you know? As I got in control of it all, I started to think: 'I don't care what you think. That's the way we are'.

So many things like that happened in the hospital and in the streets, we always got together and we stood around together because nobody else wanted to talk to us. So we had our own little thing all the time.

We got to call that Johnson's Corner in Walgett, 'Crows' Corner' for that sort of reason. I suppose everywhere we went we had a special place where everybody had to meet. We didn't go down to Walgett very much, but I remember when people came over to Colle they'd say: 'We were only standing at Crows' Corner and such-and-such happened today'. And we'd say: 'Where's Crows' Corner?' 'Oh, that's where all us Murris meet. That's why they call it Crows' Corner.' Of course, when I went to Walgett then I could see that it *was* Crows' Corner. People didn't feel so welcome in the rest of the town. So that'd be as far as they'd go, or as far as they'd want to go.

A lot of people are very hurt about things and they will never talk to those people again. Or they'll continually whinge about it. But today when I go home to Colle I see those same white people and they're so different. They've changed over the years. It's funny that. And I thought: 'They had the problem. I didn't really'. And that's why I keep saying all those things have made me a stronger person, because without feeling really hurt about that now, I can think: 'Oh well, it happened and that's that'.

There were white people who cared about the situation and the racism towards us, but they couldn't do anything about it. I suppose in communities like that it's best to not rock the boat. And that was one of the issues that could've put a lot of people offside. But any time we went to the Stallworthys, they always made us very welcome, we had to come inside and have a cup of tea. They had a truck and they used to do the mail run and the milk run and some of their boys worked in the shops. They sold the milk and we'd go down and get our milk off them. But it didn't matter what we went in there for. We couldn't go around the back and come in—the old couple would say: 'No, no, you don't come in the back door at my place, you walk in the front door. I don't give a bugger about anybody'. That's how they were to us. When I look back, I think they were really fair dinkum people then and they've always remained that way. They did know that they could cop the backlash, but I don't think it ever mattered to that family. They didn't really care about it.

We used to say: 'We don't like going down for the milk, Dad, because you've got to go in, you've got to sit down, you've got to talk to Mrs Stallworthy and sometimes Mr Stallworthy is there'. 'Well, they're nice people', Dad would say, 'they're nice people. You don't want to be ashamed of that. If they're nice to you, you be nice to them'. And that's what used to happen—we'd have to go in and have a cup of tea and they'd ask us how we were, and if we wanted to talk to them we could. They let us know that we were very welcome in their home. And that was the only place in town that I could say we felt like that. Later on, I found out there were other people who cared like that but they couldn't come out openly and do anything about it, to me that balances it—even though it was a hard time.

One of the things I remember happened round about when the war was just finished. I was coming back from Tamworth and we had to change trains at Werris Creek. We had about two hours we had to wait. So I went across to the railway café and sat down. I was sitting down there when these young white fellas walked in, about four or five of them, some girls and a couple of boys, and they said: 'Oh, do you mind if we sit with you?' I said: 'No, no, I don't mind' . . . but you know, this was unheard of. And then I'm thinking to myself: 'Oh they'll probably watch me eating and all this'; I'm getting worried about things like that. And then this girl came and she's taking the order. And she said: 'Oh, look, I'm sorry . . . ', when she come to me, 'I'm sorry but we don't serve you people'.

And I just had this sick feeling! And one fella said: 'I beg your pardon', he said, 'did I hear you right? You said you're not going to serve this girl?' She said: 'That's right, look I don't want any trouble'. So she goes in and she brings the manager out. So the manager said: 'Listen, if we don't serve those people that's our business. And we *don't* serve those people'.

I got up then and I walked out. And why I stood at the door and listened, I'll never know. These white people said: 'Oh, we just wanted to know'. And the manager said: 'Well that's the end of that'. So, they decided they're going to order up and they must have got their heads together and they ordered everything. I could see them: two pots of this and two pots of that. Then when they got the food then they're still sitting there talking. And why I'm there at the door, I'll never know. Then they said to the waitress: 'Oh, excuse me, can we see you a minute?' She come across: 'Yes what's wrong?'

This bloke said, 'We just decided, seeing that you can't serve our friend out there, you can't serve us. We don't like this stuff, it's not good enough'. She said: 'What!' He said: 'It's just not good enough'. And I'm thinking: 'Oh my God, I'm getting away from here'. The next minute the manager comes out. And he's saying: 'You'll bloody well pay for it all, you'll pay for it all right. And if we don't want to serve those niggers, we don't have to serve 'em!' And he's going on . . .

Well, I took off. Over the railway then. I'm thinking: 'Oh my God, Dad's going to say, "What you messing round with them white fellas for? What're you getting mixed up with that lot for?"' So I'm not worried about anything else, but what Dad's going to say! And I'm thinking, 'Oh God, Dad's going to be real cranky. Mum's going to probably belt me . . . '—because she did all the belting see.

Anyhow, these blokes must have went up to the shop, then the girls come along. They said: 'Hey, mate'. They're singing out to me. I'm thinking: 'Let me get right away from this, I wish the train would come'. Still I could hear these fellas saying: 'Oh she's here somewhere. Her port is still there, yeah, she's still here somewhere'. So, they found me . . . 'Oh, there you are, mate! Oh, we're gonna feed ya, the boys gone to get some stuff'. And I said:

'Oh no, no I'm not hungry anyhow'. Then the boys come back with this big load, them big tank loaves of bread and butter and saveloys and camp pie. And anyway they're saying: 'Hey, come on love', they say. And they were real happy. All I'm thinking is: 'Oh no, I can't get mixed up with these white fellas'. I was afraid the coppers were coming directly because they had a big row. I didn't want to be in this.

And these fellas are saying: 'Come on mate, come on. Now, look, Jesus broke the bread and it was still good bread. So, come on, you can break your own bread if you want to . . . come on'. And I said: 'No, I'm not hungry really . . .' 'Oh, come on you, yeah, come on we all hungry'. And he said: 'We can't help it if they don't like us over there. We like ourselves better over here'. And I said: 'Yes, but I'm not hungry' . . . He said: 'Look here . . . ', I looked, saveloys and everything, you know. And I said: 'Oh, I'll just have a little bit then' and I just had a little bit to shut them up. 'That's better', they said.

Anyway, then I could hear the train come. Oh God, I'm looking around the corner . . . and I'm saying: 'Oh, I'm sure the police will come any minute'. And they said: 'Look, if the police come, you don't worry about it. You let us worry about that' . . . But I'm still thinking what my Dad will say: 'Yes, well, you got mixed up with those young people, see you can't trust people like that'. Going through all that.

Anyway, when the train come, then these blokes wrapped all this food up together and they said: 'Here mate, you take that now, you take that lot and we taking this lot'. And I said: 'Well I'll take it, but I'm not real hungry'. And when I got on the train, wasn't I pleased to part with them!

And I was thinking: 'Oh well, Dad'll never know now'. And anyway after I got down there . . . I realised they must have given me most of the tucker. I was sitting back and I was thinking: 'Oh, I'm going to have a good feed now, anyhow'. But that was one of the worst things I ever had happen to me. Thinking about that incident, I realised many years later, that I was ashamed to mention it to anyone. I don't know why, but it was something that I kept to myself, and it was only local! But I thought all the same there were some nice people in the society when all this was happening, because those young people really went out of their way and made an issue out of it, and went about our business.

On Collymongle pastoral station, 20 kilometres outside of Colle on the Moree road, there was a unique and highly significant stand of 82 elaborately carved living trees surrounding a Gamilaraay ceremonial ground. Isabel had never been there because she understood it to be a site associated with men's initiation rituals and so it was not a place to which women could go freely. During the mid-1940s, some remote authority must have decided that these trees should be cut down and removed to museums. Most were transported to the Museum of South Australia, where they were accessioned in 1949, while some others were sent to the Museum of Queensland and the Australian Museum in Sydney. Twelve remained standing on Collymongle, but soon after all but one of these were also cut down and removed to be garden ornaments in the lawn at the homestead. There they were watered constantly with the lawn and gradually developed moss and mould. When Mick Flick first heard that the trees were going to be cut down and taken away, he tried to challenge their removal.

We heard that they was going to interfere with the trees out on Collymongle. Dad had often pointed to the area where they were and said 'That's one of our biggest ceremonial grounds. That belongs to all us Murris out here'. And he said the story was that they used to come from all around, to hold their ceremonies there. Oh, that was a general knowledge, that we owned them. Regardless of who's property they were on, they were ours. It's just as if, when the land settlement was taking place, white people who then claimed that land as theirs still allowed those ceremonies to continue. I think it's reasonable to say that, that they allowed those ceremonies to continue there, and that meant people could still know and respect that area. I think that happened, right up until the time they took them away. And I don't know what the real reason was, that they had to be removed.

Dad was so upset and concerned, he tried to get some of the Aboriginal men to go with him. But they still feared the backlash from lease holders and white farmers at that time. Dad came home and was getting ready to go out to Collymongle himself. We said: 'So where are you going?' And he said: 'Well I just went around trying to get the mob to come with me out here, but they don't seem to want to be in it. So I'm going out. I'm going out to watch them. They're cutting it down and taking it away, and it belongs to us, it's our stuff'.

And we thought: 'Oh gee, we wonder what Dad's going to do out there?' And so we were a bit concerned. But somehow too, we didn't say: 'Can we go with you?' He would've taken us if we'd said that. But he witnessed that. And when he came back in, he was very sad about it, and he was saying: 'Well, it just shows you. The people just don't care enough'. And I think he meant everybody didn't care enough about it. But even though the people didn't talk about it a lot, it did mean a lot to people. I think people didn't talk about it because they lacked the confidence to come out openly and say that. Dad didn't talk to us much for a couple of days. I don't think he went around the old fellas at the camp anymore for a couple of weeks. And so it took him a while to get back to accepting it.

I never ever went to that spot. That was a men's area. But I've encouraged other young people to go there, and mainly men. I found that after that there was a lot of students went—male and female. I guess it's all so important that that had to happen. Because it was more and more important for me. When they took the last 11 trees from there, and they put them in the Collymongle homestead garden just as ornaments, after the fact that Dad was so concerned about the cutting down of those trees in the first place, it stuck in my mind.

4
Building Pressures, 1950s

By 1950, Isabel's focus had shifted from a teenager's concerns to her adult role as a mother and worker. She felt secure within a strong family network. Working mostly on pastoral stations, Isabel preferred to work with her family, in the shearing contracts her father organised. Her son Ben was taken under his grandfather's wing, and spent his first years following his grandfather around at Longswamp and other workplaces.

The Flick family had expanded: Lindsay married Rosie Weatherall, who had been the bough shade teacher, and Joe married Isobelle Walford. Both were from Angledool families displaced in the 1936 move. The Weatherall family had moved to Collarenebri immediately, but the Walfords had spent some time in Brewarrina before coming to settle in Collarenebri. So the extended family network within which Isabel lived was sustained by a number of active senior men and women, not only Mick himself but Nanna Sylvia, Isobelle Walford's mother. These older people each took a role in caring for the younger family as well as the very elderly like Granny Ada Woods, Nanna Sylvia's mother.

Rosie and Lindsay's first two sons Mick and Lindsay had been born before Ben, then Joe and Isobelle's first child Johnny was born not long after in Collarenebri in 1950. This group of boy cousins and age mates grew up together between Longswamp and the Block, closely attached to Mick and to each other. Joe and Isobelle's daughter Barbara was born in 1951, soon after Mick and Celia's youngest child, Lavinia [Lubby], and they grew up together as very close friends, as did the succeeding sets of cousins. Barbara's birth took place in Goondawindi, because Joe and Isobelle, like Isabel herself, were travelling in that area 'looking for shed work'.

Isabel Flick

Isabel's experiences in the sheds were her introduction to unionism, as she saw the strength of collective action as well as the bitterness of internal union conflicts.

The family centred around Dad really. I think the kids got a good mateship going with Dad, none of the kids wanted to go with Mum when she'd take off. The youngest sister, Lubby—she was the boss in the house when he wasn't there. And then she'd tell him what the boys were doing. Like our brother Jimmy and the grandkids, Micky and Ben, Johnny, they all lived with Dad. And the mother and father had no control over that as they come to that age, you know. The first seven years of Ben's life . . . he went out with Dad when he was three, I think, on the fence. And oh, it's real hard . . . no trees around, just the plains. And it was hot. And I'd say to Dad: 'He shouldn't be out there'. 'Oh, he loves it out there', he'd say, 'he loves it out there'.

The other couple of kids used to go out too, Mick and John, and then in the end we had a job to get the kids to go to school. When they'd come in they'd be talking like men, you know, talking about different bosses that come down. And you'd swear that they were negotiating with the bosses and everything.

I think Ben was seven when I first got him into school, because he used to cry and play up to go with Dad. But Joe . . . Joe was a bit firmer, see, he'd say to Dad: 'No, no, you can't do that. They're my kids too'. And so we made Johnny stay in town. And Johnny used to be really ticked-off about having to stay in town. He had a good relationship with all of us really, but he just wanted to be with Dad.

Dad did a few different types of work then, mainly at Longswamp. But whatever he did he was a union man, he wouldn't miss getting his ticket and all that. The shearers were the strongest part of the union then, they used to force the AWU. I remember those strikes where, you know, one lot of people couldn't ride in one taxi or another or in the same one! Otherwise they'd be fighting in the street—I've seen that happen. In Colle and in St George. We were up in St George at the time . . . we all went up there looking for a bit of shed work and then, you know, there'd be a big blue break out there, over who had the jobs and who didn't have the jobs, over who was scabs and who wasn't scabs. So we'd move on again. And so we went around to Bungunyah and that's how Barbara was born at Goondiwindi early in 1951.

We kept moving around trying to get shed work—which is what they wanted—but everywhere we'd go there'd be a big blue over who was doing the right thing, who was doing the wrong thing. There was some really bad blues in Colle. And Dad used to say to me: 'This is terrible. You've got the black fellas even fighting one another'.[1]

And shearers were the fussiest workers I ever saw. I cooked for them and if you were a bit late with the smoko, that was a major drama. You didn't have to be half an hour late, just 10 minutes, because they've got to be back on the board. And they'd let people know that they weren't happy with it. And the same thing with all the black fellas too, they'd say: 'God, this bread is shit!' And any little thing at all, and some of the other shearers would say: 'Oh, go on! When you go home you're eating Johnny cakes, and rice!' But I think that was just the working pattern, you know, of the shearers. To complain about the cook or anything! And if the boss was late coming down to kick the engines off or something like that, that was another major drama. They'd kick up a big fuss about it. They'd be walking around as if they're going to tear the place down. And of course there was a feeling that the union could come in. So everybody had to be on guard about those things. The first thing the shearers would do when they go to the shed was, they'd go through and see if their shower was working or the taps was working. And they'd examine everything, see the mattresses was right . . . you know? They wouldn't have a mattress with a tear in it, they'd turn it over and find out. But nowadays, there's very little camp-out sheds, they're all suburban sheds.

One of the things we worked out after a while was this. There was a body of shearers organised by this contractor called Grazcotts, and they used to go all over the country. And one day Dad was sitting down and he said: 'You know, when people rang up and wanted to find out if they had any jobs going, they could have had a couple of sheds just around that town. But the contractor's tactic was, rather than do that, they'd send them to Tasmania or down to Victoria or up to Queensland. And that way, they'd get them as far away from home as possible, so they wouldn't just do a couple of days work and walk off. And then they'd bring another lot of shearers in; Grazcotts would bring another lot of shearers to the area from where they'd just sent this mob to in Tasmania.

So that was one of the things Dad used to be always whingeing about. But they kept working pretty well mainly in the sheds. And that was the way they had to do it 'cause Grazcotts was in charge of it. Sometimes they'd get a job from up in Charleville and they'd be up there, they'd say: 'Well it's way up in the scrub'. So they'd be up there for about six weeks or something like that, depending. And there might've been a shed just out from home, and those shearers would come from Victoria with Grazcotts. So that was Grazcotts' tactics. And I couldn't understand it for a long time, and Dad used to be always whingeing about it. But he was still packing his swag to go, you know. And the brothers was the same.

I started to cook for the shearers when Dad started to get some contract sheds, and then all of us mob had jobs. He'd get the contract for the sheds, so he provided the shearers and the rouseabouts and the cooks. And he'd make sure they'd be nearly all blacks. The only time he'd pick up a white fella was when he couldn't get a black fella. He had a good run there, and then he started getting sick, and he didn't have anybody to take over. He had about seven sheds for seven years, you know, guaranteed for five years.

Most of the rouseabouts was Colle and Walgett Murris. Because he used to always say the Moree mob get enough work up that way. So he'd go around and sit around the gambling schools and things like that. And pick up somebody who might be drunk, and he'd say: 'Come over and sober up'. And take them out and sober them up and get them going. He had a lot of patience like that, you know.

There's not much work like that going now, only very odd sheds that might give them a week's work and all that work is done by some of the New Zealanders that come over and the family friends. Family and friends, they do most of the shearing. And you would never have got a shearer to go out on a Saturday or a Sunday like they do now, that'd be just a no-no.

Even when working on local sheep properties, Isabel and her wider family spent much of their time in Collarenebri, living on the Block but with close relations and friends living just along the river at the Old Camp. Conditions there were much the same as those Isabel remembered from the 1930s. There was no water or washing facilities other than the river, and carrying water for drinking, cooking and washing was an arduous slog up the steep bank each day to the camps. Each family dug their own pit toilets and made their own cooking and washing arrangements with extensions to the tin houses they built scattered around the Old Camp area. Facilities and services on the Block were little different from those of the camp. The young families there had built their own houses from flattened tins, scattered around the Block but oriented towards Mick's house. These houses were built with big family kitchen areas with a fireplace and then one or two smaller bedrooms on the side. Despite being only a couple of hundred metres down the road from the hospital, the Block had no access to town services like piped water or sewage connection and was clearly regarded by the local government authorities as outside the town boundaries. Doreen Weatherall Hynch recalled the pleasures, but also the difficulties of living on the Old Camp in the 1950s:

Doreen: It was a lovely, lovely place to camp here, 'cause the kids had got plenty to do here being close to the water. I grew up our kids here. I stayed with Nanna Pearlie Mason over in her camp after I got married in the 1950s. I used to be able to walk across the river too at the bend near the Old Camp. It wasn't so deep then. And that's where we used to carry the water from. Two four-gallons [tins] on a yoke. We'd take three or four buckets down and take two at a time up the hill, full, on this yoke thing.

Then we'd have a little tin with a wire over the top and a hook always hanging beside the water bucket or water bag at the camp. It was for people to just take out what they wanted to drink and put it into their cup. I'd have to carry those buckets up from the river and I'd watch 'em getting water out with that little tin: they'd always take just two sips and throw the rest away! We used to have to carry the water up a few times each day. It all depends on the size of your washing! [laughs] We'd mainly wash down here at the river. But just imagine in the summertime with drinking and cooking and washing . . . Sometimes we'd have to boil it up first for drinking, but other times we'd just drink it.

We'd always be worried about sores on the kids' skin and in their heads then. Nanna Pearlie had a good old way to fix them, because she knew a lot about that sort of thing. And she used to get us to wash the kids heads five times a day with water boiled up with leaves from the Eurah bush. Of course that was *another* bucket of water from the river!

Friday was wood day, and we'd walk for miles looking for wood and not think anything of it. Because Friday was the day all the fathers'd be home from work out on the stations, and all the kids would be going to the pictures. So we needed the wood to heat the water for baths and Friday was ironing day too. We had to get the wood to burn the fires to heat up those old flat irons! Hardly anybody had kerosine irons on the camp in those days, so we'd heat all the flat irons up on the fires.

Weekends were busy social times on the Old Camp, with people in from working on the stations, seeing family and friends, and spending some of the cash from their week's work. Gambling was an important opportunity to do many different things, like socialising, catching up on news and gossip and even talking over community issues, as well as taking part in the excitement of the winning and losing. Isabel enjoyed gambling, and she was often at the bingo schools and dice games. She remembered the atmosphere of the big schools on the Old Camp:

Once Angledool people moved to Colle, a lot of people used to come and go, to have big gambling games and dice games. And they used to have great times, you know. I've seen blokes play for big money . . . and just lost everything they had. Come in from out in the bush working, then stony broke that afternoon . . . But the good thing was that they'd always go round, make sure all the kids had lollies and everything. And everybody had money. If they knew someone was down the end there and they had no money, they made sure they'd go and give them something.

As I got older and I started going round the gambling schools myself, I saw one bloke who lost everything this day, he lost everything. One minute

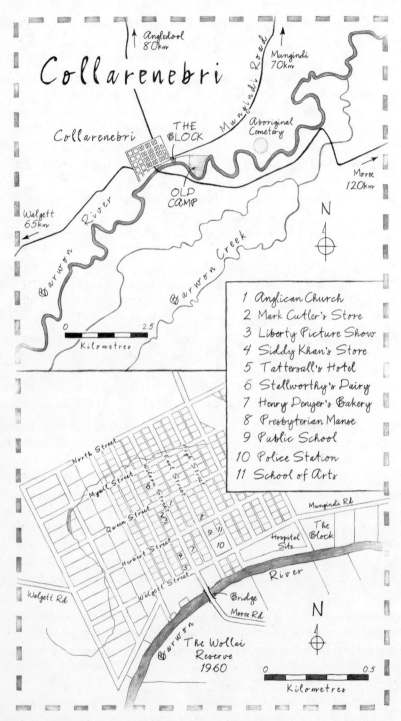

Map of Collarenebri and close-up of town streets.

he's sitting there with all these nice clothes on and, you know, really rigged out, and then, after a while, I go back there and he's sitting there with somebody else's old clothes on. And the other fella's got it all packed up. And then someone gives him money or something, he's done all that money, sold out and done all that money. He walks away laughing. And everybody was laughing at him too, you know.

The next day he'd be back there again, having another go. If someone did that today, he'd want to be swearing and fighting and everything. But then everybody'd be taking care about him, but they're not going to worry about him that much, you know. He did it. But they'd always make sure that they were giving him a fair go. You know, if somebody got a bit of a win up, they'd throw him some money, and next week he may be on top, he's a winner. There was a lot of that. There were very few women would be in the big gambling games, it would be the men, I suppose they had the money because they were working . . . But see, they weren't people that forgot about their families either. They went around and fixed up all our little debts and their family things and they went round and see their mobs, see if they all had money, and then they'd all get together and put it together I suppose you'd say. And if someone . . . everybody's going to the pictures, everybody's making sure nobody's going to miss out because of this.

Despite the pace of life within the community, the overwhelming issue for all Murris living in the town was the intrusive and frightening presence of the police. This theme overshadows everyone's recollections of life in the town in the 1950s.

I feared the police—everyone feared them because you wouldn't know when they were going to do the rounds and they could just walk in your house, it didn't matter where you were. Yes, they'd just walk in and shine the torch around if there was someone there that they thought was drunk. They only had to think he was drunk and they'd pick him up. In our little camp they could just walk in and it didn't matter whether you were getting dressed or in the bath or what. You know, we used to have old round bathtubs. Well, they never asked to come in. They never *did* ask, 'Could we come in?' They just walked in and looked around and screwed their noses up.

Dad warned us about the fact that they don't own us, so we always have to be careful, we always have to watch a policeman, because he had always this idea that the only good policeman was a dead one. [laughs] Because he'd apparently had some brushes with them! But we were just afraid because we'd see everybody being herded into little jeeps.

I saw 16 men thrown into the back of a jeep once, and there was legs hanging out everywhere, and they came along and asked us where some bloke was. And then the Murris were saying: 'But why do you want to get this other fella for? You can't put him in there . . . look, there's no room'. But all these blokes were taken and locked up, and you know, everybody would feel so disillusioned and frightened.

I think it was just a general fear, as soon as you'd see the jeep coming, everybody would be sitting around so proper. If there was a drunk at someone's place even though he wasn't doing any harm, he might've been just so happy, they'd try to get rid of him so that they wouldn't get involved with the police action. They knew it was coming up and the police could quite easily say, 'What have you got so and so hanging around your place for? It might be their uncle or nephew or whatever—it might be even their own son. I remember that very clearly.

I suppose I was about 17, one day at the Old Camp we were all playing around and the cops drove straight up to where we were. They must've known every one of us. Because they said: 'Where's this Stanley Murray?' And somebody said: 'Oh he's gone fishing'. 'So where's he gone fishing?' Someone said: 'He's just gone fishing . . .' and I said: 'I don't know. He mightn't be gone fishing'. And the way he looked at me that cop, he said: 'You *wouldn't* know, would ya?' I'll never forget that. And I thought, 'But I really *didn't* know'.

We watched those police then go from one end of that river to the other until they came back—and that was late in the afternoon—they came back with that young fella, and he was only fishing. They took him down to his mother, and then they took him to the cells. And not long after someone said: 'Oh, here he comes'. They couldn't have kept him in. So we wondered what they wanted him for. But no one ever knew what happened—whether they questioned him about anything or what.

But that's how it was. If someone wasn't there in the first round-up . . . When the police'd do their patrol in the morning, in every camp they'd know who was there and they'd say: 'So where's so and so?' 'Oh he's gone out to the rubbish tip.' 'Oh, he'll be here when I get back.' So if he wasn't there the next time, well then they'd say: 'He can't be still out there all day'. So they would take a drive out . . . just to make sure we were all together . . . that we were all mustered, I suppose that's the way to put it.

Up on the Old Camp up here, you had the police patrol coming around anything up to three to four times a day. They're probably coming around in the morning about nine o'clock, sometimes earlier than that. You'd never know exactly what time. You wouldn't get used to the time, because they'd do like swoop raids. And then they'd go around and if 'uncle so and so' wasn't there at that camp where he was supposed to be—I remember that—they used to say: 'Well, where's so and so? Did he get a job?' . . . 'No, he's not working' . . . 'So, where is he? He'd better be back here by the time I come around the next time!'

And you were sure that the bloke would be back there the next time the coppers'd come around . . . Someone would go—even if he went fishing—somebody would go and tell him the coppers were looking for him. And so when you think of it, we were under surveillance the full 24 hours, really.

They'd come around mainly on a Monday, and this is when they'd check up to see who went out to work. Then on the Friday they'd be coming around later in the afternoons, to see who came in from work. I remember once he came to our camp and he said: 'Oh, isn't your old man coming in this week?' Because Mum would always say: 'I don't know', you know, that was her main answer to everything! And then he'd say: 'Oh, you don't know much do you?' . . . and she says: 'Well, I don't know when he's coming in'. And so, you know, we felt like they watched every move that we made . . . When you look back it was a terrible rule. We are lucky people to come through it.

I suppose being roped off in the picture theatre was one thing, but the police intimidation was the worst thing—just being hounded by the cops. One of the things I wanted to talk about in this book was . . . confrontation. It's funny how our life began with that confrontation—watching it, you know, watching how the cops could just walk in through the door and push the door back. And if you stood outside and opened the door, you could see everything inside just as well anyway, because most of the time it was so open inside the door. But those cops had to push right in!

We grew up to see how our people reacted to that kind of questioning about where someone was and . . . 'When are you going to work?' 'Where are you working?' 'If you're not working, why not?' 'What are you doing about getting a job?' and all that kind of questioning. And we were seeing how everybody was very careful about what they were saying. As kids we'd learnt to be cautious when we saw the cops coming. Our parents'd say: 'Now you kids get right out of the way, so they can't see you kids'. So we learnt that pretty early.

And then the feeling of confrontation. I think when I first spoke to a policeman I was just so trembly. I don't know what the incident was, but I remember how it felt. I was so sick after just being questioned by the police about where so and so was and did I know where so and so was. Because they might've just gone to our place and asked Mum and Dad and then they'd see us and come across and ask us the same questions and I suppose they'd compare the answers after. But that kind of conditioned us as we grew up.

Oh, there was always a dreadful fear about the police, and that feeling went on right up until the late fifties when people started to think, well, you know, 'they don't own us!' And they started to stand up more and of course there was more court cases and everybody was guilty, of course! You know, they were *always* found guilty until the Aboriginal Legal Services came. But they started to stand up before that, and when they stood up or run away from the police, then they were certainly brought in and charged with things like resisting arrest and things like that. But they were 'guilty', definitely 'guilty' before they went in.

During 1952, Isabel began a long relationship with Aubrey Weatherall, the brother of Rosie and Doreen Weatherall. Isabel remained close friends with her sisters-in-law all through her life. Isabel and Aub's first child, Larry, was born in 1954. Aub had been married previously to Shirley Weatherall, from the Cunningham family, and in a small town this generated tension. Isabel developed good relationships with Aub's children, Bob, Dennis and Roma, from his first marriage, but her relationship with Aub's first wife was to remain tense and distant for the rest of their lives. This deeply complicated Isabel's work in Collarenebri in later years.

As her own family grew, Isabel's experiences increasingly focused down onto Collarenebri and to surviving as a mother. She became particularly concerned to get access to basic services for her children. In her memories of this period, the hospital and the town's medical system loom as the sites of major conflict. The hospital operated a separate and distant ward specifically for Aboriginal patients. Despite equipment being labelled with the medical term 'segregation', the Hospital Board always referred to this separate ward as the 'Aboriginal ward' and this was how Murris and everyone else in the town understood its purpose. This 'ward' was in fact a small weatherboard shed at the bottom of the hospital yard, across from the kitchen building, with room for a few crowded beds. There was a pathway joining this shed with the main hospital building. Babies born in the Aboriginal ward would then be taken to the main hospital nursery, and brought to their mothers, across the open garden path, at each feeding time, then returned to the nursery. Worried about rising costs in 1939, the Hospital Board discussed closing the separate ward and moving all Aboriginal patients to the hospital verandahs. After lengthy consideration, the Board rejected this proposal, deciding that 'The Aborigines Ward' should remain open and that under no circumstances were Aboriginal patients to be transferred to the main building, not even to the verandahs, despite the resulting financial cost of keeping extra staff.[2]

We had to fight for everything—school, hospital treatment. I remember we used to have to line up there at Outpatients at the hospital and pay the dollar before we saw the doctor, you know? I had a very sick kid one time. And this secretary at the hospital he wanted a payment before I could see the doctor and I didn't have it, whatever it was. And poor Shirley Mason, she used to have to fight him every time she went there, because she owed him . . . it might be for five visits already. And she'd say, 'If ever you shout at me again I'll smash you!' There were times when you thought you'd like to blow their head up, you know . . . But that hospital secretary was one of the real hard ones that we had to deal with.

Different ones on duty would make it hard to see the doctor even if you had paid your dollar. At one stage there I thought if I sat there in the front at Outpatients and waited, I'd be attended to. But I could sit there for hours and they would just walk back and forwards. I went through a stage of that. I waited and waited and the doctor came and did his rounds and went. So there was no point in me sitting around there anymore, so I thought I better go down to the surgery and I said: 'I want you to treat me here. If you can't I'll have to go somewhere else'. I told him what had happened and I said: 'You don't think this is happening, you're so doubtful of what I'm saying. But that is what's happening and that is the issue'. I told him I wanted all my records to be brought down to his surgery office, otherwise I couldn't have medical attention in the town at all. And that was a pretty hard time too.

All the sheets and cutlery and crockery was separate, and I had it pictured in my mind that it all had 'Abo Ward' written on it. But Rosie reminded me that what they called it was 'Segregation'. They had 'SEG' on everything. Even over the door of the ward was painted 'SEG'. And the cutlery was all stamped: Men's, Women's, Private and SEG. Everything was separate.

My sister-in-law, Rosie, was the laundress at the hospital when Mrs Denison was killed at the Camp in 1952 after her husband went mad and cut her up with an axe. They called for Rosie to go down to the hospital and the ambulance men were looking for something to wrap the body in, and they're calling for 'SEG sheets'. She told me she didn't know what they wanted for a minute. Then all of a sudden it dawned on her: they wanted the segregation sheets from the ward. Poor Lizzie Denison was dead, but they still wouldn't give her the ordinary sheets. And then they couldn't find the 'SEG' ones because they even had them stacked in a different cupboard.

There have been many occasions in Australia, and in the immediate surroundings of Collarenebri, when racial tensions were expressed in terms of fears of disease. White people would accuse Aboriginal people of suffering and somehow deliberately passing on some infection or another. Whenever serious investigation has been carried out in such cases, as it sometimes was in conflicts about school attendance, it has usually found little evidence to show contagion to the white population has occurred. More often the opposite is the case: indigenous populations have often been gravely at risk of contracting diseases brought by settlers. This has been common when government policies have enforced overcrowding in poor sanitary conditions, so that in the 1930s the reports of Education Department doctors showed that the 'missions' like Brewarrina and Angledool were far less healthy places for Aborigines to live than were the 'fringe camps' and stock route camps on the edges of towns.

The confused accusation that Aborigines were carrying and somehow maliciously transmitting infections had been a common feature of debates about Aboriginal policy in the areas around Collarenebri during the 1930s. They had been particularly demonstrated in all the debates about whether Aboriginal children should have access to the public schools of the area. The trachoma epidemics which swept Angledool mission in 1934 and Toomelah mission in 1936, and which were still being treated with bluestone when Isabel was there in 1938, were widely rumoured among the white population of the region to be sexually transmitted. This was not true, but the misapprehension was spread by local police and other officials as they relayed various white community objections to school access or to the wholesale transportation of even more Aboriginal families into the missions. The remedies proposed by local white groups invariably involved tight restrictions on Aboriginal people's movements and their exclusion from the main streets and public facilities of the townships.

The Aborigines Protection Board took advantage of this widespread public attitude to gain parliamentary approval for new restrictive legislation in 1936, lasting until 1969, which severely controlled Aboriginal people's movement in New South Wales and directed the police to enforce even closer monitoring and surveillance over any Aboriginal residence, on private land as well as on Aboriginal reserve lands. Repeated accusations about contagious disease and 'negligent' lack of hygiene were a central part of the white parents' campaigns against Aboriginal children's attendance at the Collarenebri public school in 1938, 1941 and 1947.

Fears about infectious disease were particularly common in 1956 because it was a year of severe and persistent flooding, with floods passing over the Collarenebri area in February, May and June. This increased problems with mosquito and waterborne diseases and meant that septic and pit sewage disposal was not working properly as all the surrounding blacksoil ground was waterlogged.

It was in this context that the Collarenebri township heard the news in 1956 that one of the small children in the Flick family homes on the Block had developed an unusual infection. The new doctor in town was Frank McGarn, an ex-serviceman who had graduated in medicine after his return from World War II and who had arrived in the town directly from an urban practice in February 1956. He was unprepared for the town's hostile insistence on prolonged quarantine. As his uneasiness over the situation increased, he became more open in voicing his concerns to the Flick family as the quarantine period was extended and extended again.

We went through a real crisis in 1956 there when we were quarantined. One of Rosie and Lindsay's daughters was about three or four and she got sick with big purple blotches on her skin. They never did find out what it was, but they thought at first it might be scarlet fever or meningitis. So they put us all under quarantine and we couldn't leave the Block.

The doctor said to us: 'One of you people could pass it on. You've picked this up somewhere and you can pass it on. But you can only pass it on to children. So, in my books you should be able to go down and shop, normally. I don't think there's any need for this quarantine. But that's what the police ... what they all decided. They had a big public meeting and the towns-people decided that you people had to be quarantined. And that adults can talk to one another, but you're not to talk to any of the kids, any kids that might go past'.

I forget exactly how long we were in quarantine. I think it was something like six weeks. We weren't allowed to go down town and all our shopping had to be brought to us. I was having Brenda, Claire was having Gregory, Rosie was having Gavin and Isobelle was having Joey. It was a really dreadful time for us you know, because of all these big bellied women and all that. And of course Dad and Aub and Joe was out of town, they were all out working. And when they came in they weren't allowed to come in to the Block, as if that could stop the infection spreading! But Dad used to bring us stuff and used to come in nearly every day and made sure we had plenty of everything.

Joe decided he'd stay in there with us for a while. And the milkman, Walter Stallworthy that had the dairy, he used to come there every day and make sure we had milk. He was really pissed off because of the quarantine. He'd tell Joe what they were saying downtown and he said: 'I don't think there's any need for this'.

And there was a couple of old drunken fellas who'd come right in there. They'd say: 'I don't give a bugger'. And we'd be saying: 'Oh don't come in now, you'll get into trouble' and one old fella, Old Uncle Bungie, says: 'No, I will not. They won't stop me. They put me in gaol all the time anyway. So it doesn't matter'. Poor old fella, he used to get picked up and gaoled just because he was too drunk to go home. So we'd sit outside with them then, so if it really came to the crunch we could say: 'Well, they didn't come *inside* the house'. I don't know what they expected of us. But anyway, we used to sit on one side of the fence and talk to Dad on the other side. Barbara was five then and she can remember talking to her Pop through the fence.

Another fellow, Robert Mundy, he came in from out at work. I always thought that showed a real concern for us. He was out working at one of the stations and he heard about the quarantine. So he told the boss he was going in to see his people and see what was going on. And we thought, what a nice thing for him to have done. He was the only black fella that did that. And he used to come there every morning, and we'd say: 'Here comes Robert now'.

And all the kids would say: 'Oh Uncle Robert bringing us something' . . . Uncle Robert would always bring fruit and lollies. And he'd be back and forward to the doctors, asking the doctor what's going on. He'd say: 'Went and seen the doctor today, and the poor little doctor he can't do nothing about it'. And the kids used to just idolise him after that. We said, 'Well at least one fella really cared about us'.

Dr McGarn came up and said: 'Look, another public meeting coming up'. We said, 'Oh? What happened now?' And he said: 'Well, someone down town reckoned they saw Jimmy downtown'. 'No, no, no, Jimmy wasn't down there. No', we said. And we knew that was so. No one'd left the Block . . . you know . . . illegally, as they say. So he goes through this big inspection of all the kids. And he comes up and says: 'No need to look at these bloody kids, but I just want to make sure you're all right. I'm not on the other side of the fence really'. And then we got to know him. And he said: 'I'll keep you posted'.

So next morning he comes up and he said: 'Well, they agreed that, to safeguard the town . . . Now this is just to make sure you don't infect the town. We need to put another two weeks on it'. And he said: 'And I tried to convince them that legally they couldn't do that to you. But of course, I'm just the doctor here'. And we said: 'Okay Doc, we'll do exactly what they say. And no harm done. We're right'. He said: 'You're lucky you've got your own little piece of land here that you're on. I asked the meeting what would have happened if someone in the middle of town would have got the same thing. And it could have happened. Of course, no one answered that'. And that's where we left it.

To think it didn't have to happen, but it did happen. And all those things are there now in the past. I think that they've made me a better person when I think: 'How can people just do that and then be so nice to you when you go downtown?' And then I think: 'Well, that's their problem it's not mine!'

And in the middle of all of this, Brenda was born but I didn't even get into hospital. So she was born at home. It was a rough little camp, all flattened tins, but that's where Brenda was born, in that rough little camp. And they sent Rosie [Weatherall Flick] for the taxi. Rosie rips down and gets the taxi and she's standing outside then when I said to Dicky Hansen, 'Oh, it's too late for you Dicky, I'm going to have this baby here, you'll have to go and get the ambulance'. And Rosie's saying: 'Oh no, Dicky, don't do that'. Poor Dicky, he didn't know what to do! So he realised then, yeah, that I was having the baby. And anyhow he goes back, 'cause he was the taxi driver and the ambulance driver all together, and says: 'Come on Henry' to Henry Denyer, 'cause he was the ambulance driver too.

I had to go back inside to have the baby. Oh dear, it was a turn. And Isobelle was saying: 'Oh look Sis, you can't have your baby here now, you know you can't have it here. Oh you must be feverish'. And my little sister Rose said she remembers she was in one of those two little rooms off on the side and she could hear all the commotion. And she was frightened to come out, because she would have had to come out of the side room into this big kitchen where I was. So she had to stay there! She said to me later: 'I'll remember this you know. You'll never get me wanting to have a baby'. And she went on to have about seven of her own I think!

And poor old Nanna Pearlie Mason was walking down the road, going to town and they dragged her over because she was the midwife out at Angledool, and so she calmed them all down, and cut the cord and all that, just when the ambulance officers came in. But we had a bit of a difficult time with Brenda because they really had to work on making her cry. Anyhow that was my experience with home births. I had a home delivery and all the nurses in the world around me!

I was so weak then, that as soon as I got to hospital, Dr McGarn says he'd decided to send me straight on to Tamworth. Brenda had to stay behind with Isobelle and Rosie and Clare. Now there was Henry Denyer, the main ambulance officer and old Dick Hansen the taxi driver was his sidekick. And they had a little Volkswagon ambulance and we had a sister travel with us too. And when we got to Moree, the big flood was happening then, all around. And they said: 'I'll just go around and get a big truck to follow us out over this area where they say we might get caught, because we'll get swamped for sure if it comes over us'. And sure enough, this bank broke just when we got there. And it was just turning towards dark, and we could see this wall of water coming towards us. So they got me up into the cabin of the truck, I was only about seven stone then, can you imagine it? And then with this wall of water, they'd just got me up into the truck and it hits them, and it went straight over the little Volkswagon. And sure enough, we're stuck in that then . . . oh, for hours in the dark.

Dickie Hansen had to go back to get some help to come out and take us back to Moree. And that's what happened then early in the morning. And they're keeping me awake, one of the main things they told me was, 'You must not go to sleep. You're not allowed to go to sleep'. So, there we were, playing 'I Spy' . . . me and Henry and the sister, because Dick's gone to get help.

It was just on the daybreak then, and Dickie comes back with this big grader. That's how he had to get us out, by grader back to dry land and another ambulance and then back into Moree Hospital. And gee, I admired Henry then. He said: 'Now all I want to know is: will she make it to Tamworth? I want to fly her to Tamworth'. And apparently they said no, so

I was treated there. And it's funny how I seem to have waited until there was a decision made and then all of a sudden the room was going all around and I was out for about four days.

But I woke up after a little while and there's this helluva row going on with the matron and the staff there. Henry was saying: 'We've got segregation down there in Colle. But this is not segregation, this is a boiler room or something!' They'd put me right out the back, because they didn't know what kind of disease I had. So, he really went on until they said: 'Okay we'll shift her up into this room'. When I woke up properly, I was in this nice little room with flowers. So he'd really done his job, and he came over and said to me: 'Well, I'm off home now. You should be pretty right now they tell me. But you're just going to have to stay here a while'. So I stayed there for weeks in Moree until we caught the train back.

Now with all the floods, Aub couldn't bring the baby over to me, so they had to bottle feed her. Oh don't talk about it, they had such a time. Of course, this was the first bottle baby in our family. We had all kinds of visions about that. And by the time I get back there, everybody is nearly a nervous wreck, because they've got to put so much of that milk and so much of this milk and Pentavite, so many drops of this . . . And when they actually brought her home from hospital, they're doing it all at home see.

And this day I'm watching Geoffrey making it, Clare's husband. Everybody was having a turn at making up the bottles. Geoffrey was making it, with the measurements really right, and then someone said something to him . . . oh, he went off. He said: 'You know, I was counting this . . . ' He really went off about it. And then he had to put all the milk back. And he said: 'That's no good. I have to throw the milk out now'. In the end then I think Lindsay came in to town. I think it had to be that Lindsay had to stop working, come in here and take over, and that's what happened. He was the fella to do the bottles and everything.

Now after I'd come back, the others were nearly ready to have their babies. They had to have their babies in the segregation ward, the little shed down the back of the hospital yard. There was room for a couple of beds inside the shed, and there was a little sort of back verandah where the babies were actually born. I had Ben in that SEG ward in 1949, and my sister-in-law Isobelle had Johnny in 1950 and Patsy in 1953 in there. Then in 1954 I had Larry there too. The babies'd be born in this little room no bigger than a bathroom at the back and then they'd take the babies up to the main hospital to the nursery. Then they'd bring them down along this little open pathway every feed time and afterwards they'd take them all the way back again. The only time you'd get into the real labour ward was if something was going really wrong with the birth.

By 1956, they were still putting Murri patients in the SEG ward and this is where I would have had Brenda if I'd had time to get to the hospital. Clare went in with Gregory, and Rosie was nearly ready to have Gavin. Then Isobelle was ready to have Joey, but they'd all had enough by then. This was the time when she said: 'We're not going to have our babies over there any more, in that segregation ward!'

Dr McGarn must have had enough too. Isobelle said: 'I refuse to have my baby out on that back verandah'. And she kicked up a big fuss about having it over there. Joe had gone back out to work on the stations by then. And this little Dr McGarn said: 'Well I'm going to refuse to deliver your baby down there, girl. You need to keep refusing to have your baby in that ward. And if your husband's got to come into it, well, he's got to come into it'. And so that's how that started, she refused to have it over there. So he said he refused to deliver the baby there, so, don't worry about the meeting . . . every day they were having full Board meetings. They said: 'Oh, Mrs Flick you'll have to get your husband to come in'. This is getting serious see.

And the funny part of this, the old minister was one of the Board of Directors, you know. So, next minute the Chairman of the Board come up to the Block and tried to sort it out. No, that was the stand. Then the full Board come. They said: 'Oh well, someone has to go and make sure Joe comes in. We'll talk to Joe about this'. And so I think that's when Joe came back in and they stuck to their guns. I think Joey was the first black kid that was born in there without there being an emergency. But that's how that changed.

From there on then we used to be in beds on the verandah of the main hospital, and have the babies in the labour ward. So we were still not *in* the main maternity ward, just outside it. It had fly screen, but it wasn't too warm! But we weren't in the segregated shed then. So that little bit changed there.

So, we stood up for a lot of things in the town here, and this was one of them, over Joey, over having him in the labour ward. There was a lot of hostility, I think they found it hard to accept, but they eventually had to deal with it. And I might add, the doctor didn't stay there very long. He had to go . . . he didn't have a real good time in Colle.

I was very sick when I got back to Colle after I'd had Brenda. It was just after they'd closed off that segregated ward and put us on the front verandah. And the only time they'd take us in was if it rained or if it got windy. And so that was a sort of graduation from segregation to . . . a bit of an Annex in the hospital, just like the old Annex with the school in the 1940s!

When you were there for a while like I was then, you could hear the sisters making snide jokes about people, always about black people. One sister in particular used to say it in front of me just to get me cranky because I'd started to react to some of the things she had to say. She used to always make a point of being out on the verandah when the kids were coming past going to school and she'd say: 'Oh here's that lovely little golliwog girl there. Look, isn't she just like a little golliwog?' And I used to get so mad, I used to say: 'You'd never say that to her mother, but you say it to me because you know I won't tell them. I won't tell them because I know they'll come in here and they'll slap your face and they won't care what the cops say'. There were lots of things like that. I'm sure the others must've suffered that kind of stuff too. She used to talk about the blacks when they used to go past the hospital because they used to have to go that way to go home from town to the Old Camp.

It wasn't something you could go and talk about. And in that time when you look at it, it wasn't all that long ago. This sister would see one of the old fellas coming in to see our patients. She'd say: 'Oh here comes Sambo again ... Oh! ... It takes him all day to say three words'. I used to say to her: 'If only you had the guts to say that to his wife, she'd knock you clean over'. And she said: 'Oh you can tell her'. I knew I couldn't tell her because she would come and tear her down and anyone else with her. I didn't want to cause trouble like that, so I had to put up with a lot of that. But she was the one that stood out like that. The others I couldn't say treated me badly. But I didn't feel I could tell anyone. There was no one that you could talk to. Half the time this sister was sister-in-charge anyway. And when the matron came around and did the rounds, that's all she was doing, just doing her rounds with the doctor.

That same particular sister knew I was very sick, I was really sick. I didn't have visitors all the time because our mob would just send in the kids from school to pick up my washing and take it, because they were all busy trying to survive over there. I remember when I was there, I started to get worse and had to have a transfusion, and she tried to make out that I was bunging it on. When Dr McGarn came he said: 'Why have you got all these blankets on?' And I said: 'Oh, well, she put these blankets on me'. And he said: 'But why? You don't need all that'. And I said: 'Well, ask her'. And so they walked away, because he was working with this sister you see, I could hear her saying: 'Oh one minute she wants all the blankets on and the next minute she wants them all off. I just don't know what's going on with her. I can't read her at all'. And I thought: 'Bugger you'.

Now he had to monitor the transfusion, and so he used to come around every now and again. So the next time he comes around, he said: 'You haven't got anything on now'. She'd take everything off. And he'd be feeling my pulse and he started taking my temperature again. I looked at him straight in the face and said, 'She wants you to believe that I'm just bunging this on, but she's not telling you what's really going on'. He woke up then. And I heard him say:

'Listen sister, this transfusion has to go on, and it has to be done tonight. And she's only got so many hours to complete this. So if you don't mind, I'll get my wife to come and sit with her, because she's been a bit unsettled, well, you can't handle her apparently'. So his wife came down and she sat with me, because I was feeling so ill.

And she was even kinder than he was. And anyhow, the next time then he'd come and sit while she went and did her packing. Because they were getting ready to leave. And she said to me: 'We're in the middle of packing . . . we feel we have to go. We couldn't believe what was just happening with you. We wouldn't be able to report it to the police. The police would not listen. So it'd be best for us to move on'. And he said to me: 'I couldn't have this going on all the time!' So they moved on. They went to Quirindi soon after and then I heard he went back to Canberra.

You were really at the mercy of the nursing staff. Like, eventually I told that little girl's mother about how that sister used to talk about this little 'golliwog girl' and I told the others and they used to go: 'I don't like her'. But that's about all they could say, they couldn't do much else. But you were better off to keep fighting. And you know, to overcome stuff like that you've got to gain something from the experience, you know? I still say, that poor sister had the problem, didn't she? I can't even remember her name. So see how insignificant really she was to me.

The tensions in the town and the Murri challenges to the local authorities were not evident to outsiders, even to sympathetic ones. Archie Kalokerinos was the doctor who followed Frank McGarn to Collarenebri early in 1957. Archie's autobiography makes it clear that he already saw himself as a loner, with little interest in cultivating social approval. From the beginning he refused to comply with the petty segregation of the hospital and medical structures of the town. He was horrified by the physical conditions of the Aboriginal camp and by the poor health of the Aboriginal community. But Archie appears to have had no inkling at the time of the turbulent months which had just passed in the town and he was not aware of the tenacious protests which had forced the school open in the forties and had so recently gained access to at least the hospital verandahs. Instead, he saw a downtrodden and, in his view, a passive community, with no one other than Mick Flick confident enough to express protests at the discrimination which was still so evident.

But Isabel, the other Flick families and the wider Murri community, saw themselves in an ongoing and indeed escalating struggle with the township. To them, Archie was a surprising and welcome ally whose support might tip the balance in the conflict. His presence in the town from 1957 to 1964, then again from 1967 till 1977 allowed new hope to emerge that decent conditions could be achieved, and that alliances could be made with outsiders which could challenge local power.

And it wasn't long after that that Archie came and a lot of things changed then that made it so much easier for us. We had had to fight for everything—school, hospital treatment. I remember we used to have to line up there and pay the dollar before we saw the doctor, you know? Until Archie Kalokerinos came here and then he started saying: 'Well, don't worry about that then. You're all getting upset about that dollar . . . just come across to the surgery and we'll work it out there'.

Archie had a hard time at the hospital a lot of the time. He couldn't work with one matron, he went through a time when he was just 'a black doctor' and we said 'that can happen, the doctor can come here and he can be seeing more blacks than whites, so he's got to be a black doctor'. But I don't think he was very happy there. He wanted a lot of things brought into the community too and what he wanted was too expensive, the government wouldn't even consider some of the stuff that he wanted to do there.

We put on a turn there at one stage when we didn't want Archie to leave. And that was a difficult time for Murris too. And he said to me: 'I have to leave, because if I don't leave they'll call me too late and it'll probably be one of your kids or one of the people that I'm dealing with, and that can happen. We can't overlook that. And I wouldn't take that risk'.

As Archie Kalokerinos recognised, Mick Flick was a well known and active partici-pant in town affairs. His war record was acknowledged on Anzac Day and he regularly contributed to town activities and charities, as the Collarenebri Gazette *reported, often bringing in fish to be raffled or sold to raise money for the CWA or the hospital. Mick's personal sense of disillusionment with the white townspeople deepened over time, as his family became aware, but his pivotal role within his family intensified as he became the focal point for his grandchildren in the busy Block community.*

After Dad's boss left Longswamp to retire to the city, Dad did all kinds of things. He could put his hand to any kind of work. He was doing that shearing contracting for a while and then he was always fencing or shearing right up until the last thing. He was what they call 'an expert in the shed' on grinding tools for the shearers. That was a pretty easy job, so right up until the last he still did things like that, even though he was entitled to a service-men's pension. But he got to really hate the system—the repatriation system—so much that he kept refusing to apply for that pension. They still wouldn't let Murris into the RSL club. And they haven't done it either, not till very recently . . . So there was an exclusion from the other facilities that RSL men had access to. There's a lot of Aboriginal members in the RSL club now. Some of my family are members. But I still remain one that . . . you know, I think that it wasn't good enough for my Dad, so I don't think they're good enough for me.

Joe and Isobelle's son, Joey, did some research for us a while ago, and found out how to look up Dad's war record. Then my sister Rose got Dad's file for us, and she got a better idea about why he didn't want to take a service-man's pension:

> *Rose:*   When I went down looking for his records with the number that young Joey told me, '4292', the army bloke doing the research said: 'I can't find it, are you sure of the number', and he went over and over it, and he said: 'Just a moment'. He was in there for a long time and he came back, and he said: 'This man was trained for two positions, and that was Lighthorse and machine-gunner, and he also carried out duties as an Ambulance man . . . and he also volunteered to stay over there' . . . And he got paid . . . what? . . . twenty pounds. Then he came back and they chased him around the river trying to take his kids off him.

But in those days, his old mates used to think it was such a great thing that he was a soldier and in the march each year. And we grew up thinking that too. And then, this old friend of his died. It was after the Old Camp got moved in 1960, across the Walgett bridge to where the Wollai, the reserve, is now. The first ANZAC Day afterwards we said: 'Oh, Dad, aren't you going down to the march today?' and he said: 'No, I only used to go because my old mate used to want me to go'.

And I said: 'Well, it was great', and we started to say: 'Come on . . . ', we thought it was terrible, that he didn't want to get involved. And he said: 'Hey, listen, you know, I'll tell you what war is all about . . . it's about people killing each other. We must've killed some really good blokes and they must've killed some really good blokes on our side'. And he said: 'And then you look at the way these white people treat us, they won't care about me tomorrow. They only want me just to make out that we're all good mates together and all that'.

I don't think we really wanted to accept that, we just thought he was just being a funny old bloke. 'Oh, no', he said, 'I'm invited out for my dinner over at the reserve today, and that's exactly where I'm going'. We said: 'Oh, what are you going over there for Dad?' and he said: 'Look, I'd rather spend my time with my people. There's Shirley and Freddy asked me over there for lunch and I'm going over there for my lunch. They think that I'm important and it's important for us to have dinner together'.

So, we said: 'Oh. Anyway, they'll be marching soon'. He said: 'Yes, I know which way I'm marching—I'm marching straight across the bridge and

Joe Flick with Joey on truck running
board, c. 1958. (Photo: Karen Flick)

Brenda and Amy (on left),
Isabel's daughters, and Marjorie
and Stephanie (on right), Rose's
daughters, at Mick's house on the
Block at Collarenebri, c. 1961.

nobody is going to stop me'. And that's what he did, you know? He put on his
medals and he marched down the street in the opposite direction to the big
march, across the bridge to the reserve. And from there on he always went
across the river then, and they always made a big dinner for him. And everybody used to make a joke about him going over to the mob while he should
be up there with all the *wandas*[3] you know? And they used to give him a bit
of a ribbing: 'Go on, you used to go before', and he'd say: 'Oh, yeah, well I had
a reason then—my mate, see, my mate wanted me to go so I went to please
my mate'.

But I have the strongest memories of Dad in those later years from the way he got on with the grandkids. I used to spend a lot of time with my grandkids. But I haven't got all that time that he used to spend with them. See, they just see me as Old Gran that comes now and again and says 'G'day' to them, and 'hello, how you going'. But I'd have liked to be able to do the same thing that my father did—he spent a lot of time with his grandkids. More so than with us when they started to grow up and become his mates. So that was another wonderful part of our life too. I think a lot of those things have become so important to me now that I must get this down in this book so that at least my grandkids will know something about me too.

For a long time now I've been thinking about the way Dad was able to get on with those kids. I suppose all grandfathers and grandparents develop a different way of working with the kids. But after they got to a certain age—about nine or 10—they'd be with him more than us. So he'd be organising for the big events for them, like cracker night. The kids would know that he'd be coming in from work specially for cracker night. And they'd go out to the rubbish tip and the boys would pick up a couple of motor car tyres and bring them back to burn them, to kick the fire off. That was a really fun time. First, I didn't bother getting involved. But then, after a while, well Isobelle was always there and old Granny Ada[4] would be with us. And she'd say: 'Oh, you wanna come. You watch how he goes on with the kids. And he can hand them one cracker and that'd be fine. But if we give 'em just one cracker, they'd be looking to see why they didn't get the same as the other kids'. So he had a way of controlling how it all worked.

He probably had a yarn to them before I'd realised what was going on. But they'd get these bloody crackers, and he'd be the fella to take them shopping. And on the afternoon, they'd be expecting him, whatever time. And they'd be all out the front, playing and watching down the road. And the first one that sees him sings out and then they'll rush out. And we're saying: 'Oh, it's on now'. And all the kids, they'll *all* want to go in the car. He'd always have some kind of old bomb. When he got the truck they'd be all on the open truck, going down town, and pointing out all the new crackers that's coming out.

I don't know how much he used to spend on the crackers, but I'd say the full week's wages. Then when they all came back, someone'd make sure they had tea ready for him over at his camp. It'd always be someone, might be Barbara or the little sister we lost,[5] or sometimes the boys would go and make sure they had his tea ready. And he'd have his tea there while they're making the bonfire.

And we just said, 'What a relationship he had with them', because he'd pass out all these crackers. Someone would always have the say on who gets

Mick Flick with the truck he drove the kids around in.

all the throwdowns. And he'd say: 'Okay, whose turn is it?' And someone'll say, 'It's my turn', and they'd be okay. And they'd make sure all the little ones got the throwdowns. The bigger ones would want some too, but then he'd say: 'Oh no, I think you're too big for a throwdown'. And there'd be no squabble about it.

And Isobelle and I, we used to just look at one another when he'd say: 'Oh no, he's too big for a throwdown. And so he's into the big stuff now', he'd say. So I suppose he used to be building them up too, like growing them up. But the big sky rockets, he'd say: 'Okay, this is real stuff now, we've all got to be careful'. And long before they put the ban on all these big sky rockets, he had that relationship with the kids and he was controlling the safety of that night.

Then there'd be something like the football grand finals in the region and they'd want to go. They'd be all really doing everything for Dad. And he'd come in and say: 'Hello, something's going on'. And they'd say: 'Footy on in Mungindi'. 'Oh, right.' So he'd end up taking them if it was the big game. Most of the other kids would be gone. He had a little 'T' Model car and that used to be packed. How he got away with loading it like that, with kids on, I'll never know. But he'd let the kids out as he drove past the oval. He'd let a couple of kids out and then he'd let a couple more kids out. So when he drove into the football ground he'd only have two or three in the car. We used to say, 'He's going to get caught'. But he never did.

Camp children at a farewell for a well-liked local policeman. Lubby (Isabel's sister) is third from left with bow in hair and in spotted dress. Patsy (Joe and Isobelle's third child) is in front looking at camera. Late 1950s.

And show times, he'd organise the girls one year. Never missed the Moree Show, or the Walgett Show. So one time it'd be the girls going to Moree. And they'd be fussing around, making a big fuss, just tormenting the boys. They'd walk back and forwards. 'I forgot something'. And he'd be sitting in the car, just waiting. 'Oh, we went through this last year'. Or the boys, the boys do the same to the girls. And I used to think: 'I don't know how he had the patience to just do that with the older ones', especially when they were 11 or 12.

So he just had a little unit of mates. And when Mum would take off, she'd be gone for months and months. And the kids would all move in with Dad, to stay with him in his camp on the Block. Especially if Joe got a bit solid about something. He was a very strict father and if he took the strap around one of the kids, they'll take off over to Dad's. Not that Dad tried to interfere, but he'd say: 'Oh dear, I should have belted him when he was little', or something like that, to make the kids feel better. I even saw him at one stage telling the kids to cry, so that we can all go out with him. At that time we were all on this property where he was managing, the Wilgas. So everybody had a job. We used to often go up along the river, fishing or something. The men didn't want to go out fishing this time because it's Saturday morning and they would rather have gone to town, only about 13 miles away. But Dad wanted to go out fishing and the kids all wanted to go too. So he said 'I can't take youse all, see? I can only take the three big fellas'. But he said to the other kids: 'Now, when I go up there, about where that tree is up there, you've got to start crying and see if that works. It mightn't work, but you've just got to see if it does'. Sure enough, didn't they put on a turn when he gets up to that place and he's taking his time filling the radiator with water and checking the tyres.

We were in a hut just across the road and I'm watching him and thinking: 'Well, he really needs the mates. He wants everybody to go with him'. How the kids started crying! And everybody started getting chipped off about everybody and oh, they're going off at the kids. All the time he's still rattling things up at the tree . . . and kids running up the road and kids on his arm.

At last everybody said: 'Oh well, we might as well go with him I suppose. Go on, pack your dinners. Pack something up'. Lindsay used to get really cranky. And Joe. And Old Aub would say: 'Oh well, we might as well go I suppose. Doesn't look like we're going to town. Anyhow, we'd better pack something'. Then Larry said, 'You don't have to pack nothing! Grandfather's got all those'. I said: 'What?' He said: 'That's true, he's got it all'. And he had meat for a barbecue and he had all these fishing lines and everything. He had all the tucker packed, enough for everybody. Everything was ready. And I thought, 'Well, this bloke can't be true!'

I didn't say anything to the others, I just said to Aub that's what I saw him do. And he said: 'Oh well, he must really want us to go with him'. So away we went. Lindsay had one truck and Joe had another old bomb. And so we had to go in the big lorry. All these kids on it.

And, you know, he was teaching them all the time, when we were going along. He said: 'Nobody knows how to knock a goanna, do they?' And he'd pulled up then. By that time he's pulled up and talking about how he saw this big goanna up in the tree. He said: 'So we've all got to be careful now because the boys are going to have a shot at it'. The boys are taught how to load the rifle. Had to take it in turns at having a shot. And when I look back now I can see that was what he was doing. Showing them then how you put the gun back in the car. And as I went along I noticed that the boys learned how to handle all these guns.

Anyhow, when we gets out there, two volunteered to make the fire and he's showing them how. And this was a big lagoon where we were. And Dad said: 'This is the best place to get fish I ever knew'. 'Oh, right.' So we had the fish net and everything and we got on that to drag up and down. And Lindsay's getting a bit suspicious then. He'd say: 'You knew all the time we was coming out here. What about us, we wanted to have our weekend off, we wanted to go to town'. He was getting a bit shitty about it. And he said: 'No, no, we'll just give it a couple of runs with this net. I just had it on the truck, I should have took it off'. Away they go. And they drag it up one side of this muddy lagoon, then they dragged it back. Lindsay said: 'Now they must be stirred up, because we're not getting any bloody fish'. He's getting really worked up about it. And Joe and Aub trying to get it over and done with.

Well, Lindsay has two goes at it and he says: 'That's it for me'. So he sits over there and he's got a cowboy book, and that's it for him. And so the third time it went up, Old Aub said: 'Well, that's it for me, there's no fish in this lagoon'. Dad said: 'Well, that's funny that, because I always thought this place had plenty of fish'. But then the kids started crawfishing, so they're catching a lot of crawfish. Oh, he said: 'Wow, we're going to have a big feed of crawfish'. Which we did. And then he showed them how to clean this goanna and cook it. So he used to do things like that, and it's just as if he wanted to have the kids around him a lot, you know.

We just knew that he was always there if anything went wrong! We'd just have to ring him up and say: 'Come and get me Dad', and he'd be there. He'd always come across to see if we had food in the house. And when Rosie and Lindsay were in St George, he'd always be going up to try to coax them to come home. He always had his truck full of kids. *All* the kids. Landrover full of kids, sitting on top of one another. And then he got that way that he had white kids and all. He'd laugh and say: 'Oh, look, this is too much'. I wondered how Dad got the patience, you know, to have *all* the kids. My sister-in-law Rosie used to say, 'Old Mick, he'll look after them. He'll take them under his wing'. And they knew Dad would protect them. They knew that they could bank on it.

5
Confrontations, 1960s

This decade was an intense, formative one for Isabel. It witnessed events of deep distress and a rising sense of tension. But Isabel also felt growing confidence that she and her community could challenge the racism of the town.

Isabel had often talked about these events of the 1960s when she first came to live in Sydney and was trying to explain to me and others why it was so urgent to make changes in Collarenebri. Much later, when she was recording for this book, she would usually recall episodes of her earlier life piecemeal and out of sequence, as memories crowded in on her. She planned to come back later and rearrange them into the order in which they had happened.

But this group of 1960s stories was different. Isabel arrived at my house one day in mid 1999, for what turned out to be the last recording session we were able to have. She was excited and eager to get started because, she told me, she had sat up the night before working out exactly how this part of the story should go. She wanted to explain how confrontations had educated her. So we got started recording and Isabel dictated the core of this chapter virtually fully formed.

'I really want to talk about all those confrontations we've had to have. You can't think what a terrible feeling it is when you've got to argue the point over something. And you know that everybody is thinking: "Oh Christ! Here she goes again".' Isabel 1999

Tension was rising in Collarenebri by the late 1950s. The full employment of the decade had allowed Aboriginal people a degree of economic independence which had *previously been difficult. There were already changes occurring in the pastoral industry, such as the increasing use of machinery, which would mean that eventually there would be fewer jobs. But there was still plenty of work around while the wool boom continued. The sense that Aboriginal citizens were missing out on the benefits of the strong rural economy had not only angered Aborigines themselves. Urban campaigners had begun to pay attention to conditions in country towns, and in 1957 a union-funded deputation visited nearby Walgett and made inquiries about discrimination and poor housing for Aborigines.[1]*

The response among Murris in Collarenebri was cautious. Mick Flick had warned Isabel: 'I reckon you don't want to get mixed up too much in this mob because you don't know who they are or where they come from. If it was black fellas I'd understand, but these white people involved there, that's what's got me mixed up'. But the persistent colour bar in Collarenebri continued to enrage Murris and there was a growing air of defiance among them. Isabel remembered the late 1950s to have been the time when Murris started to stand up to police harassment; while this brought heavier charges against themselves, they persistently asserted 'they don't own us!' As Isabel's children and nieces and nephews began to grow up, it began to seem intolerable to her that this new generation would have to face the same suffocating racism which she had experienced as a teenager.

A major entertainment focus in Collarenebri was the local picture show. Mark Cutler had run an open air theatre for many years. Aboriginal people were not prevented from attending, but they were seated in the far back of the viewing space,

The Liberty Picture Show in 1998, faded from its glory days of the 1960s.

without chairs, and a long way from the screen. Isabel remembered having gone to this picture show only twice as a teenager. In 1955, Mark Cutler opened a new, indoor picture show,² grandly and ironically called The Liberty. The Aboriginal population was now booming with many children and teenagers fascinated like the rest of the town by the images they saw in the movies. The price of their tickets made a good profit for Mark Cutler, but Aborigines found they were still segregated in the new building.

When we went to the pictures we always knew that we would be lined up and we got in the certain little section. All the blacks were herded down the front and all the whites at the back. We were right under the screen—there we were, screwing our necks up—they even had ropes around us. That kind of exclusion in the picture theatre went right on till 1962. Until I said it was time to cut the ropes!

You have to fight for everything, everything you want you had to fight for. So that was one of my first fights. How it happened was the girls wanted to go to this picture, Barbara and Lubby. It was one of those great big shows—*Ben Hur* or something like that. Lubby would've been about 11 and they'd just done their first Communion at the Anglican Church. Oh yes, if you would've seen those two girls every Sunday morning. And our little sister used to be ready and Barbara would still be dragging the chain, and she'd be out the front saying: 'Every Sunday morning this happens'. Every Sunday morning she's walking around. And we'd be saying: 'Well why don't you go along by yourself?' And she'd say: 'Barbara will get cranky then'. She was such a dear little thing. They were all churchgoers—Barbara and Lavinia—they never missed Sunday morning at the Church of England . . . they were confirmed and all. And they used to sing with the old fellow that owned the theatre.

Now those girls wanted to go and watch *Ben Hur*, but they knew they were going to get pushed into the seats under the screen. And sure enough, the usher came up to them when they tried to sit in proper seats and said: 'Come on you've got to move on. You've got to get in your black seats, where the ropes are'.

Now I was there and I felt hurt for their sake. I think that's what prompted me to question that. I said to the usher: 'Hang on, you bring your manager down here. Bring the boss down'. And he wasn't able to do that, so I went up to the boss, Mark Cutler. And I stood in front of the ticket office and he said: 'Look, I'll talk to you in a minute'. For a while they didn't want to react. So I kept standing there in front of the ticket office, and by then my sister-in-law Isobelle was there too. The two of us, making trouble!

And I said to this old fella at the ticket box: 'I want you to come and fix this. Take these ropes off! What do you think we are? Our money is as good

Lubby and Barbara dressed for church around the time that Isabel and Isobelle broke the picture show colour bar. (Photo: Barbara Flick)

as anyone else's and we want to sit where we want to sit'. I was terrified when I stood up there, but I said: 'Look, my sister and my niece go to the same church as you and we should be treated the same as everybody else'. And my poor little heart, I don't know how it stayed in my chest, but it did. Even though I said it as calmly as I could, I was so sick within myself.

I heard my own mob saying: 'Oh God, she's making us shame . . . oh God!' And then one of the Stallworthys and someone else said: 'Good on you Isabel. It's about time that happened'. I thought: 'Oh well, somebody does care'. Here's my own mob saying: 'Oh God . . .' but they were afraid of confrontation too. And then old Mark Cutler could see I was just going to stand there and keep standing there. Sometimes I think if he'd waited just a little bit longer I'd have gone away. But then he said: 'Oh, all right, you can sit anywhere then!' And that's what happened.

The next morning the minister came down to see me and he said to me: 'You know, I wasn't aware of what you raised last night. I wasn't aware that you people had to sit in those roped-off sections'. And I said: 'Oh weren't you?' And he said: 'No. I want you to know that I disagree with that. And we'll talk about it'. I said: 'I don't want to talk about it anymore'. And he said: 'Well I'll go down and talk to him'. I said: 'Oh well, he said we can sit wherever we like now. Whether the people will want to sit like that or not . . . well good show. I don't want to talk about it anymore'. Because I had this dreadful feeling about it.

But I went down there the next morning to Mark Cutler's shop. I'd gone there to buy a box of matches just to see how he was going to treat me after that. And he was just as cheerful as ever. He said: 'Oh good morning Isabel. How are you today?' And I said, 'Oh, I'm real well thanks'. He said: 'What are you going to buy today?' I said: 'I'll buy everything in your shop . . . no, just a box of matches'. And he starting laughing. I admired him for treating me no differently to the way he'd always treated me.

It's important to see how to use something like that. In a confrontational thing like that an issue was dealt with and that was it. That was the end of it, you know. We didn't have to do that anymore. But most of the people today still do the same thing, they'll sit in the little section where they've always sat, and I'll go and sit somewhere else.

I said to my grandkids the other day: 'Well, I won't have much to leave you, but at least I'll be able to leave you some part of my life'. In this book I want to make sure I've got a photo of the Liberty Theatre, because it's one of the things that figured in *changing* my life, you know. I *was* terrified when I stood up there that night, but I did it because I was hurt for the kids' sake.

And I think a lot of people can't understand that that bitterness didn't stay with me. I think the bitterness about us not being allowed to go to school stayed a long time. But things like standing up at the picture show helped me make the change in my life. And so they were the people that directed me to where I am today.

Barbara Flick has written about how these events looked to her when she was 10:[3]

> *Barbara:* When my Aunty Is teamed up with Mum she was a force to be reckoned with in the small conservative town of Collarenebri . . . My father was a shearer and spent most of his time on the track working or looking for work. So it was Aunty Is and Mum.
>
> In the [early] 1960s, these two women took on the establishment and desegregated the picture theatre at Collarenebri. The picture theatre was divided into two sections. One for the whites and one for the blacks. I didn't understand why. It was a strange feeling to see all the white kids from school walking past us with their noses in the air. They knew what segregation meant. It meant they were better than us. Didn't it?
>
> So there we were, divided by ropes. The theatre owner and his assistant would walk around and if they found us (they sometimes did) sitting low in the white fellas' seats, they would belt us on the head with their torchlights.
>
> Then *Ben Hur* starring Charlton Heston came to town. The whole town was turning out to see it. Mum and Aunty Is decided it was time

for political action. They stood at the small ticket window and demanded the theatre be desegregated. Troublemaking blacks? Wasn't that what he called them? Well they told him that they would block his patrons and prevent them from purchasing their tickets until the ropes were taken down. There they stood. Defiant. Two black women in that crowd of whites. Talking calmly. Can't you see how proud they were. Their heads held so high.

This may seem like a small thing to you, but in Collarenebri in the sixties it was a big event. This was the way that Murri women took responsibility to try and make a more equitable society for their children to live in. This story makes my heart big and full. Tell us again Mum, Aunty Is, tell us again. And the lights in their eyes show the pleasure.

As Murris started to demand access to the town's services and entertainments, the discomfort of many white townspeople re-emerged, once again in the form of accusations that Aborigines were a threat to white people's health. The target was the Old Camp on the police paddock on the Mungindi road, where it had stood since 1924 and which had offered Isabel such a sense of security. One of the goals of Collarenebri's white population during their strenuous campaigns to keep Aboriginal children out of the school in 1938 had been to have the whole Aboriginal population removed to another town like Brewarrina where there was a Board station. This plan was abandoned on advice from the local police because all the men were fully employed in the immediate district and would lose their steady work if forced to move. Since then, the population at the Old Camp had risen significantly to 175, swelled by ex-Angledool families moving away from the oppressive managerial control of Brewarrina into which they had been transported in 1936. Town anxieties surfaced late in the 1950s with an accusation that the Murri camp was polluting the water running downstream towards the town. Doreen Hynch joked with Isabel in 1999:

> Doreen: 'Well they say they moved the camp from this side to down the other side because we put disease in the water. Oh dear yes, but they had the hospital pumping its sewage and things like that in before the water got to the town! But you had no say in those days. Nobody would stand up and talk!'[4]

The camp residents were shifted unceremoniously in 1960 to a piece of reserve land on floodprone low ground on the Walgett side of the river, a long walk across the bridge from the town and much further away from the Block than the Old Camp had been. The conditions on the new reserve, called the Wollai by Murris, were identical to those on the Old Camp: people built their own houses from flattened tins and there was no water supply or sewage service when the camp residents were dumped there. A year later, the Welfare Board recruited the Collarenebri Apex Club to volunteer their labour for the erection of an ablution block with three cold water showers, a tub and a tap, which then constituted the only running water on the Wollai from 1961 till after 1975.[5]

Not long after, Isabel's young sister Rose had unexpectedly married Jim Fernando, a local man who already had a family with grown-up children. The tension surrounding their relationship in Collarenebri led them to decide to leave, heading for the distant fruit-picking town of Leeton, where they reared a family and worked for many years to buy a property. Isabel missed Rose intensely and carefully saved all the letters, cards and clippings which recorded Rose's life and her children's doings.

As a community in which poverty and ill health were common, death came frequently and affected many people among the close-knit Murris in Collarenebri. The need to travel for work, and the continuing interest Murris took in travelling around the region to keep in touch with people and places, meant that death fairly often occurred away from home, and yet burial 'at home', in the Murri cemetery in Collarenebri, has remained very important. So the cost of funerals often included the high cost of transporting bodies home, and for many families in precarious financial positions, this was crippling.

During 1962, a death like this occurred and, as often happened, the community chipped in and the cost of the funeral was eventually covered. But Isabel started to think about a way that families and the community as a whole could build up their own capacity to cope with sudden and expensive funerals. She talked it over and gained strong support from some people and later in the year they launched a funeral fund. They needed to raise a body of capital and they needed to convince families to join and make regular contributions. Neither of these was easy. But this handful of people began going from door to door, as Joe remembers well! Soon they worked out other ways to raise money, from street stalls to a percentage of the takings in the bingo schools held at different people's camps or on the Block. In many forms, the funeral fund has continued to the present, and years later Isabel wrote about its beginnings when its management was being reviewed in the 1980s.

In 1962, one of our people passed away in Tamworth, and the cost to have that funeral here in Collarenebri was £400 at that time. We went door to door in this town to collect that money and I can assure you that that wasn't an easy thing to do.

However it was the start of my struggle to get people to think about setting up a funeral fund and I had the support of a few other people. But there wasn't many because such a thing wasn't easy to even talk about! Much less talk about having dances, street stalls and raffles to raise the money we needed. Those people were Josie Thorne, Linda Hall, Isobelle Flick—my brother Joe's wife—Doreen Hynch, Walter Stallworthy, Nookie Ryan and the Reverend Roy Randall, and many more of our people who have since passed away. As we went on, we worked harder and harder. Those people involved handled the funds with absolute honesty and respect. And we got more support as people were able to see the benefits of such a fund.

No one could possibly know the hurt I felt from time to time, when I had to say: 'No because you are not in the fund!' I will never be able to shut those times out of my mind. However, we built that fund up to £1500!

In 1963, the Flick family was hit by a series of tragedies. On the Block, as in the camps, there was no electricity. The only sources of light other than the fire were fat lamps—milk tins which burnt a wick and were fuelled with fat rendered down from sheep. Kerosine was also used for irons and fridges. In many Aboriginal communities living under these conditions, there were frequent serious accidents with fire.

Early in the year, Joe and Isobelle's daughter Barbara was minding a baby at her grandfather's house. She told me the story years later, remembering that it was twilight and all the other kids were playing outside to catch the last of the light. The baby needed a drink and Barbara carried it inside to the kitchen, lighting a fat lamp to see in the dim room. Mick was lying down in the upper part of the house, boots off, resting after supper. Suddenly the belt of Barbara's dressing gown trailed into the lamp and caught fire. She had time to throw the baby to her cousin Ben who was sitting reading in the doorway, then she struggled to reach the water in the rain tank at the side of the room and to tear off the burning clothes. But the flaming belt made it impossible. Her grandfather reached her, skidding on the lino floor in his socks, and wrapped her in his blanket, but the cloth was burning so fiercely that the flames kept bursting to life again. Barbara was severely burnt despite Mick's attempts to save her, and it was not thought that she could survive. She was kept in Collarenebri for some days, so gravely ill she could not be moved, and still remembers the agony of being bathed to clean her wounds. The family attributes her survival to Archie Kalokerinos' dedication in the days before the ambulance could take her, with Joe and Isobelle, on the long drive to Sydney.

The doctors at the Children's Hospital announced that Barbara was out of danger, but that she would not walk again. Her parents reluctantly had to return to Collarenebri, where their baby, Karen, and the rest of the family needed them too. Barbara began the long and painful months of recovery in the Children's Hospital, often needing to be anaesthetised to have dressings changed, receiving skin graft after skin graft, and being confined to a wheelchair. She was surrounded by children in the wards each day, so she doesn't remember feeling lonely, and the nurses were good, giving her the run of the ward once she had surprised them all and stood up to walk.

But she was a long way from home, and it was especially important for her to have some familiar faces. The Murray sisters from Collarenebri, Bertha and Myrtle, were maids at the hospital and shared a house with Hilda, a white woman who was a hospital cook. So Bertha and Myrtle would drop in often with treats for Barbara from the kitchen. The town of Collarenebri sent her a box of toys for Christmas, and visitors from home would drop in whenever they came to Sydney and keep her in touch. Out of the blue, as it seemed to Barbara, Rosie Lamb came and asked when Barbara could go home. With a flurry of phone calls and some fast organisation, she was put on a train with Rosie as her escort to finally take her home.

But by the time Barbara reached home, life there had changed forever. The accident had left Mick Flick devastated, worrying that his grandchildren's fondness for staying and keeping him company had contributed to Barbara's injury. He tried to limit their time with him, but his grandchildren refused to leave him and were always there through the winter, looking after him as much as he looked after them. When he suddenly fell ill himself late in the year, he was surrounded by his family.

Dad's little house was in the middle of the Block. And we had a little top camp, middle camp and bottom camp set up there, all around his camp. And this is where the older kids would be allowed to stay over there with him. After Barbara's accident he made a rule then, he wasn't taking that responsibility, or so he thought. But they still all moved over there anyhow. You couldn't rouse on them in front of him or anything, because he could never say no to them. Even when we lost him he had kids staying with him . . . they were trying to wake him up.

But it happened so suddenly, none of us were prepared for it. He said one day, 'Oh gee, I didn't think I'd be here this morning. I thought I was dead last night—I thought I was gone'. And we said, 'Well if you're sick, Dad, you ought to go to the hospital'. But he said, 'No, I want to go down town—I haven't made a will, I want to go down and fix up a few things'. And we thought he was joking, but he said, 'I don't want you to laugh about this, but this is something I should have done. And I just haven't done it'. And we just said, 'Now, look, Dad. Don't worry about that today. Today's Saturday. Think about it Monday'. 'Cause we could see by then that he was quite serious. And on the Sunday morning we found him at home, dead in bed. He died in his sleep from pneumonia.

Well, the RSL committee came up and said, 'We'll handle all the funeral arrangements' and . . . we just went along with that, because we knew a lot of people'd be happy about that. We still thought about the times when Dad would remind us that he was treated differently, because he was Aboriginal. But we always had our instructions that there wasn't any point in us crying and going on. That was one of the things he said, 'I want you to promise me that you won't go on like that, and you've gotta accept the fact that's the end of my life, and when I was born that was the beginning. And you have to look at life like that'. And even though it was a very hard thing to do, I think we did that very well. We were able to say to each other we carried out that wish. Just exactly as he said, you know.

So the RSL organised it and what was involved in the ceremony. He was given a full military burial. A guard of honour and all that. We had a church service for Dad, I think the RSL talked to my brothers about the church and they just decided, oh, Church of England will do. Dad never really practised any religion. He never ever encouraged us to go to church. If we wanted to go that was all right.

But that brings us back to our cemetery. No religion separates you. You're not buried in Christian portions. We're buried in the family unit there. There's a small section of people that are Christian, but at large, I think that we have a spiritual sense all around us. I think our church is all around us, really. I always feel that that's how we've always been and it's been our spiritual directions.

Then we started to think about his grave. At our cemetery, people have got different ideas of decorating different graves. Their own family style. That persists, even now. It's carried on from the past—some of the people alive today don't know who the people buried in some graves were, but they know that they were their people and a part of their family because of their type of decoration, or where the graves are, and so they carry on the same kind of work. I think, myself, it was a combination of two things. First of all it's about identification, it kept in mind which family you belonged to. And then I think it meant something to be working to make that particular grave look nice—it was a labour of love, shown in a lot of the work.

Different people have different needs. I think about the very first grave to be here in this cemetery—and it's reported to be one of the Mundy family, which is one of the main families, descendants, to go back a long way. And this boy's name was Hiram Mundy. And he was reported to have been four years old. And the people at that time lived on the lagoon and his mother was a young mother who'd just lost her first child and she wanted it closer to her so she could spend as much time as she could there—and they say that she did spend most of her days there. And that took the graveyard from the old one, which is deeper in the scrub, further from the lagoon. Working on the graves helps us to cope with death, I think. We get a stronger inspiration, I think, we get a lot of spiritual strength from the fact that we still have a closeness to the person whose grave we are working on.

I'd known about the cemetery from when Granny Fanny first showed it to me and explained how people looked after the graves. But I hadn't gone up there too much until Dad died. So we didn't really notice a lot of what other people were doing. I think it happened—once you lose someone—the need's there—it *needs* to be done. And I think that's what throws everyone into being able to do this themselves. They know that it's their responsibility.

People often wait a year or so after a burial to start work, mainly to let the grave settle itself. Some people like to do it earlier than that and that means that they have to do a lot more work, and more often, because the grave is settling down all the time. And sometimes that's what people need to do—I think to help us to adjust to that death.

We finally felt that we needed to get in and really start to do it—to burn the bottles like they did years before, to make crystalled glass pieces to cover the grave. There was my sister Clare, and myself, and my sister-in-law Isobelle and my brother Joe. We looked at the bottles that were on the older graves and we thought, 'Oh, we can do that', and we started this great process of learning how to do it.

We used to make this big fire. We went about it all in the wrong way. We didn't ask anyone, we just thought we could handle it. So we used to make these big fires and throw the bottles in, and they'd all turn out black and the ones that didn't turn out black and burnt would be all melted. Oh, we must have gone through this process on every weekend for about four months, just trying to get this process to come to us. Nothing was happening.

One day when we had this great fire going and one big piece of coal— fire coal—was out on the side, and Joe stepped right on it with the sole of his foot. He stuck it in the cold water, he was dancing around and he was going to give up on it. He had to go and get his foot bandaged up and went out to work with a bandaged-up foot.

It was a couple of days afterwards that Granny Ada, my sister-in-law's blind grandmother said, 'Gee, you must have a lot of bottles up there now . . . how are you going burning the bottles?' Isobelle said, 'Oh, look Gran, we've got a fire going and then . . .' and Granny Ada said: 'Do you just throw the bottles in, then?' And we said, 'Oh, we've got a big fire', and we thought we were doing all the right things. She said, 'No, that's not the way you do it. You're supposed to dig a hole'.

'Oh, yeah, we've got a hole, and we throw all the bottles in and make a big fire on top of it and . . .' and she said, 'Oh no. That's not the way'. She said, 'You're supposed to make the fire, let it burn down, then you're using all hot ashes and hot coals after that. So you put your bottles in and you have your cold water there, where you can dip them straight into the cold water. Just try it like that and you see what happens'.

So we finally got the idea of how to start off doing it. And it still took us a long time to get the temperatures right with the fire and the temperature of the water. And how long you leave the bottles in the water. You quickly dip them in and out.

But it still took us a long time to really get them right—well sometimes now we don't even get them right—but we can say we're pretty close to being qualified to do that now. And we try to learn the other young people, because we said, we had a terrible experience trying to learn it. I don't know how we'd ever have picked it up if Granny Ada hadn't started to think there was something wrong because we were burning so many bottles.

It helped us a lot, working on our father's grave. I feel it helped us to accept the fact that he didn't just die and go off and leave us. He left us a lot of valuable things to continue to do. He left us not ignorant to death. He told us that he wanted us to accept his death as the other part of his life. That was the end of his life like it's the end of everyone's life, and to accept it as sensible people. He wanted to remind us of this as we listened to his church service and—and it was very hard for us, because those were his instructions. He didn't want us crying and really feeling that he's gone away and left us for no reason.

He left us a lot of direction. I'm sure he felt that if we got into a situation where we needed a friend—we could think back to situations in our lives with him, which would help us overcome it. And we did. That really did happen to us all through our lives.

Within a year, another strong older member of the family, Sylvia Walford, died. Her granddaughter Barbara wrote:

> Barbara: Nanny. Sylvia Walford. My special protector. She would wake me late at night to feed the possums Sao biscuits and water. She taught me to fish. She took me to the circus. She kept my school work. She wrapped me in a cocoon and talked to me about the magic of the river. Her death taught me about mortality.

And then only a year after Sylvia's death, Sylvia's mother died. Ada Woods, although blinded years before by German measles and very elderly in 1965, had continued to be a central figure in the family network. Despite her blindness, she had taught her great grandchildren how to sew rag dolls and pillows, and how to find a good spot along the river to fish. Granny Ada, who had taught the families to burn the glass for their graves, was now herself buried in the Murri cemetery.

Isabel and her grieving family found those years difficult, but the growing confidence of the Murri community in the town was an important source of strength. The school was a place of intense meaning for Isabel's generation who had been kept out of it or made miserable within it, and now they were not going to stand quietly by when their own children were treated poorly by teachers or other students. So the school once again became a place for fighting out the battles of small town racism.

*The Flick children who were at the school gratefully remember their parents'
presence to back them up, but they laugh now too at the sinking feeling they used to
get if they saw their mothers marching towards the principal's office in their good
dresses. They would know their mothers were going to take on the headmaster over
something and they'd think, 'Oh no, not again!' But Isabel played a special role at
the school because she went to work there as a cleaner which allowed her to actually
be on the grounds to observe problems and step in to help children. Barbara has a
vivid memory of seeing her Aunt sweeping, quietly and unobtrusively, but able to
sweep her way close to where any trouble might be brewing. Isabel's very presence
offered security and support, and increasingly she would intervene and speak up on
behalf of any Murri children she saw being victimised.*

I was cleaning in the hospital a bit then, and also sometimes in the hotel,
before I started at the school. You had to join the union, and I didn't mind
that, I went straight into it anyhow. We joined the Miscellaneous Workers'
Union. The only place where I wasn't covered with that was at the hotel,
when I was cleaning there. Of course I wouldn't be a bloody barmaid . . .
they're flat out giving black fellas barmaids' jobs even now . . . But I've had
some jobs in my time, I'm just about jack of trades, an all-rounder.

Then when I started as cleaner at the school, it was back with the Missos
again. Seven years I did that. Seven years. You've got to be there to start right
on six. You'd finish at nine. You'd go back at two and you finish at six again.
And it was pretty heavy work all the time.

But it started to seem like it was good for the kids just to have another
Murri around. For a while you know, I don't think I'd really say anything if
I saw something happening to black kids. Then I started to do that and they
began to realise that, yeah, I was going to say something. For instance, one
day I watched them doing the headlice check. And they're going through all
the black kids' hair with a pencil, and I'm supposed to be sweeping and then
I stopped, and I thought: 'I'll just sort of watch this now'.

And they went through all the black kids, and then there were other kids
that were black, but they didn't identify as black, and the teachers just went
past them. And I walked over and I said: 'Why didn't you check those kids
there? Because those kids are cousins of my kids. And so I would think you'd
do them too'. And he just said: 'Oh look . . . no, Mrs Flick, now we don't
want any trouble'. Straight away just 'didn't want any trouble'.

So he got these two little black girls sitting out the front there, all shame
and crying. I said: 'I take offence to that. So I'll take them home to their
grandma, because that's who they're staying with'. And he said: 'No, they
usually go home when the others go home'. And I said: 'No, I'm taking them
home now. I'll get a taxi and take them home now'. And so, little things like

that I began to do. And I guess they started to become aware that I would say something and take it a bit further, you know? So I did take the little girls home and from then on, if they did head inspections, they did it very quietly because I didn't see it anymore. So it was a very hard job, but an interesting job.

There were all kind of issues at the school that I started to talk up about. But the one time where I didn't handle it was when one of my kids once got a cut across the hand with a ruler—a great big welt across his hand. So I'm going up there to talk to this teacher about it. And you know, I had a sick feeling because I knew they were going to work it out somehow. I walked in to that teacher and I said: 'You fucking try and hit *me* with that ruler!' And it was terrible. I just lost it.

That's the only time I remember losing it. Then the headmaster came in, he was my boss because I was the cleaner at the time. I said: 'I don't care what you do about this, but I'm not having you or anyone else belt my kids. I don't belt them'. He was so apologetic. And he was so afraid I was going to get the cops!

I was sorry after that I didn't take action against that fellow because my son had a real big mark across his hand. And I've thought since: 'Why the hell didn't I? Because I was serious about it . . . But the headmaster was so apologetic then, he said to the teacher: 'This kind of thing can't go on'. And he really got stuck into him. But the teacher of course was deputy principal so I thought later it was just a set-up anyway.

But that was that feeling of confrontation. Over any issue that you wanted to bring up, the feeling of confrontation was always there. You could never sit down and talk about the issues. The welfare officers when they came, everybody had to get their act together so they were knowing what they were saying. And they might only be just coming to do another survey or something and asking questions. And everybody is wondering what the hell the questions were for and who's done something now?

Isabel was extraordinary in that, by 1966 she could steel herself to carry out a confrontation if she needed to, but she could also negotiate through an issue with the people on the other side. The school authorities and the Parents and Citizens Association began to draw increasingly on her knowledge and skills. Isabel could see common ground with the school principal and with white parents on the appallingly limited resources which were available to all the school students. She joined with the local Anglican minister and the owner of Collymongle station to petition the Minister for Education to provide urgently the better classrooms the school needed.[6] The irony that Isabel Flick, who had not been allowed to enter the school in 1938, was now a spokesperson on its behalf, probably did not strike anyone at the school except Isabel herself!

But we did a lot of things against the odds. Like when we started to have dances and things, oh, we had some great dos! I think we got started when young Aub was about five, in 1965, because that was when I got the cleaner's job at the school. So we were all raising kids and I was working nearly all the time. The oldest of my kids would have been about 13 or 14. Joe and Isobelle's older kids were around about the same age and then we'd have a couple of kids on the tit and dragging in the pram and all.

And in between jobs and stuff like that, I'd find out that Roy and Joe were raffling something. Now I'm not real trusting and I'd say, 'Well someone has got to get those raffle books off them. I don't know what they're raffling, and where the money is going'. And it'd turn out to be towards another dance!

I remember when Isobelle and Joe were first getting home, and she was coming there from Walgett see, and Dad said: 'Oh, this is going to be your new sister-in-law, they tell me'. Because we used to go out gambling together. And he said: 'Oh well, I'll tell you what, there's no doubt Joe's a good worker. He'll look after you like that'. But he said: 'You know, he can get you in a situation where he'll get you hung, this bloke, you've just got to watch him'.

Lindsay and Rosie never went to these dances much, they used to keep more to themselves, but we'd get drawn into everything—Isobelle and Joe and me and Aub. And Aub wasn't real keen to get mixed up either you know. But Joe would go down and he'd meet up with Roy and that'd be it, they'd organise something. And the next thing they'd run into Freddy Mason and they'd say: 'Oh, Fred's going to help us and this other one is going to help us'.

So we'd book the Town Hall and Roy and Joe would want everyone to sit down and eat. And we did that a couple of times, and then we said: 'No, we'll just make sandwiches. You can cook all that stuff'. By that time we were able to stand up to them, you know. It was supposed to be one job for each person. But Josie said: 'I don't think it'll work out like that because this one isn't going to be in it now, and somebody else isn't . . .' Roy and Joe had just nominated people that was going to be working there, but those people just didn't want to know any part about it all. Or we'd get some friend or other involved and then she'd get the shits about some little thing and we'd be going around to her place, to make sure it was right with her again. And then we'd find out her old bloke didn't want her to do anything, say because he was older than her and he was getting jealous. And later on we were able to talk about things like that, you know, but a few women couldn't do it because they weren't allowed.

And on the night it'd be just us working. Everybody else having a ball of a time and we'd be there just ourselves trying to watch that there's no grog coming in and all that. Josie Thorne and I would be scared stiff someone was going to break a window or something was going to be broken, so we couldn't enjoy ourselves. And Isobelle would be saying: 'Who kicked this dance off anyhow? Oh, Joe . . .' she'd say. 'Roy and Joe! They went around telling people about the dance. And now here we are, no good trying to pull up now!' And she'd laugh and say, 'Pop used to tell us about that! Well I'm not getting mixed up any more. This is the last time for me'. But sure enough all the dos would come off okay.

We were on our toes all the time with Joe and Roy, because you'd never know what they'd come up with next. But one day I said to Josie, we still had a good time organising things! And the kids used to look forward to it too. See, everybody would go—the kids and the grown ups—and they'd have little beds made up in the supper room part there, and they'd just put the kids down to sleep there. And the taxi drivers would be waiting for their fares home after. So it all worked out well. And yeah, it was good times.

When we look back on it, we started to organise it better and we used to have 'the belle of the ball', and all that kind of stuff. It got that we would have two every year. And they'd be big dos.

Some white fellas came, just a few, but not a lot. And some others would come and make a donation at the door. And we thought: 'Well, that's good enough'. That was really good. And sometimes a taxi driver would say: 'Well, I'll take the book of raffle tickets, because I'm going to the club tonight. I'll sell something at the club'. And we used to get a lot of help like that then.

Sometimes what we made on the tickets we'd put into the Far West or the funeral fund. Sometimes it mainly just covered the expenses! But then if we had anything left over we'd say: 'Oh we'll give it to the hospital'. And then when one of the matrons was leaving we'd organise a do. Then another time when they needed a fridge for the nursery we ran a dance and we bought that. And that was a good do, too. See, there was the little local band, Gordon Kennedy, and Vicki, his wife, she used to play the accordion, and he used to play the guitar and sing. So they'd be singing to us. It was quite a band and quite an event. And a lot of Walgett people used to come over and they used to really liven it up.

Just things like that we used to do. It all made the organising we did later on for the Legal Service and Land Rights look pretty easy! And these dances and giving money to the hospital or whatever was all happening at the same time that we still had segregation, eh!

The political scene in the state was changing rapidly, with a number of legislative changes which significantly altered the context in which Isabel and her community could hold social events like their dances. In 1961, the Federal electoral laws were altered to ensure Aborigines could vote in national elections. Aborigines in New

South Wales had always legally had the vote in the state and therefore in the federal electorate; but many people had been either confused, misinformed or intimidated against exercising their rights during the long decades since the Commonwealth had denied Aborigines the vote in 1901. And others had refused to vote in protest at continued discrimination. Of far more immediate impact, the laws prohibiting the supply of alcohol to Aborigines in New South Wales had been repealed in 1963. It was now legal for Aborigines to purchase and to be served alcohol, although clubs and publicans still controlled completely who was allowed to drink in which areas, if at all, on their licensed premises. Dress codes replaced race as the tool used to exclude Aboriginal patrons. Urban interest in rural conditions was escalating. In 1964, an Australian Aboriginal Fellowship delegation visited Walgett to inquire into conditions there, and in 1965, the 'freedom ride' came through Collarenebri.

The Freedom Ride bus went straight through Colle and everybody was shitting themselves! The news about what had happened in Walgett was travelling like wildfire. The white fellas had nearly tipped the bus over just out of town. Murris in Colle were saying: 'What are we going to do if they come?' And I said: 'If they're going to Moree they've got to come this way'. They could have gone Wee Waa way I suppose, but then the white people started saying to us: 'You fellas don't want to get mixed up with them'. And I remember one old woman, Dorrie Combo, she said: 'You know, these white fellas have been saying to me: "You don't want to get mixed up with them people on the bus" '. And she said: 'How can I get mixed up with them? I'm 59 now. I live at the camp, they're not going to come over there looking for me'. And I said: 'Why don't they want us to get mixed up with them anyway . . . because they're only talking about what's happening. They're telling the truth'. Now old Dorrie she had a couple of run-ins with those white fellas. But at that stage I wasn't in it. I'd had Dad warning me against trusting a lot of white people.

That's why I admire old Harry Hall,[7] you know. He was a shearer, but he was prepared to stand up and he really stuck in there. He went out and fronted them in the town after those Freedom Rider fellas went. And I think about that now, looking back I think: 'Gees, a lot of these other fellas who run organisations now would never ever put themselves out like that'. Then when he started to build that hall for the Foundation[8], he came over to Colle and he was asking for donations. He's going door to door, I thought to myself, 'I wonder if this fella is going to the white fellas' places too?' So I watched him and he went through every house in Colle, the white fellas' houses too. So you've got to admire him. They built that Foundation in Walgett. It was pretty important in its day, it showed that Aboriginal people could do things.

When the Freedom Riders came out, everybody went quiet, you know, everyone was scared I guess. And one thing old Henry Denyer said to me was: 'What are you going to do now, Miss?' And I said: 'I'm not going to do nothing'. Because I didn't know how he was going to react, or anyone, you know. Because I knew I wanted to know more about how we could do some of the things that these Freedom Riders were saying. Some of the women just didn't want to have anything to do with them, they said that they wouldn't even let them go over to the Reserve if they came there. So I thought, well, I couldn't interfere with that because I didn't live on that side of the river. Even though I belonged to Colle, I didn't live on the Reserve where it is now. But I think that was one of the beginnings of me getting involved.

And later on, Henry was the fellow that more or less pushed me into going to meetings and getting involved in that way. I used to try and shy away from it. But he used to say: 'There's nothing stopping you from coming to the meeting, you know. You can come with me. You come with me and I'll soon show you the ropes'. Because he was in everything. He was in the Apex Club, or whatever was there. And President of this and member of that. And so I think he took me along to one of his Far West meetings in 1965, and that's how I started to get involved in meetings and committees.

And then, when the Parliamentary Committee came out there in 1966, well he reckoned it was time for me to meet politicians, and know that they're just men. I remember that old fella said to me . . . 'Wake up to yourself, these fellas talk about you all the time, they talk about you Murris all the time'. He pushed me over to a tree there, old Henry, and he said: 'Oh, the big *Wanda*[9] is coming up again tomorrow or next week, they come up to talk about you Murris again now . . . they're going to talk about the great things they're going to do. You know what you're talking about. You just come along with me and I'll show you how to handle them'.

And he said: 'They've got a couple of old hens with them, writing things down. But I'll show you how to handle them'. And he did. Because there was a lot of us all standing around and one of the questions was: 'How do the police treat you?' And the police were all there. And Henry said: 'Oh well, they don't get it that easy'. And then a couple of other women said: 'You're right there too, we don't get it easy'. Then Henry said: 'But that's not the place to talk about it here, they'd rather talk to you by yourself. Then they can tell you exactly what goes on between these mob over here and them'. And so he set that up so as we could talk about the curfew and all that. Even though people were dreading it when they went to that meeting, 'cause they were still scared stiff that the cops would retaliate against them.

And I remember, another one of the first meetings I went to with him was the Parliamentary Committee investigation into Aboriginal living conditions. And I've thought back over the years after about how those people must've treated him, too, because as soon as he said a couple of things they'd look at him straight away and look at each other because, you know, he was making it a bit hard on them.

Like, when this big politician said: 'Well, I think if we got into building some houses and we did this, and that would look all right there, and . . . ' Then Henry said: 'Oh, but that mightn't be what the people want. See, you're not giving them a chance either, you're saying what's good for them, they're not saying that'. I think that's the first time I heard someone saying: 'Yes, *you* say what's good for these blacks, but what do they want?' When you look at it, you know, people are still saying things like that . . . they're still playing games.

Henry himself was in a hard position. He actually said to me one day: 'When these big politicians come here, they send us a letter, all us business-men, to tell us they're coming and that they want to talk about the Aboriginal issues as well—so what can we do for them?' He said: 'Sometimes when I say something I get offside with my own mob, see. That's why I need you to start coming along and you saying something. You're not silly, you know what you're talking about. And you know what's happening'.

Because at that time we'd been saying things about segregation in the hospital and in the picture theatre and stuff like that and he was becoming aware of that. And I wouldn't blame him if he thought: 'I don't want to get mixed up in that, let them do it' We'll never know what he was thinking, but that was how he started saying to me: 'Look, you know old Mrs Combo, there she is, she'll say what she thinks. You have a yarn to her, she knows a lot too'. And I used to go and talk to her a lot. And she'd say: 'Yeah, you know, we should be saying something about the way they treating us at the hospital and things like that'.

As Isabel became more confident in speaking up on behalf of the Collarenebri Murri community, she retained a strong respect and affection for her genuine allies like Henry Denyer and the Stallworthy family. But she was cynical about the newfound attention she received from some other white people.

But it was hard too when we started to talk up for our mob. I reckon, when you go back to people like, say, Gran's people. My great-grandmother was a tribal queen, Queen Susan at Welltown, eh? And that family had a different kind of treatment, because she was treated a little bit better than the other Murris because she was a key person, you see. And then when you look through it all and you follow the line, white people was treating other people . . . even right to me . . . differently, you know? Because people still say: 'Oh, but you're not like those other people', you know? . . . Yes, they give you the shits.

The Flick families on the Block moved their houses around after Mick's death. Many Collarenebri families feel strongly that after a death the person's belongings should be burnt and their dwelling either dismantled or at the least smoked, with burning Budda bush, to cleanse it of pain and protect the living from any ill effects of contact with the dead. Mick had advised his family not to burn his belongings and his camp after he died, and they had tried hard to follow his wishes. But each family ended up living in a different place on the block of land over the next year or so. Isabel arranged for a loan from the Welfare Board so that she could build a house on the Block for her family and her mother Celia. This house had a living room, separate kitchen/dining area, two bedrooms and internal bathroom, a verandah with a laundry at one end, but an outside toilet.

Joe and Isobelle had moved across the gully and built another tin house on a piece of high ground which their brother Jimmy called Wildflower Ridge. There were often visitors to the existing houses so camps were built around the land as needed for members of the family network. The Block was detached from the main Murri community, particularly after the Old Camp residents had been moved across the river, and so it offered some people a respite and refuge from conflicts on the Wollai.

Isabel's strong involvement during later years in speaking out to protect women and children from family violence was deeply rooted in her community and family experiences in Collarenebri.

I'll never forget the ones there at home in Colle. There was about five women there leaving their husbands, and dragging their kids all over the place. And ending up at my place. One night old Aub came home and he said: 'Twenty-three kids in that lounge room sitting on that floor, eating there. I counted them'. And of course, I got defensive straight away. And I said: 'Oh did you?' And I said: 'Well, I wasn't going to kick them out'. And the old bloke said: 'But you know, I only *work* out there on the station. I don't *own* it'. And I had the cheek to get really upset over that, and I said: 'Well, your sister there too, you know?' And then we'd have their friends and their friends . . . There was often people running away . . . So my house was a real refuge.

The Murris of the northwest needed the Royal Far West Scheme. Set up in the mid-1930s to meet the needs of isolated white country children for seaside holidays as well as medical treatment in Sydney, the scheme's support had been increasingly drawn on by the families with the heaviest burden of illness, the Aboriginal community. When Barbara had to be in Sydney for so long in 1963 and 1964, the Far West had offered support, and by 1965 one of Clare Flick and Geoffrey Mason's children was in need of continuing medical treatment. So Isabel's involvement in the organisation at Henry Denyer's invitation was strongly supported by her family and the wider Murri community. They began running street stalls selling scones and ran raffles to support the Scheme. In 1966, Karen Flick remembers being taken as a young child on a train trip from Pokataroo to Merrywinebone with her family all loaded up with boxes and bags. Once there, her mother and aunts set up a stall and sold food they had cooked to workers harvesting wheat, all to raise money for the Far West.

Isabel continued to go to Far West meetings and travelled with Clare to annual Far West conferences in Sydney. Her articulate expressions of the concerns of her family and community was noted in the caption of the press photo of Clare and Isabel taken around 1969: 'Mrs I. Flick of Collarenebri added emphasis to the discussion on underprivileged Aboriginal children'.

Back at home, Isabel began stepping more often into the day-to-day conflicts she saw taking place around her. She was frequently caught up responding to police actions and to the use of the courts against Aboriginal mothers in order to remove their children.

Things like what happened to Robert Murray in the sixties happened all the time. He was drunk the night before but no one knew, he just went home and went to bed. He used to live on his own and the next day, then, he was home cooking his lunch and the next thing the copper comes along and says:

Isabel and Clare at the Sydney conference of the Royal Far West Scheme, c. 1969. Isabel had addressed the meeting, bringing 'added emphasis to the discussion on underprivileged Aboriginal children', following Dr Barry Nurcombe's address.

'Come on . . . I want you, you smart arse!' And he said: 'What are you wanting me for Constable?' . . . because he was feeling pretty good about it all because he wasn't drunk . . . 'Yeah, what do you want, Constable?' He said: 'Come on, you get in here. I'm arresting you. You were drunk last night . . . Now, I heard you was drunk . . . come on!'

And then I walked over there and I said: 'But you can't arrest him because he was drunk last night'. And he said: 'Oh, yes, I can . . . Oh, yes I can, Isabel'. And see, Mum was the only one that walked over as my witness. She came over . . . and I said: 'No, listen, this is not right. You can't do that to him'. Just when this copper started to realise, yes, I had a witness . . . and I could see he was thinking along those lines, he said: 'Well, Robert, if I've got to come over here today', and of course, Robert started to get a bit cheeky then, see, and blow me if he didn't let loose and he kicked the bloke . . . My God . . . So there Robert was charged then with hitting a policeman. Now Robert was only about six stone-something, and this big copper, he's about 16 stone.

Anyway, this assault charge comes up on Robert, this was a couple of days after that, and Robert is just sent straight off to Narrabri to do six months. Then the police in Narrabri must've got a bit suspicious about this, and he rang this Church of England minister here at Collarenebri at the time. And the minister came over to me and said: 'Oh, listen, I don't want to get mixed up in this, but a police sergeant rang me from Narrabri and he asked if he could speak to someone that might want to talk to him about Robert. Now, I don't want to get mixed up in this, so I told him that you'd ring there and here's the number you can ring, reverse the charges'.

So, I rang the cops in Narrabri and got onto this fella, and he said: 'Yes, I just want to ask you something. How good is this Robert as a fighter?' I said: 'Oh, I don't think he's much of a fighter. Why? What's he done now?' And he said: 'No, I'm just trying to work this out. What kind of trouble does he get into?' I said: 'Oh, well, look I don't know . . . just getting drunk'. And he said: 'Well, he must be a real nuisance because . . . and he must be able to fight a bit because he bashed this copper up and he's 16 stone they tell me . . . and Robert is about . . . what would you say he is? I reckon he's about six stone wringing wet'. And I said: 'Well, you'd be right there with the weights. Yeah, well, as for Robert not fighting anyone, I don't think Robert *could* fight anyone'.

And he said: 'Well, that's my opinion too. I want to work with you', and that's one of the ways that I got involved in things. Because he said: 'Look, somebody has got to say something, so I'll come up there. I'm coming up there to have a look at that station'. And he came up one weekend and he started to tell me how I must talk to people like the minister to be able to help Robert stay in the town because they were going to kick him out.

See, they could work the law to move you on or bring you back or whatever. And so I think that was one of the cases that I got involved in where, if he was staying at his mother's place, and I was to see that he stayed at his mother's place they couldn't do anything about making him go somewhere else, and the minister had to be brought in as a witness.

And so, my job was getting to talk to the minister. Now, see, I could get around the minister, and the minister didn't want to have anything to do with it, of course. So when I rang the policeman again I said: 'No, the minister doesn't want to have anything to do with it'. And he said: 'Oh, yes, I just rang him and I asked him to do a special favour for an Aboriginal person in his congregation. And he agreed to do it'.

So there was all kind of things happening. People were trying to do things and you know, it didn't get a lot of support. But I suppose all the way along there would be people that wanted to say something and couldn't say anything because that's the way the law was, and that's the way they'd govern the Aboriginals, I suppose.

By this time, I started to feel really good about myself and how I could handle it. I knew that I could call on other people and that was good too. There was an incident, which I suppose played a part in me becoming confident. This woman had just had twins on the Reserve. It was summertime and we only had tin huts. She'd had the ten days in hospital and then went home and I suppose she was finding it hard to get the babies to settle down and then they developed diarrhoea and, of course, then the Welfare was on them all the time.

At that stage we had almost weekly visits from the Welfare officers, even though they had to come from Moree. Anyway, these two babies were put in hospital and they were kept in hospital for a long time and they were about to send the kids away. They said that she was a bad mother and that she had never reared any of her kids. But in fact she had, she's reared all of her kids before that. And then they said that she never used to visit them in the hospital. Well, she wasn't allowed to. And I was able to say to her: 'Look, you can go and see your babies. They're your babies. You insist that you see them'. And she said: 'Oh, no when I see the doctor he says: "You better see the matron". When I see the matron she says: "Oh you've got to see the doctor"'.

I suppose they thought they were doing the right thing by the babies, too. But then we worked it out that they'd given her some milk when she went home, and the Welfare officer wrote it up that she'd sold the milk around the camps, which she hadn't done. So this was building up the case to send these babies away.

Now just a couple of years before that, I'd got a loan through the Welfare Board to build my own home and I used a lawyer in Walgett. Now he happened to be there this day when they were taking these babies into the court, and I just went around to see how the mother was going at the court. The lawyer came over to me then and said: 'How are you going?' and starting talking to me. I told him I'd just come over to see how Mavis was. 'Her little boys are going to be sent today.' 'What do you mean?' he asked and I said: 'Oh, the Welfare has got a case against her with the twins and they're going to send them away'.

These poor little fellas were in their bassinettes, real done up too. I remember they had blue suits on with these little bow ties. And poor Mavis still wasn't allowed to be near them. Now to get this lawyer to think about it, I said to him: 'She wouldn't have much of a chance on her own anyway'. And this was long before we had legal services.

So I could see he was thinking it over and then he said: 'I'll tell you what I'll do with you. I'll have a look at this case'. I said: 'We wouldn't have any money. She wouldn't have any money to pay you'. And he said: 'No. I'll do a deal with you. One day you might hear of something that might pay me. And we'll do it that way, eh?' 'Okay' I said, and then to Mavis I said: 'God, Mavis, this fellow might do this case, you know?' 'Oh I don't know . . .' she said. We had no confidence of course. And when we went back in, he was talking to people.

We could see him going in and out and talking to different people. And we were saying: 'Look at them, they're all putting their heads together'. We had him in the same pot as the others. And she said: 'Who's he?' I said: 'He's a fella helping me with my house. We had to have a lawyer'. So when he comes out he said: 'Listen, would you be prepared to go in the court and dispute what they've said about the milk and about Mavis not rearing her kids?'. I said: 'Yes'. He said: 'I'll get it adjourned and at the court, then, I'll have you as a witness'. 'Okay.' And that happened then. When it came to court again, he came around to the school where I was working as a cleaner, and he said: 'It doesn't look as though we need you to come in. They've quashed that case'.

So, just having a lawyer to argue those points made all the difference. He must've just said: 'Well Isabel said this is not right. And that's not right or whatever . . .' and let them know that I was going up there. And the good thing about it then, I had to work with those people at the hospital again because I had sick kids and I was going back and forwards too. And I had to go back there, but they never treated me any different. I said to Mavis: 'We've really got to be careful because these people mightn't see us. We might be sick and go there, and the Welfare will be on you from now on to make another case'. And so we always had to be prepared for another lot of confrontations. But it never happened . . . Those kids grew up and sometimes I used to joke with them: 'Oh you're getting into trouble again. I should've let them take you'. And those boys say: 'Yeah, you're the one, you should've let us go . . .'

But the thing was that you always had to be ready for a confrontation. And it wasn't a good feeling, I can tell you. All those kinds of confrontations, you think what a terrible feeling it is when you've got to argue the point over something. And you know that everybody is thinking: 'Oh Christ! Here she goes again'. And I've had this said to me: 'God Isabel, not again'. But someone has got to do it. I learnt how much respect I got from people after I was able to say to them: 'I don't care what you think'. And I was starting to feel more confident how I was dealing with it. Of course, I had some good trainers. I was getting mixed up with so many different people—black and white—that I started to gain my confidence from outside of Colle.

What was happening at the hospital was still really worrying us, and we thought things might be better with Murris working there. So about this time, Joe and I stuck up for two Aboriginal nurses to be taken on. There were two Aboriginal girls from the Reserve and we'd said to them: 'If you really want to have a go at nursing you've got to go to the secretary and you've got to ask for a job. The matron and the doctor told me that there's four nurses aides' positions there, so you should be pretty right. They're willing to train you'. Right. So they go up there.

Well the secretary made all kinds of excuses for these two girls—'I think you should apply for Walgett because that's a training hospital . . . Moree is a training hospital' . . . And so this went on for a while. We used to tell them every week: 'You go up there and ask that man for those jobs, because we know they're still vacant. Those jobs are vacant. The matron and doctor are telling us. Okay?' The girls used to do that—every week they'd go up there and ask for a job, and that they particularly wanted to do nursing. He said: 'Look, I can make arrangements for you to go to Walgett or Moree if you like'. But the girls stuck to their guns and said: 'No. We're not in for that'. Anyway, the Annual General Meeting was coming up soon and the matron said: 'Well, the AGM is coming up why don't you bring it up there?'

So, sure enough Joe and I go around telling everybody: 'Now we've all got to go to this meeting'. And who turns up? Me and Joe and my sister-in-law. It comes to the part in the meeting where they said: 'Now is there anything else we can do about our hospital to improve our hospital service?' Joe said: 'Yes. We think that you're being very racist towards us, because two girls want to do nursing here and . . .' 'Oh righto . . .'

And so, the minister was on the Board at the time. And he said: 'Did you want to move a motion Joe about that?' Joe said: 'Yeah, I want to move a motion that these two girls be given an opportunity to work at the hospital as nursing aides'. 'Oh right. Can we have a seconder?' 'Oh yes, I'll second that', I said. And, oh God, then he wanted to see if it was going to be carried or not. I don't think it could've even been considered. No one wanted to go on . . . and three little hands go up. So you can imagine that. The board was full of just town people. We were the only blacks there. Nobody wanted trouble, see, everybody was scared of getting in trouble, black and white. I don't know whether we ever thought about that.

Somehow, someone said: 'Are you accusing the secretary of being racist?' And Joe said: 'Yes. Of course I am. He can't be anything else'. The secretary got really cranky and went on about having good Aboriginal friends. So we said: 'Oh well, we can't do anymore'. We walked out. On the following Tuesday the girls got the message that they could start work on the Monday. They probably thought: 'Okay we'll put them on. They won't last long'. And what happened was that those girls stayed there for years, and they were as good as any of them. We had to get clothing—stockings and all that stuff— they were probably thinking that we couldn't come up with all the requirements that they had. But we did.

And then we thought to ourselves, now these girls have got to hang onto these jobs. And it was so good that they stayed on. One stayed on for seven years. I forget how long the other stayed. But they were there through all the crisis times, and they were really good workers. And they used to go to work all done up nice and all that. So in a way you win little ones . . . you can't win them all.

During 1969, Isabel met a group of university students who had come to Walgett on a fact-finding tour for Abschol, the organisation which had taken up many of the strategies of SAFA [Student Action for Aborigines] which had organised the Freedom Rides. These students included law student Peter Tobin, who reported on his return about the normal but seriously discriminatory practices of the police in Walgett and Collarenebri.[10]

I met Peter Tobin when we'd gone to what I think would've been the last meeting of the Aborigines' Progress Association—the APA. They had a branch there in Walgett and I'd only gone to about two before that and this was the last meeting that they had. Peter was still studying law and he came to this meeting and asked everyone to have their say about what was happening to them everywhere. After it was over, I was sitting on this verandah and Peter came over and he said: 'You know, I just find it so hard to believe all this'. I said: 'Oh Peter you've got to believe it'. And he said: 'Oh yeah, I'm not saying you're telling lies. But I'll tell you what as soon as I get my degree I'll come on out and work with you'. I said: 'Oh well, that's one way of having a go at it, eh?' And he said: 'Yes, we'll see what kind of difference we can make'.

And sure enough, he did too. Well, he was a great man, eh? So that's when I first started to meet and trust white people, you know? Because he was the first fella who sat down and talked about what we could do. He'd say: 'Oh no, they can't do this', and 'They're not allowed to do that'. But they do. Everything was cut and dry before they went into court. He knew before they went into court just about what they were going to do. Everybody that was charged, nearly always got 30 days. And that's to clean up the yard at the police station and put in more plants in and make their garden and that's what they used to do. They'd have a garden all over the police yard—pumpkins and everything growing there. And it worked out when you looked at it, one lot of things out of season would be ripped up by these prisoners and then the new garden gets put in by the next prisoners . . . all the work, wood-cutting and stuff.

The economy had begun to change dramatically in the northwest by the late 1960s. Jobs had dried up in the grazing industry, where mechanisation had cut down the size of the work force and subdivision had cut the size of the properties. Aborigines had moved into the seasonal harvesting circuit, including bag sewing for the wheat crops on the western slopes, but again new technology, like silos, was beginning to eat into those jobs as well. Cotton was first planted in 1969 at Wee Waa just south-east of Walgett. In its first few years there was plenty of seasonal work available in summer after the spring planting. The job involved 'chipping' the hardier weeds out from between the rows of newly sprouted cotton plants, which would give the crop maximum access to sun and water. Aborigines formed a major part of this work-force of 'chippers', gathering from across the west and from the coast to work on an hourly casual rate for contractors. This was a new way to work for people who had previously been union members in the highly organised shearing and pastoral industry; but many people went down to Wee Waa to try their luck in this new job, and pick up a bit of spare cash, particularly just before Christmas. The chipping season saw hundreds of Aboriginal workers converge on Wee Waa from all over New South Wales, many of whom retained a degree of suspicion about strangers. Some of the largest fights in the cotton camps were between groups from different regions of the state. But these camps, as well, saw the beginnings of new personal and political relationships—for example, between people from the north coast and those of the northwest who, separated by the Great Dividing Range, had previously had little social contact.

Isabel's memory of her experiences on the cotton field and her actions to challenge the conditions there around 1970 give a glimpse of her role in the network of Aboriginal activists—mostly men at that stage—which had developed across the larger north-western towns of Moree and Walgett. A similar network was developing just to the west, between community leaders in Brewarrina, Goodooga and

Bourke, and the pattern was being repeated on down the Darling through Wilcannia, Broken Hill and Menindee. Campaigns like that around conditions and wages on the cotton fields were one of the ways these local networks linked up to allow the regional co-operation so evident in the next few years. One result was the creation of the first rural branch of the Aboriginal Legal Service, set up in 1973, with Peter Tobin as its first lawyer. Based in Brewarrina, he served the area from Collarenebri and Walgett in the east through Broken Hill and right on down the river to Dareton on the Victorian border.

A lot of the Murris went across to Wee Waa, thinking they were going to get a lot of money out of it, but when they got over there they realised they weren't going to get much money anyhow. But it was the social contact, and they'd play cards and sing all night. We used to have some great times there. All the young boys in that age group went. A lot of kids used to jump onto that too. And Harry Hall was very active too then keeping an eye on issues all over the place.

Well that's how we started to find out who we could talk to about the conditions in Wee Waa. There was a lot of us involved in that and a lot who started to get angry about it. And I'll tell you why, because we were only getting a dollar an hour. They used to work ten hours for $10.

I thought I'd just go over and have a look around. And me and Aub went over, with Josie and Roy, we decided we're going to earn a quid, see what it's all about. Well, I wanted to see what it's all about, but they wanted to earn a quid, see. So we go out and when we got out there I could see that the weeds were well over your knees and the cotton's only a couple of inches high. And he's showing us what ones you've got to chip out. 'And you'd be better off pulling them out with your hand,' he said. And I said: 'You've got to be joking'. And he said: 'No, I'm not joking. That's what we've got to do. That's what we're getting paid to do'. Anyway, my old man and Josie and Roy said: 'Come on Isabel, come on, let's get into it. Don't make a fuss'. And so they could see I was getting a bit agro about it. And I said: 'No, no, no. Go on, you fellas can go', I said. 'How much you say you're going to pay us?' He said: 'Look, ten hours, $10 a day'.

And I said: 'So . . . I don't believe this. So you reckon that's good wages?' I called out: 'Eh Aub, you think that's good wages?' 'Oh, come on look, we're out here now . . .' So away they went. And they're crawling through this! You could see them crawling through the bloody weed. And it was like a big mistletoe thing. You couldn't see them half the time, you could only see the grass moving. And so I sat back, I was leaning against his truck. And he said: 'You shouldn't even lean up against the fucking truck. I bought you out here to work'.

'Oh well, fuck you.' I said, 'I don't want to lean up against your truck'. And so I went and sat down in the shade of the truck tray, and I said: 'So you're going to whinge about me sitting down in the shade of your fucking truck now?' And he said: 'Well, I don't like it'. And I said: 'Oh well, you can move the truck then'. Look, all day he rowed with me over the fact that I shouldn't have got on that truck to go out there.

And I said: 'Well why don't you just run me back to town? Because I'm not going to be fucking silly like that and walk through that stuff'. And he said: 'Oh no, you wouldn't'. He said: 'You're one of them trouble makers'. And I said: 'I didn't think I came out here to make trouble. I thought I was going to earn a quid. But I'm not going to work for a dollar an hour'. And he said: 'Look, everybody else is doing it. Everybody else is quite happy. You're the only one that's putting on a big turn. Look at everybody else'. And sure enough everybody's going. All you can see is the bloody grass going . . . the weeds waving like that.

And I'm sitting there, and I said: 'Well, what a stupid lot of bastards'. Every now and again I'd say this, you know. And he'd say: 'I don't want to hear what you're fucking talking about'. And he'd walk round the other side of the truck. So we spent the day rowing, see. Anyway, when the day was over and, oh, I could see them coming back and they were buggered. And I said: 'I just don't believe this, you know'.

They were all standing up, lining up, getting their little money, signing for it. And I'm standing there saying: 'You say all you fellas agree with this one dollar an hour stuff?' He said: 'Well look, we're having a good old time

Cotton chippers' camp, Wee Waa, c. 1972. (Wee Waa Echo.)

here. We all get together'. That's all the Murris wanted you know, for us to just get together.

And, oh, we used to have big gambling games and everybody from every-where was there. And it was just a great time to meet up really. And they might send two or three kids out and so they're getting their little $30 a day, or $40 a day stuff. And anyhow, I went back to Colle then. I left Aub there, and Josie and Roy. And anyway, I get in touch with Harry Hall in Walgett and old Lyle Munro in Moree. At that time they were both reps on the National Aboriginal Congress.[11] And I said: 'Have you been over there?' 'Oh', they said, 'I just drove through'. I said: 'I went out into the field. And that's what it is, one dollar an hour. Working 10 hours a day. You're no good at going out for two hours, because you only get the $2'. And so that's how they started that movement then. You know, a lot of other people, from Brewarrina and different places, they were saying the same thing.

And there was no accommodation. You were just jammed anywhere. If you didn't have a tent, well you just slept down in the flat. Or if you can, you might get a caravan in the caravan park. But they were very dubious of taking black fellas into the caravan park. We had a caravan . . . We had a little old car and we got a little caravan. But, well, by the time you paid out your expenses for the day, you had nothing. So I said, 'Bugger this! I'm off home'. But a lot of people stayed. And, as I say, they stayed for that community gathering thing.

So that's when we started to make a fuss about it. Harry Hall and Lyle Munro and young Lyle Munro and Billy Craigie and all started kicking up a fuss and after a couple of years they called that strike.[12] See, a lot of people would just think it was only one or two in a group, but it turned out to be a lot of people once they saw that someone was going to take it up.

And that's when things started to get a bit better, even though the con-ditions haven't changed that much now. When you look at the fact that they might earn $80 a day, $80 or $90 a day, then they're taxed, then they're charged travel out in somebody's vehicle. So their expenses for the day would total about $40. So really they're only getting $50. And, well, by the time they go and get their food and that for the next day, they're not getting very much out of it. But they couldn't pull out and do what they did before with the strike because you're not supposed to be out there. Most of them try to get a bit of extra cash on top of their Social, for Christmas. And so they're not supposed to be out there. So you don't get any union support again now. You wouldn't get any support. They're in a no-win situation.

But I'd gone over there a year or so before the strike just to see what it was all about. And then a few of us started to say: 'Now this is no good'. And then everybody started to say the same thing. In those days we had a common thing between us. And that's how we started meeting up down in the Foundation in

Sydney and we met the unions there. We used to hitch-hike, that's how we had to get around. If someone had a car, we'd put in a bit of petrol and travel down that way. We were going to everybody. I think we started to go to any meetings where we thought someone might listen to us, and they did. The Builders Labourers were one that was around. They all took it up then and as I say they've got some changes made.

So that's really what started me big-noting myself. And I just sort of went on from there. I started to get gamer and gamer and started travelling to Sydney for meetings, you know. And the good thing about it was, we'd all pitch in and whoever had a car could go. Or whoever heard that we could get a ride if we got to Dubbo or wherever, we'd all head off there and we'd all be lining up there and we'd hitch-hike to wherever we wanted to go.

There were just so many confrontations. After I went to Sydney in the early 1970s—I've been on a lot of deputations—with land rights and whatever—we started getting involved in finding out how we could get Land Rights legislation into parliament. That meant we had to go right around to all the communities, and meet politicians and confront people really opposed to what we were saying.

But it was much harder at home because you knew you had to work with those people the next day or the next week, or you needed their service or whatever, you know? Yes, there was a real difference there. It's attitudes, I guess, because racism is people's attitudes. People have different attitudes now. And a lot of those Collarenebri people just live in their own little world, and then all of a sudden if something happens in the town they're all there. They know where they have to go and who they have to talk to, and it's like a big family. And it's funny to find that I've overcome all that kind of slur and stuff that used to go on. I used to feel so hurt sometimes when I'd hear them talking about different ones having babies and even myself, when they were making snide cracks at you. And then to overcome it all and to be just able to walk and hold your head high.

It's funny that. A lot of Murris are very hurt about all these things happening and they will never talk to those white people again. Or you know, they'll continually whinge about it. But today, when I go home I see those same white people and they're so different, they've changed over the years. And I thought: 'They had the problem. I didn't really'. And that's why I keep saying all those things have made me a stronger person, because I can— without feeling really hurt about that now—I can think: 'Oh well, it happened and that's that'.

When I think back and I can talk to those people who were like that with us, you wonder where they're coming from over the years, and even now, they're all on-call. Any emergency in that town, every one of them are committed people, you know? And I suppose that happens in all little communities. But I often say that to people, when you're in a little community like that everybody has got a role to play and even if you know nothing about it, you can go there and someone will tell you what you're supposed to do. We've had drownings and things like that and searches for lost people. And oh . . . lots of tragedies, murders . . . and everybody gets together and always someone is doing something to support someone, you know. And yet these are the same people who've had these confrontations over the years, the same ones who wouldn't let us into the school or into the hospital . . .

But then, it doesn't matter how we look at it, non-Aboriginal people are reared in a different way. I was only just thinking about that the other day, because I thought . . . they were coming out from a military rule and everyone was trying to find their place in society too, I suppose, just as we were becoming aware slowly of what our status was in the community.

So, we all live under an act that governs us all, and then everyone was caught up in it. Because I later spoke to non-Aboriginals there, and I thought: 'Gee whiz, this person knows so much about this town, why aren't we . . . all of us, you know, recording what she has to say?' But people seem to look at her as a little old gasbag and I even spoke to some of her family and said: 'You know, we should be recording what she says, because she had the whole history of our town in her head'. I don't know if that was ever done. But I'd like to research that too, because that all fits into my life.

And when I look back, there were those people in that community that cared, but they weren't free enough to speak out because they'd become . . . you know, 'nigger-lovers' or they'd be seen in a different class then, I guess. And I suppose all my bitterness has turned into so much affection and what I feel for Collarenebri and that area because I think it gave me everything that made me today, I reckon. You know, it gave me the opportunity to stand up and say: 'Hang on, this is not right'. And to start challenging systems. And I'm still doing that today.

6
Entangling the City with the Bush, 1972–1978

Isabel's most complete recordings about her life covered the years until she left Collarenebri in 1972. She recorded memories of separate events from later times and kept boxes of letters and papers, which allow us to learn a lot about what happened after that. But we don't have enough to complete the story fully in her own words. So the main voice of storytelling at this point must pass over to me. I met Isabel when I was a student about a year or so after she arrived in Sydney.

The city had seemed a hostile place for Murris when Isabel's children were young. Isabel's close friend Josie Thorne had taken one of her children to Sydney for medical treatment in 1966. She wrote to Isabel on a postcard showing the imposing and alien architecture of St Andrew's Cathedral and the Town Hall, about as far away from Collarenebri as you could imagine:

> C/- Travellers' Aid, Elizabeth St, Sydney
> Dear Isobel,
> Well, mate, here I am stuck in the big smoke and hate every minute of it. But Joan has four more tests to have. We have to go back on the fifth for the last lot and I am hoping to get the results then it is costing a fortune to live down here even though we are getting our board paid. How did the stall and the meeting go? I have been to housie a few times but couldn't win any thing. We are seeing a lot of Sydney.
> Time is running out mate,
> Cheerio
> Love Josie

The difficulty of surviving Sydney when children needed medical treatment had been what made the Royal Far West Scheme so important for Colle Murris. It had been why they had put so much time into the stalls which Josie mentioned, raising money for the organisation.

Yet things were changing by the later years of the decade. Not only were more outsiders coming to Colle, like the university students who followed the Freedom Ride, but Murris were travelling further for work. The grazing industry continued to slow down, cutting out even more jobs. People were finding they had to travel longer distances for any sort of casual work, like going to the Murrumbidgee for fruit picking and to Dareton for the grape harvest.

Family matters became tangled up with these wider changes. Rose's life in Leeton seemed very far away from Collarenebri for the family who missed her. But her new location in the fruit picking area made her home a link into the lengthening cycles of work travel which northwestern Murries were beginning to make. Ben Flick, Isabel's eldest son, travelled there by train in 1969 along with others for the picking, a trek which had became more and more common as work for young people became harder to find in the northwest.

Barbara had left already, winning a scholarship to complete high school at a boarding school in Armidale in the northern tablelands. Leaving for education was also becoming more common, although financial support to do so was very rare. Barbara struggled with loneliness in Armidale, trying to focus on studying while she was still recovering from her burns and the extensive scars she was left with. But she soon had company.

Other Murris were leaving Collarenebri because they had had enough of the suffocating conditions in the small towns. The stronger job market in growing regional centres offered not just work but a way to escape. Isabel's youngest sister, Lubby, chose this path out of the town she had come to hate. She left Collarenebri in 1966 to live and work in Armidale, which also gave support to Barbara while she was there. Lubby worked as a maid in the University of New England's Wright College, putting herself through a dressmaking course at the same time and learning how to drive. Then she got a motorbike and really began to travel. She rode back and forth across the eastern half of the continent, and fascinated her family with stories from places with fairytale names, like Daydream Island. Lubby's relief at her escape can be read in the letter she sent home to her mother, Celia, around 1969:

Dear Mum,
Just a few lines hoping that you are well and happy. Well how are things going?
 If you ever want to leave Colle just write and say, for I'm sure we can rent a caravan in another town. So Mum please get Isabel to answer for

you. We could have a great time, maybe Isabel would come and stay with us too.

I'd love [to] live with you again, but not in Colle for there'll never be peace in that hole.

Well Mum that's about it so please think about it and write or get Is to write straight away.

To my darling Mum,

love Lubby

XXXXXXX

Another chance of escape beckoned in the new industry of irrigated cotton which had started up just to the east at Wee Waa and Narrabri. While Isabel had been angry at the conditions she saw there for Aboriginal workers, others saw the rising prosperity of the cotton towns as a place to make a new start, to create a fresh relationship between black and white residents, free from the shackles of the old grazing hierarchy of squatters and stockmen and maids. This was the hope that helped Joe and Isobelle Flick decide to move their family to Wee Waa in 1969. And it drew others, like Arthur and Leila Murray and, for a while, Roy and Josie Thorne a few years later in 1972. They all knew they would have to fight to build that new future, but they were willing to take the risk. They just didn't know how hard they would have to fight or what the cost would be . . .

When Joe and Isobelle left, those still in Collarenebri felt their absence badly. For Isabel the loss was intense. Joe's energy and enthusiasm and Isobelle's unfailing and courageous support had been an enormous factor in her rising ability to challenge the repression of the town. Without them, everything looked harder. The networks she had begun to build with people in Sydney began to seem like they offered a stronger hope. While her relations had moved to larger rural towns, Isabel began to look to Sydney itself.

The education of her children was now a major question for her. Her frustration with the schooling available in Collarenebri and in the high schools of the district had reached a peak with her sense that the schools were failing her older children. Hostels had opened in Sydney offering a supportive residential base for rural Aboriginal students. Isabel began to see this as a way to escape the despair of education in the northwest and by early 1972 she decided to take the chance and move. Ben was independent, now well advanced on a high profile regional football career, playing with Narrabri and then Bathurst, and he had married Lorraine Peters. Larry was working and had begun a relationship with his future wife, Jedda Adams, although both families worried that they were too young. Larry and Jedda were defiant and so they stayed in the bush. But Isabel hoped the city might offer new opportunities for Brenda, Tony, Amy and young Aub.

Her announcement at the school that she was leaving generated a flurry of organisation with a farewell supper organised by the Parents and Citizens Association at their regular meeting in April. Isabel collected a whole swag of character references to arm herself against the nerve-wracking task of job hunting when she reached Sydney. Despite the intense pressure which she had experienced as she had tried to change the town, Isabel had already made an extraordinary contribution to the school and the community. The degree to which she had established real relationships with some white townspeople are clear in the warmth of the endorsements in these references.

Dawn Stallworthy, then the hospital matron, wrote of the 'Extremely high sense of responsibility' which Isabel brought to everything she was involved with, while Peter Swane, the Anglican minister in the town, spoke of the privilege of working with her on the school P & C: 'Isabel is respected and trusted in this community and we are very sorry that she is moving on'. Archie Kalokerinos described her with insight: 'She has a natural ability as a social welfare worker, being able to spot problems, talk to people in all circles, and act in a practical manner to overcome the problems. She has been of tremendous value to the community, universally respected and there is no doubt that she will be sorely missed . . .'

There were some Collarenebri people already living in the inner suburbs of Sydney. Vera Roach from the Murray family was one, linked to Isabel by traditional kinship, and Bertha and Myrtle were still there, working at the Childrens' Hospital in Camperdown where they had been when Barbara was in the burns unit for so long in 1963. Barbara herself had returned to Sydney to begin nursing training at the Children's Hospital, drawn to the work by the warm memories she had of the nurses when she was there as a patient. And Isabel had now met up with a number of Sydney political activists, from the unionists she had been meeting with Harry Hall to the young lawyers like Peter Tobin who had come to Walgett in 1969.

At that stage, the greatest concentration of Aboriginal people was in the inner western suburbs, and so that was where the family headed. They struggled to find accommodation, camping around with family and friends for a while in Bridge Road, Glebe, before moving into 102 Johnston Street, Annandale. Isabel began applying for jobs doing what she had always been employed to do, clean and cook. Like Bertha and Myrtle she applied for hospital work and was taken on at Royal Prince Alfred, just up the road from the Children's Hospital. Isabel was to be a maid in the 'assembly room' of the kitchen, where the meals were put together to be sent to the wards.

*Amy and Brenda's baby
Bernadette at the rear of Isabel's
house in Annandale, c. 1974.*

Isabel's initial reaction to the job and to the city itself was a sense of release. It was a new beginning for her. The work at the hospital, where she was just dishing out food, was much lighter physically than the school cleaning at Colle had been. And the atmosphere was different. She felt that the pressure of constant confrontation was no longer on her shoulders:

> *Isabel:* Yes that changed. Of course it wasn't easy to get accommodation. But we didn't come across the hostility so much. I don't know, everyone treated you differently than at home. I don't suppose they had any thoughts about anyone, because they had so many different people—it might've been that. At home you knew everyone, you'd grown up with them and you had to face them next day or you needed to deal with them, so having that hostility to you or confronting their attitudes was much harder. I know we didn't suffer that much in the city even though I always felt more comfortable in going to the Aboriginal Medical Service after that was set up because they had sympathetic doctors there, and people who cared about what they were doing. And that's still the same. Once people started to talk about setting up our own legal service and medical service, I think we started to feel a bit more confident that we could call on different people because there were people advising us about legal issues and we were starting to get to know a lot of people like lawyers, and then we were feeling a bit more comfortable with what we were dealing with.

Isabel arrived in Sydney just as the wave of activism of the past decade crested in the emergence of militant shopfront organisations which were independent of government control. She was already familiar with the Foundation for Aboriginal Affairs, set up by white and Aboriginal activists in Sydney during 1964 and the organisation on which Harry Hall was modelling his Walgett work. And her involvement with the attempts to get better conditions on the cotton fields had introduced her to Sydney unionists, many of whom had a history of involvement in the more left-wing Aboriginal Australian Fellowship and in supporting the trips by unionists to Walgett and Moree even before the Freedom Ride.

But by 1972 many of the younger Aboriginal people who had come to Sydney for education and jobs, and who had spent time at the dances and offices of the Foundation, were becoming more interested in American models of urban community activism. The work of the Panthers in California, for example, had met urgent needs by setting up shopfront agencies which drew on white professionals and students to support communities struggling against racism and poverty. These young Aboriginal activists were building on an urban movement which had already been established in Sydney, so the outcomes did echo the American experience, but were also very home-grown responses to particular Australian conditions.

The movement away from small country towns had been happening across the state, and had brought many Aborigines to Sydney. Some had followed relations into Leichhardt and other suburbs, but Redfern and Waterloo were often the first stop for the flow of rural immigrants in the 1960s. Ken Brindle was one of the activists who had started organising social football and dances for the newly arriving immigrants in the 1960s and who ended up challenging the ways local government and police had been trying to control the growing Aboriginal population by harassment and brutality on the streets.

Young Aboriginal law students and their lecturers worked together through structures like the Council for Civil Liberties and drew on the body of support built up by the Aboriginal Australian Fellowship. They began to mount challenges not only in the courts but on the streets themselves, with night patrols of lawyers in Redfern to observe and report on police behaviour. Similar networks had begun to form between activist doctors, like Fred Hollows, and Aboriginal people in the inner urban communities, including those like Barbara Flick who were working in the health system. Campaigns against racism, like the Anti-Apartheid Campaigns against South African sporting teams during 1970 and 1971 galvanised and educated a wider range of white students than had been involved before, leading to a larger body of volunteers to help staff the fledgling agencies which set up in the run-down shopfronts of Redfern to give free legal and medical aid to the Aboriginal community.

So this was the scene into which Isabel arrived, a whirl of newly formed and energetic organisations, struggling to identify and address urgent legal and health needs with no funds and poor facilities. But what they did have was a body of enthusiastic Aboriginal people and professional and student volunteers. Some of them were young people Isabel had met in the bush, like the lawyer Peter Tobin, now graduated and still committed to working for the communities in the west. Almost before she had unpacked the family's scanty ports Isabel was invited onto the committees that were setting up these organisations, really making up the rules as they went along for organisations which had never been seen in Australia before. They tried many models, and the traces of their experiments can still be seen in the way the organisations are shaped today. A formal structure as a basis for an organisation seemed reasonably important in itself, particularly for those Aborigines with a union background, but it rapidly became a necessity when later in 1972 the Whitlam Labor Government came to power at the Federal elections and for the first time promised substantial funding to Aboriginal community bodies. But funds could only be handed over to bodies which were legally set up to receive government moneys.

A common early model was the co-operative, drawn from the contact between union and christian socialist traditions which generated Tranby Aboriginal Co-operative College, an organisation which became increasingly important to Isabel. This model had been tried out in Aboriginal community enterprises from the mid-1950s in Queensland and in northern coastal New South Wales and it was valued for its protection of the rights of all shareholders in the co-operative. It had been championed by Tranby's Reverend Alf Clint because it seemed to reflect the egalitarianism of traditional and contemporary Aboriginal culture. Another early model was the commercial company, and despite concerns about its ideology, it was seen as a quick solution. The young lawyers who were volunteering to assist the fledgling Aboriginal Legal Service organised it as a company; but they also tried to work out ways in which the complexities of company law could be made manageable for the urban and rural Aboriginal communities which could now apply for funds to build houses only if they had a properly set-up housing company to hold the funding. The result was a body of 'shelf companies', empty but legal bodies which had already been registered and which could be rapidly modified with a new name and a set of local directors to fit the circumstances in any local rural community.

The learning demands were enormous for everyone on the committees of these new organisations: they not only had to develop a political and professional strategy for running a new medical or legal service but they had to learn the rules of company procedure and come to grips with the responsibilities of directors of companies, the rules of formal meeting process, and the financial dealings of major government departments. Union experience helped some people, but the community base of these organisations, with tensions arising from family differences and the competing loyalties of different areas of origin, was a very long way from a body of individual union members. On top of this were the particular challenges for Aboriginal community members on committees. Like Isabel, many of them had been denied even basic education in a racist 'public' school system. Now they were faced with hiring, managing and firing a workforce of [mostly] non-Aboriginal professionals.

These few short years in Isabel's life were tumultuous. She was faced with the intense pressure on her family of urban life along with the exhilaration of the new and exciting politics of the period and the tough learning necessary to make those organisations work. They not only had to deliver services effectively but do so in a principled manner which would strengthen Aboriginal communities, not weaken them. While Isabel was immediately drawn into these new bodies—particularly to South Sydney Community Aid in Regent Street Redfern, then in the Medical Service and then at Tranby—she did not have to take on major managing roles. Instead, she was an observer at close range, watching and learning and considering everything she saw in terms of her experience in community organising in Collarenebri and her continuing close links with her family back there in the bush. Whether co-operative or company, these community organisations all faced the dangers of corruption, nepotism and the concentration of power into too few hands. The big questions she saw in Sydney in the early 1970s were just as relevant for those rural communities. They were questions she was to grapple with for the rest of her life: how could communities fight for what they wanted and then organise themselves to carry out their goals in ways that not only got things done but were representative of all in the community—both sustainable and democratic.

Isabel laughed years later about her rapid induction to Sydney politics and her early caution with the political activists she met:

> *Isabel:* As soon as I came down here I got mixed up in all kinds of organisations. First there was the South Sydney Community Aid, with that girl that got that Human Rights award, Vivi Kostanardi, for working with the Greeks. And her parents had a café down there, not far from the South Sydney Community Aid. I did a little bit with them and that was more working with the people working in the churches, and they were trying to see whether they could help Aboriginal people. And we used to

go down there and nut out what we were going to do. And me and Richard Pacey were the only two Aboriginals on it then. And then I think old Bob Mazza came on it.

When the Tent Embassy was being set up in Canberra, I went along to some of the meetings where people would work out how they could support the Embassy and they were talking about getting an Aboriginal flag. I used to try and go along to all those kinds of meetings then. But I didn't want to get mixed up with those 'freedom fighters' too much. I was a bit cautious about that at first, but once I settled in down here and found out what it was all about, I often started to think: 'Why aren't we out there again?' I think it should've been done on a yearly basis. We might've got somewhere then.

I think I had first become aware of Tranby in the late sixties, late 1969, or 1970. It was one of my first visits down to Sydney and I was staying in Glebe, and I just sort of wandered around this way and the sign out the front just caught my eye. There was three students from New Guinea inside and I just knocked on the door and said, 'Mind if I have a look around?' And they said, 'Oh we're setting up co-operatives for Aboriginals, that's one of the things that the brothers are doing'. And they talked about some church organisation that I didn't have a lot to do with . . . but I kept hearing about Tranby, 'Oh the church has got some kind of thing going for Aboriginals around here', and I think Tranby kept flashing back into my mind.

Then in 1971, I dropped in and Lester Bostock was one of the first Aboriginal blokes I knew that was doing some voluntary work with the books. So I sat down and talked to Lester and I said, 'Oh you know this sounds like a very good place, and if you could keep it so Aboriginal people are havin' the most say . . .' And he said, 'I think that'll come'. By the end of 1972 when I was living in Sydney, I started to come in more often. Kevin Cook was involved by then and I began to do a lot of things with Cookie. I was meeting all the different groups that were starting to say, you know, 'Hang on, we want to do things for ourselves and we have rights!'.

So I became involved in the movement in earnest and it was then that I saw other Aboriginal people coming down and we'd start to meet at Tranby. So often we'd all be busy going about our work at home and in our communities. We were trying to put it together down here in Sydney so we could take it back there to home. All our knowledge and energy was going back into our communities.

Kevin Cook had started to co-ordinate meetings. We needed that co-ordination to say, well this is some of our plans that'll work and we'd run with that. And a lot of our people become directors on the Board of Tranby, like Jacko Campbell. So after a while, we were not only just blacks sticking up for their rights, we became like brothers and sisters. Kevin had a way of putting us at ease in what we were doing, this is how I see Tranby and Kevin and you can't isolate these two.

As well as her new friendships, Isabel caught up with young Aboriginal people whom she already knew from the bush, like Lynne Craigie from Moree, who was living in Surry Hills with her husband, Peter Thompson, a non-Aboriginal archaeologist who had also grown up in Moree and who was then working in the Australian Museum. Lynne and Peter, with Lynne's younger brother Billy Craigie, were activists in the Sydney Aboriginal and anti-racist movements. Their tiny house in East Sydney was lined with posters of the Native American icons and the famous images of the Black Panthers, and it was always busy with the Aboriginal students and friends who had been the footsoldiers in the campaigns to stop the sale of the Eveleigh Street houses, to protest about the South African Springbok tours or to demand Aboriginal Land Rights. Lynne was involved at the grass-roots level in the newly established medical and legal services, doing the night rounds in the tough back streets of Redfern looking for Aboriginal people in trouble with the law or in need of urgent transport to the emergency ward of the nearby Prince Alfred Hospital. Peter Tobin was a constant visitor and so were other young white friends drawn into the networks by Lynne or Peter.

Some time early in 1972, Isabel met up with Paul Torzillo, a third-year medical student at Prince Alfred where she was working. Paul was already volunteer driving for Lynne Thompson on her night rounds and was beginning to learn about Aboriginal politics as well as health issues. Isabel remembered being surprised by his interest when she went to an outpatients' clinic where he was a student observer, and she was amused when he was able to usher her in far more quickly than she was used to being seen:

> *Isabel:* So, that's where I met Paulie. I went to the hypertension clinic and so I was taken straight in! And that's when we started to talk about, oh, all sorts of things. I suppose Paulie must've been a bit like I was with Cookie, see. Cookie knew a lot of the people that I was starting to mix with. And he was able to steer me in the right direction, because I didn't know the people. I think that's how we built up a relationship too. And that's what I could do with Paulie. Then you'd start to mooch around with this one, that one and the other one. So it's become an ongoing thing I think, where we keep learning from each other. And that's a good sort of life to go on with, eh?

So Isabel took Paul under her wing, like she did with so many other young people she met, black and white. Paul had already heard about the outspoken local doctor, Archie Kalokerinos at Collarenebri, through his contacts with Fred Hollows and the Aboriginal Medical Service. He had a 12-week elective term coming up and had been thinking about doing it under Archie's supervision in Collarenebri. Isabel encouraged him, and offered to catch up with him there if she was visiting home during his stay. Isabel hadn't stopped thinking about the bush, despite her hectic time in Sydney. In fact she had begun to draw on the whirl of optimistic ideas in the city to begin planning to make a difference in Collarenebri.

Characteristically, Isabel did meet Paul in Colle on her repeated visits, and took the opportunity to draw him into a larger project she had begun to think about. This is how Paul remembered his experience:

Paul Torzillo: In retrospect, I think that Isabel had already seen the possibility of me going to Collarenebri as an opportunity. She wanted to upgrade my education and to 'school' me about Aboriginal communities. But she also wanted to get me to help her to get some change happening on the Reserve at Collarenebri. She felt that the Reserve was an urgent priority and she was trying to find a mechanism to make change happen.

Living conditions on the Reserve were horrendous. Housing consisted of tin humpies with only two water points on the whole reserve. One of these was a single tap and one was a structure which had been built in the sixties as an ablution facility. When I saw this it consisted of a few pieces of galvanised iron over an area with a couple of broken tubs beside what was supposed to be a washing area. This was a small piece of concrete with a drain that was completely blocked so that the whole area was continually flooded with dirty and contaminated water and could not be used for anything.

The Reserve had quite a mixture of inhabitants. There was old Mrs Bessie Khan, a quiet but always smartly dressed old woman. Shirley Weatherall lived there with a big mob of kids. And there were a range of other families.

The whole situation was really a microcosm of many communities facing huge environmental problems, but with a whole range of obstructions to organisation that many people would not understand. Isabel, I realised later, saw all these difficulties quite clearly. She recognised that change was going to be difficult not just because of the problems of moving the bureaucracy, but also the difficulty of getting people organised and lobbying together. As in most communities there were some long-held family differences between people, and Isabel herself had some difficulties in approaching everyone. Another thing I did not realise was that it was necessary to organise people, both in the town as well as on the Reserve to be supporting a general principle of change. But what I did begin to see was a talent of Isabel's that I was to see many times in her career. This was the ability to utilise white support very astutely. She was aware of the potential value of white supporters, as well as their hazards. I also think that she was someone in whom the politics and the social justice of situations was really the dominant issue and so this allowed her to form friendships and comradeships with white supporters which few other Aboriginal leaders were able to do. The presence of a young, fairly naive, quite inexperienced but energetic white medical student for three months was an opportunity rather than a nuisance for Isabel. In the weeks after I arrived I underwent a really amazing and intensive training course in what would probably be called 'community development' nowadays, but in reality was training for political organisation and action.

Two processes began simultaneously through which Isabel began introducing me to almost the whole Aboriginal population in the town. I thought that all of this was happening through some random process, but in retrospect it was really quite orchestrated. It was done carefully, sequentially and with deliberate briefings which nevertheless seemed quite spontaneous. We would be sitting on the step of her house and she would just start talking about someone. She would talk a little bit about the person—she might mention where they had worked or what they had done in the past and would invariably highlight some skill. 'So and so, he is always good with the funerals—you know he organises the things, gets the grave digging to happen and always manages to find a car . . .' Or: 'So and so was really great on the fences, you know he fenced that station out at such and such'.

She would always tell a little introductory story to 'place' the person. Then she would outline how he was related to her or other people I might know and usually say something about what she thought that person might be able to contribute. Another device she often used was to relate a conversation she will have had with the person as a way of demonstrating some point she wanted to make about them. Sometimes it would be an actual conversation she had had, but sometimes, as I realised later, it was an amalgam of experiences she had had with that person which she related by enacting it as a conversation. She gave me this background for men and for women, for young people and old people, and she clearly had a view that everyone had some potential to contribute to the struggle.

Of course, in a small town like Collarenebri she could also 'place' the white fellas in the same way and provide a similar background. She certainly did this for sympathetic figures like Archie Kalokerinos and people like Henry Denyer and his son, Harry, who was following his father in his quiet support for the Aboriginal community in the town. And she could do it for those white fellas who were antagonistic as well!

The next step was to organise me to meet the Aboriginal people she had told me about. Sometimes she would do this by going to visit the people for some reason and just having me tag along, or sometimes she would construct some other circumstance where I would get to meet that family. She would sit back and just observe how I performed in this circumstance. If I had stuffed up at the beginning then she could have stepped in to cut the process off, but this was a way of assessing my potential.

Early on Isabel got me to the Reserve. Doreen Hynch and Les Adams were living there at that time and I got to know them early. They were fantastic supports and incredibly helpful and soon became my base on the Reserve. My first real political issue was to take on the ablution block. In those early days we had unbelievably modest claims. Certainly Doreen was just trying to get another couple of taps on the Reserve and get some way to drain the ablution block. I was of course naively optimistic about the outcomes, because the case for change seemed so strong. I was later to realise that just getting this humble goal to happen was actually going to take a few years. Over my time in Collarenebri this involved innumerable phone calls by me from the local public phone box to Walgett Community Welfare Office, letters being drafted, discussed and sent, and eventually a couple of visits from the Walgett officers, who travelled over to the Reserve with Harry Hall, by then working as a liaison officer with the department.

These were great educative experiences for me. On their first visit, the Welfare officers told me that the only reason the drains were blocked was that Aboriginal kids would push tin cans down the drain. Even at that stage I was able to look at the grill, rusted in over the drain and with at best one-centimetre gaps in it, and realise that no one could push a tin can through it. This myth of blaming health hardware failure on vandalism is a tradition in Australian politics. It reappeared so often in my later work that by the 1990s I became involved in a long-term study of Aboriginal housing across the country which has finally disproved the myth. We have now studied over 5000 Aboriginal houses in every state except Tasmania and Victoria. We have shown conclusively that problems exactly like the ones I first saw in Collarenebri are caused 98.5 per cent of the time by poor design and faulty construction.[1] They are almost never caused by resident vandalism. All this work arose in a very real way from that experience on the Wollai at Collarenebri in 1972.

The process of organisation around this little action was a fascinating example of how Isabel worked. After getting me established and friendly with Doreen and Les, Isabel began the process of introducing me to the rest of the people on the Reserve. This was not easy. Most of these people were not in the habit of talking to strange white fellas for a start. They were quite reasonably suspicious and most of them recognised that it was pretty unlikely that they were going to get much benefit from talking to me. And for my part, I was nervous and uncertain. However, Isabel guided me through this process, usually by teaching me to do things in a slow fashion and one at a time.

As the talking around about the ablution facility went on, the issue of actually forming a housing company was raised. I think that Isabel just dropped this into the conversation one day as Doreen and I were discussing the environmental health and housing issues. This planted the seed, so gradually we were moved from focusing just around two extra taps and unblocking a drain to the idea of forming a housing company. In retrospect, I think that this was something that Isabel saw might evolve and that she really recognised quite early that we had to have some start-up issue to get the whole thing rolling and to get people involved.

We decided that in regard to the ablution block we needed some sort of letter or petition that would be signed by everyone on the Reserve, or at least supported by them. As time went on, this process merged with the idea of getting support for establishing a housing company. In any event, this gave me an excuse or a reason to be talking to people. We kept going through the same process. Isabel would just suddenly raise somebody's name one morning. She would give me one of her briefings and then tell me that we should go over to the Reserve at a particular time. On some occasions we would both go and she would walk up to the camp, sit down, just start generally yarning and then casually introduce me through the process. I had a little clipboard with a draft letter on it and we would gradually start to talk and then we would discuss the issues. She did this a few times and then would sometimes change the style. She might send me on my own. Sometimes this seemed to be because she thought I would be okay to cope or because she thought it would be good for me.

On other occasions there were clearly strategic reasons. I remember her explaining to me in great detail Shirley Weatherall's role in the community and how it was very important to talk through these issues with her. Then as usual I drove Isabel down to the Reserve. When we were about 200 metres from Shirley's place, Isabel said 'just pull up here'. I stopped the car and then she said, 'Look I've just got to walk over this way. Why don't you go down there and see her?' I was a bit nervous about this and asked Isabel if it wouldn't be better if she just took me down to introduce me. In a very off-handed fashion she just said, 'Oh no, you go down there. You'll be right'. It wasn't until a long time after this that I realised that Shirley had been Aub Weatherall's first wife. This was the reason that Shirley would have felt uncomfortable if Isabel had come. It was a great example of mixing the personal and the political!

Probably the next stage in the process was Isabel getting Barbara and I together. Both Barbara and I often recount the story of our first meeting. In 1972 Barbara was living in Wee Waa, and had driven across to see Isabel with her young baby, Dezi. Isabel had not mentioned to Barbara that I was actually in Collarenebri and often staying at the house at that time. I remember walking back from the hospital up to the Block and there was Isabel on the step with Barbara sitting next to her and Dezi breastfeeding. Isabel said, 'Barbara, this is Paulie Torzillo. He's a young medical student from Sydney'. Barbara looked me up and down and her first words to me were: 'So this is the young doctor come to save the poor black fellas'. Normally I would have been intimidated by the sarcasm of that comment. But Isabel brushed it aside by saying something mildly reproving of Barbara and then asking her a question about what she thought we should do about the upcoming campaign around the Reserve. Barbara immediately responded to that and addressed it seriously. She managed to include me in the conversation and it kicked on from there.

I am sure now in retrospect that this was part of Isabel's schooling of Barbara too. She had clearly recognised even then that Barbara would not just be a protégé of hers, but be someone who was going to really make a big impact. I was somewhat in awe of Barbara over the following weeks and months, but actually very quickly she swung into action around the housing company.

Things moved pretty fast then. Almost without me understanding why, we had a community meeting of everyone on the Reserve one night where we discussed the establishment of the housing company. A few old fellas decided on the appropriate name: they chose Mangankali, meaning sand goanna, which is an animal particularly associated with Collarenebri. They felt it was the right name to link the organisation, the people and the place. In typical style, Barbara produced all the essentials. She typed them up on an old typewriter and in what took only minutes, we had a submission for the establishment of a housing company in front of us. It was probably almost a decade before that process actually resulted in some housing coming to Collarenebri, but it was an essential step on the way. I guess that like Ho Chi Minh, Isabel realised that sometimes you had to be prepared to wait for victory.

This whole episode allowed me to learn some things about Isabel which I realised over time were fundamental to the way she did every-thing. One was that she was a political strategist and organiser. Isabel was always able to have an overview—to facilitate, encourage, organise and sometimes manipulate other people to undertake action to get to a goal that she had already predetermined. Another was a talent I suspect was related, and that was the ability to be doing several things and running several agendas at the same time. Thirdly, was her ability to develop and maintain incredibly close friendships. I think these were more than friendships: they were really examples of comradeship because of the way they evolved and were sustained.

Collarenebri wasn't the only place where Murris wanted changes in 1972. The bush communities across the northwest were each raising demands for change and the volatile situation Isabel had witnessed on the cotton fields in Wee Waa blew up late in the year. Her brother Joe and his family were in the thick of it. The summer of late 1972 and early 1973 was hot but wet as well. The many Aboriginal people from all over the state who had come to chip in the fields faced the worst conditions imaginable. The 'camping' area at Tulladunna was well situated to be close to pick up spots to meet employers and get out into the fields, and it was next to the river so water was available. But the campsite was virtually unserviced, with no taps, no showers and no toilets. This was of course just like the Reserve at Collarenebri and in other towns, but it was put under even worse pressure with the massive influx in numbers which the cotton season brought. Heavy summer rains that year turned the black soil campsites like Tulladunna into deep quagmires in which families camped around their bogged cars trying to dry soaked bedding by draping their blankets over the open car doors or hanging sheets on fence wires. Over these months, the local paper was full of reports of large numbers of fish found dead inexplicably in the lagoons. Aboriginal chippers were being sent into the fields with no protection from the aerial spraying of concentrated DDT being delivered frequently to try to beat the boll weevil plague which was ravaging the crop at the time.[2] The conditions on the camps led to a dozen Aboriginal children being hospitalised early in December 1972, and an outcry was raised by the local doctor, leading to a promise to install a bore and get electricity to work its pump to try to provide clean water at Tulladunna. It is not clear if work had even started on this when, two days before Christmas, in the rising atmosphere of anxiety that all these events combined to generate, an Aboriginal woman dropped to her knees and died in the middle of the cotton fields as she chipped weeds in the heat. A couple of weeks later, early in January 1973, another Aboriginal man died while he too was chipping.[3] Joe Flick has described the situation over that terrible summer:

> *Joe Flick:* When the cotton started, the Aboriginal people came in from everywhere for the employment. And there was about, I suppose, two to 3000. Mostly Aborigines and Torres Strait Islanders who used to come in for the work during the chipping season. Mainly Aboriginal workers, there was hardly any European people on the field until later years when we got the award wage, then you'd see the Europeans come in. When the chipping started each year it was coming Christmas time and they'd do anything for Christmas. And it used to be lovely to see all these beautiful people from all around, it was really great to see the big gathering, but the conditions were terrible. The Murris had about a 20-mile radius with little camps here, there and everywhere. Then they made a main camp in Tulladunna close to town.
>
> They used to get their water from the river, because they didn't know anything about it then, about pesticides in the water, they didn't know a thing about them. Once they got more aware of it, they had to carry their water from the town tap, they used to get the water up in the town. No one to take it down to them, they had to carry it down with their containers. There were no toilets, no showers . . . nothing. They had to dig their own pit toilets, probably go down three to four foot and put a bag around it.
>
> The growers were spraying the cotton, spraying while the chippers were on the field. But the Murris weren't aware of how the spray could affect them then. There was no protective clothing. What you went to work in that morning, that's what you'd come home with at night. It didn't make any difference, they just seemed to think it was all Aborigines working there, so they just thought they were nothing. The growers were using these little kids to chip there, and some of the Murris thought it was a great family affair to go onto this cotton field. But it was very dangerous at that time for kids to go onto the field because those kids would be in among the cotton when they were spraying it.
>
> But the growers didn't seem to understand that, as long as they got their work done. And they were only paying a dollar an hour . . . ten dollars a day. So you had to work ten hours to get ten dollars, and it was cheaper before that.

They didn't care whether you were on the field or not, they'd spray you. When it was time to spray, they'd spray just the same. I remember one poor chap, he saw the plane coming in and he started to walk fast, and as the plane came closer he started to run; he couldn't get away so he just dived into the cotton and the plane just went straight over and sprayed him and the whole lot of us. That used to be a common thing.

I wasn't aware of it for starters too, because I was just like the rest of them. But at the finish I started to sing out about it and bring the newspaper into it at the time . . . Well, with them, once you started to sing out about it, you were a bloody agitator or something . . . you were interfering with them. And of course, I wasn't very well liked then, because I got under the skin of the cotton growers. 'He's a bad man that Flick'. I had the worst name in Wee Waa.

And the bloody contractors were as bad as the owners. Even today the contractors are as bad as the owners . . . They might take us off the field and say, 'We're going to spray this', and about two hours later they'd said, 'Oh, we've finished spraying there, go back on the field', they want us straight back on. And the cotton was wet with the spray, so I didn't go on. I just picked my spade up and shot through. The contractor was saying: 'It's all right, it can't hurt you now it's all finished'. But you can smell the bloody thing. It's a terrible smell.

Of course, diseases were breaking out—these women were having miscarriages and all this business. And blokes were getting cancer and some other diseases we never ever heard of, they were new to us. See, when the strike started I was trying to think of these things, and I was trying to look at these poor little kids—10 year olds, walking all day, up and down the water line, up and down handing out water, and then in the cotton the same as the men and the women, and they must've been affected too, it scared me.

Well, in the strike, we didn't want to see any kids go out there.[4] And we didn't want that poison to be put on the field while the chippers were on the field. And we wanted better facilities for the people, toilets and showers and all those sort of things for them—to come home and have a good shower and have your hands clean when you're having a feed. And to stop the council from kicking them around from pillar to post—which they were doing. There were a few from each camp in the strike, but . . . half the people didn't have food . . . then we set up some food relief . . . Social Security had to come there. And we put in the money and we gave them food rations.

There was me and Michael Anderson, Harry Hall . . . I think that's the only three. We went to Sydney, and we saw the Waterside Workers to help us out with the strike, to fund us, because the people never had any money to buy tucker, so that was the only way we were successful with that strike. The union wage came in and they said: 'Well, we'll knock off all the kids, the kids can't work anymore'. Well, I felt real pleased about that because I didn't want the kids to be there. But there were families who said: 'Well, I'm going to miss out, my kids are not going to get paid and we're not going to be getting that amount of money'; but they were the ones thinking about themselves and didn't care how their kiddies were going to get hurt.

In that strike, we had to try and get things on a more even scale. So we had to set up these campsites. The Advancement Association got going and we set up three campsites there for them. The council had to come to the party sooner or later.

The strike achieved a minimum wage for the chippers, and the exclusion of children from the fields. The Wee Waa Aboriginal community, with strong support from nearby Walgett and Collarenebri, set up the Wee Waa Aboriginal Advancement Association, and they campaigned for immediate improvements in the facilities in the camps and for more suitable camping grounds. But throughout the rest of the summer, the spraying continued and the local paper kept reporting sightings of dead fish in the river and reports of confirmed pesticide poisonings among both workers and residents affected by spray drift as the pesticides sprayed on the crops was blown over the town and nearby grazing properties.[5] The tensions at Wee Waa—about cotton generally and between black and white residents—were not going to go away.

Joe Flick (on right), Roy Thorne and Harry Hall (third and fourth from left) at an early meeting of the Wee Waa Aboriginal Advancement Association, c. 1973. (Photo: Wee Waa Echo and Karen Flick.)

Isabel followed the Wee Waa saga closely, saw Joe when he was in Sydney for meetings with the unions, and was in constant touch with Collarenebri as well. Isabel was a great letter writer, sending off short notes and cards just to keep in touch and for every occasion from birthdays to illnesses to anniversaries. Her main family focus was in Collarenebri because her mother Celia was there, living in the house on the Block with her sister Clara. Their brother Jimmy had a house over the gully, and Lubby had come back home.

Relenting in her determination never to go near Colle again, Lubby had returned to see her family at about the same time as Isabel was preparing to leave in 1972. But instead of a short visit, Lubby stayed on, falling into a relationship with a Collarenebri man which rapidly became tense and violent. She had a son, Deakin, early in 1973 but towards the end of that year the situation deteriorated and Lubby was desperate to get away. Her family knew she was in trouble and supported her when she boarded the train at Pokataroo, heading to the city to take refuge with Isabel and Barbara. But her bloke heard about it and raced the train to Wee Waa in his car. He pulled her off the train there, and after a very public argument they disappeared. Lubby was found shot dead outside the town.

The family were distraught. Isabel rushed up to Collarenebri and helped with the funeral as best she could. Baby Deakin was brought into his mother's family, cared for by all his aunties, but really settling with Joe and Isobelle in Wee Waa. The family had no peace as they waited on the outcome of the police investigation. For Isabel and all her brothers and sisters, the years of watching police intimidation and abuse of Aborigines in the area had fostered a deep distrust. Their worst fears were confirmed when the long, distressing inquest at Wee Waa ended in nothing but frustration. The family were convinced Lubby had been murdered, but the coroner's open verdict suggested suicide. It seemed like an easy way out for a justice system which didn't want to take the trouble to find out what had really happened to this young black woman.

Isabel was shattered by Lubby's death and its aftermath. She was haunted by the feeling that she could have intervened had she still been living in Colle. It began to suck the energy out of her. Her unresolved grief was overwhelming and on top of the sense of things being out of control in the new city environment, she felt she was having a breakdown. This was an episode of the deep depression which was periodically to overtake her in the years to come. It changed the way Isabel saw life in the city, which instead of a new beginning began to seem like a series of ever worsening trials for her family to drag themselves through. Her blood pressure became more difficult to control, interrupting her ability to work and look after her busy household.

And the Flick house at 102 Johnston Street was busy! It was a semi-detached single-storey house on a wide street near the Annandale shops, larger than many in the inner city and with a laundry downstairs under the back of the house. There were usually people staying, along with the immediate family. Barbara Flick and her husband, Bill Kennedy from Walgett, and their baby son, Dezi, were often there after they moved from Wee Waa to Sydney. Isabel's eldest daughter Brenda had had a baby, Bernadette, and so there was a whole new generation of Flicks to enjoy and worry about. Clara Mason's daughter, Jacqui, was living with a supportive church family in nearby Burwood, but she welcomed Isabel's visits. In 1975, Clara's youngest son, Noel, also needed visiting as he lay in a St Ives hospital, immobilised for months in a cast to correct congenital hip problems.

The house was a hub of contact too with the other Collarenebri and northwestern families in the city. Aub's eldest son by his first marriage, Bob Weatherall and his wife Patty, lived close by and were regular visitors and comrades in the campaigns Isabel was involved in to improve the local city schools for their kids. Another regular Collarenebri connection were Bruce and Pat Mason with their children. Bruce was Clara's brother-in-law, brother of Josie Thorne, and the youngest son of Nanna Pearlie Mason; he had grown up on the Old Camp with Isabel. His wife Pat was a sister of Mavis Rose from Walgett, another strong and active woman in a nearby western town in which Aboriginal politics was dominated by men. Both Bruce and Pat remained Isabel's staunch friends, as did Mavis Rose.

So the northwestern connections shaped the way the household worked. There was often a crowd of people at the house, sometimes in a big card game of Eucre, sometimes getting ready to go to housie to meet up with other Murris, or just sitting round and yarning. But there were others as well. A quirky demonstration of the generosity and empathy which Isabel and her family showed to anyone in trouble was Col, the old down-and-out white bloke whom Amy had found in the street and taken pity on, bringing him home a bit like a lost dog. Isabel had agreed that he could spend the night in the downstairs laundry, and he had just sort of stayed, unobtrusive, respectful, and probably barely able to believe his good fortune.

Isabel found the space to invite some of the new friends she had been making in the political movements. Peter Tobin was there and Paul Torzillo began to drop in, partly to continue the work Isabel had got him started on, partly to keep an eye on Isabel's health, and partly just to pass the time, sitting and talking on the end of Isabel's bed because her bedroom was the one quiet place in the house.

One of those visits early in 1974 was my first introduction to Isabel. I'd been hearing about her since Paul had first met her and I was nervous as I was introduced to this woman who had so inspired him. And it was easy to see why. Isabel was extraordinary as she talked with Paul about Collarenebri;

astute and shrewd, and hilarious as she parodied the obstructive officials with whom they had had to deal. And as she talked she never stopped analysing the situation and seeking out practical ways they could try to get through the bureaucratic maze. Isabel was cautious with me as she sized me up, but she became more interested as I asked her about my project.

The idea had grown from a conversation I'd had with Peter Tobin, whom I'd come to know well by then. I was being offered an opportunity for post-graduate research and Peter advised me not to waste it on a distant, esoteric topic, but to grab the chance to do the urgent work of recording the memories of the older members of the Aboriginal communities around the state. Isabel knew how powerful these stories were and was interested in the possibilities of having them brought together. Before long she started to suggest people I could go to for more advice and things I could ask about, many of them the formative experiences of her own life—like colour bars in schools and police violence. So I became one of the visitors to 102, dropping in for a cup of tea and, recruited to do some driving every now and again, I'd catch up on a talk with Isabel as I dropped her off to one or other of the many appointments she had to keep after work, like visiting little Noel Mason or going to one of her meetings.

She started looking after me like she looked after Paulie and Peter and the other young people she took under her wing. I can't even begin to count the times I was deeply grateful to her for it. For some of her city friends, the bush environment was familiar, but for others like me, country white society was just as alien to us as her Aboriginal bush communities were. Isabel was a guide and navigator into the untracked wastes of rural race relations. The delicate negotiating and communicating skills she had polished in the tough years she had lived in Collarenebri were what she was teaching from as she suggested the most likely people to approach with questions, how to tactfully avoid confrontations if we could, or to face them where they were unavoid-able, when to expect attacks and when to confidently pursue the secrets she knew were locked up in country council minutes and school files. She kept an eye on us, suggesting useful work we could do, pushing us into challenging situations because she knew we'd learn that way. She gave us advice so we didn't make fools of ourselves too often, worried about us and defended us if, or when, we messed up, laughed with us later to ease our regret and embar-rassment, and gave us a chance to talk about it and learn from our mistakes.

Despite its warmth, Isabel's household wasn't peaceful and it wasn't always happy. She was working hard because she had one of the few stable incomes in the family and her spare time was often soaked up by political meetings. Her children felt her absence, struggling to deal with the tension between their resentment at what they saw as her lack of attention, and their admiration and support for her political work.

Tony Flick at Kirinari Aboriginal School Boys' Hostel. Tony is sixth from left in a checked shirt. His cousin Joey is fourth from left.

Tony had had a mixed experience at Kirinari. His cousin Joey, Joe and Isobelle's son, was there, as were many teenaged boys from other north-western communities like Brewarrina and Bourke. But the arrangements for schooling had just changed, as Tony has remembered:

> *Tony:* All the other Kirinari kids had gone to Gymea High, but me and Tommy Stewart from Bourke, being new, they thought they'd put a couple of Kirinari boys at Sylvania just for a trial. We were the only two there, whereas if we'd been at Gymea, we'd have been among maybe 22 kids. And because we were only young fellas, we were way outnumbered and outclassed! Lucky Tommy could fight, believe me . . . 'Cause I was always skinny! . . . But it was good. I was glad I went to Kirinari. At least it gave us a chance, and I think I took advantage of the chances I've had, 'cause I've worked all my life.

Tony completed his School Certificate at Kirinari, but the apprenticeships he looked for to meet his interest in mechanical work were impossible to find. The factory jobs which were open for him and his father in the city were alienating and short term. Isabel's partner Aub was unhappy in the city and he worked less and less and began drinking more often in frustration. Amy and young Aub had a hard time at the local high schools and Amy particularly ran wild in the unregulated spaces of the city.

Amy's exploits became legendary. Her activities were victimless crimes, but outrageous and provocative ones. She dabbled with stealing cars, but never ordinary cars. Her attention-seeking behaviour was deeply worrying for Isabel, but it was also a cry for some sort of help. The apprentice filmmaker Phil Noyce was interested in making a film about her called simply *Amy*, which became a talking piece at the time about the dilemmas facing Aboriginal families in the city. For Isabel, it was a worry that she didn't need but she was at least able to draw on the resources of her friends:

> *Isabel:* Amy went through a really bad time growing up. I think I was trotting up to the court all the time; she was in all kinds of misdemeanours—off with a bunch of kids in a car. And ended up stealing it and driving through Coonamble, four little black girls in a Mercedes! One time, she'd given her age as 18 and she ended up in Silverwater Women's Prison. And that friend of ours came over and he said: 'Wipe your legs over, put your shoes on. You've got to go'. Poor Peter Tobin, he was such a great worker. And getting to know people like him gave me more confidence as I went along.

Peter Tobin had fulfilled his promise to Isabel and taken up the job as the first country solicitor with the Aboriginal Legal Service in 1973. He served as legal adviser for Aborigines across the whole western half of the state for an arduous and exciting 18 months before returning to Redfern as Principal Solicitor in the Aboriginal Legal Service. He saw her both in her visits to Collarenebri and in Sydney: he continued to give her legal advice and she continued to give him personal and community advice in a friendship which was sustained despite their geographic distance and travels. His support for her family and community was important to Isabel as she tried to work out how to make it through one crisis after another.

Problems about her own house in Collarenebri were worrying Isabel. Since she had moved, the Block wasn't just a house for her mother Celia, her sister Clara and her family. It had a heavy symbolic value for all the family—wherever they were living—because of the struggle Mick had had to secure the lease in the first place against the racism of the town and then because of his success in making it such a home base for them all.

The western lands lease over the Block itself was held in perpetuity, with only a relatively small annual lease fee. But Isabel had borrowed money from the Aborigines Welfare Board in order to build the house there in 1969. From 1972, there was little money going into paying off the loan: there wasn't much left from Clara's and Celia's pensions after Clara's seven children had been fed. Isabel's family was struggling to make ends meet to pay their rent and to support their teenaged children in the expensive city. The mortgage payments fell into arrears and by December 1974, the Directorate, successor to the Welfare Board, demanded that Celia and her grandchildren move out of the Collarenebri house so it could be publicly auctioned to recover the debt.

This meant that not only the house, but also the land on which it stood was going to be sold. Isabel was appalled at the thought of losing this link with her father even more than she worried over losing the house. She called on Peter Tobin, then still based at Brewarrina, to take up her case. He wrote to the Directorate on behalf of Isabel and the Aboriginal Legal Service, pointing out how important the house was to the wider family and how damaging the loss of the land as well as the house would be for them. The Directorate eventually called off the auction, and grudgingly agreed to rene-gotiate the mortgage repayments, taking the immediate pressure off Isabel, but leaving her with the continuing task of meeting the payments.

For the moment, the house and the Block were safe, but the disrespect in which Isabel's home was held by local authorities became apparent the next

Isabel's house on the Block at Collarenebri, c. 1976, showing the newly constructed water tower, built by the Shire without consultation with Isabel. The hospital grounds are immediately to the right, just out of the picture.

time she went back to Collarenebri. On the boundary between the hospital and Isabel's land, no more than 20 metres from her front door, the Shire had built an enormous water tower, 50 metres high and 15 metres in diameter. They had not sought Isabel's consent, nor had they consulted her about the position of the tower. The message was clearly that Isabel's consent or otherwise was of no consequence to the Shire, her house was invisible to them and her Block was considered as outside the town limits, 'beyond the pale' in every sense.

7
Reinventing Isabel, 1977–1980

Isabel's health deteriorated as she struggled to keep an income coming into the Annandale household and to meet payments for the house at Collarenebri. She was still deeply disturbed over Lubby's death. At the same time, she found herself exhausted and on repeated sick leave because she was facing complications from worsening gynaecological problems. She'd relax with a smoke, but she was starting to realise that cigarettes were worsening her hypertension and her recurrent chest infections. But trying to give up smoking in an environment where everyone else smoked just added to her worries. She needed to call on relations and friends to get through:

> *Isabel:* I think with Amy, a lot of people were always available to take custody of her when I was very sick. I had to get more strength as I went because I was just going through one crisis after another, after I lost my little sister—and even before that, because I knew that she was in trouble and that she wanted to get away from that bloke of hers.
>
> But after being so sick since I lost my sister, I don't know how I coped. I just went from that breakdown into the fact that I needed to have a hysterectomy. And that was a mental smash. Because I know I didn't want to have that. I was so scared. I thought surely I could have something other than the hysterectomy. But then they finally said: 'No, this is not going to go away, it's going to get worse'. And when I went to the specialist in Macquarie Street, he said: 'Yes, you've got to have a hysterectomy and you've got to have it done very soon'. I go down there

> [to the hospital], they stuck me in. They put me in one afternoon and
> operated on me the next morning, and the next day after the operation,
> the fella who gave me the anaesthetic said: 'I didn't know that your chest
> was as bad as it is. If I'd known I wouldn't have given you that because I
> could've killed you. You very nearly didn't make it'. And then I went out
> to a rest home for a while that time, because I was having all those
> problems with Amy and everything . . . I don't think I'd have made it
> otherwise. But, it strengthened me to deal with a lot of issues—all my
> own personal stuff. It's marvellous how I kept getting mixed up with
> other people as well, and going on and doing other things, because I had
> a full-time job dealing with my own personal problems.

But she did keep getting mixed up! As her strength gradually returned after
the operation, Isabel began to get involved again in community politics. She
had resigned from the Prince Alfred Hospital and in mid-1975 took a job as
community health worker with the newly established Aboriginal Health
Unit in the NSW Department of Health. Her wide knowledge of north-
western Murris living in Sydney allowed her a base to extend her network,
developing friendships with people from across the state.

Her focus remained strongly on the bush, despite her work in Sydney,
and her involvement with Tranby deepened as it became the centre of
building momentum for the campaign for land rights in New South Wales.
Isabel's concern about land security had been awakened years ago by the
dumping of the Old Camp population at the unserviced Wollai Reserve in
1960. And she had learnt how hard it was to protect important sites when her
father had witnessed the uprooting of the Collymongle trees. These concerns
had only been sharpened by the near loss of her father's block. So the swell
of land rights' agitation was intensely interesting to her and allowed her to
make the direct links between city and country that were so close to the way
she was living.

Land had been a major public issue for Aborigines in New South Wales
at community level all through the nineteenth century and it had showed in
the statements made by the earliest political organisations—the Australian
Aborigines' Progressive Association in the 1920s and then the 1930s'
movement led by Bill Ferguson, Jack Patten and Pearlie Gibbs, which had
mobilised the north-western Murris in the demands for citizens rights, an end
to enforced movements like that from Angledool to Brewarrina, and for land
security. It was these activists, Ferguson and Bert Groves, whom Isabel had
seen as a child at Toomelah. And she had come to know Pearl Gibbs well
during the 1950s and 1960s as she campaigned from her Dubbo base as
well as from sitting on the Welfare Board.

The land issue had simmered, but had often been put on the backburner in New South Wales in recent decades as campaigners tended to focus on ending legislative discrimination and on building up community organisations. But it had been the land issue, and New South Wales activists, which had sparked the Tent Embassy in 1972, and the question of land rights was high on the agenda of the incoming Federal Labor Government late in that year.

Australian Federal arrangements meant that land remained under the power of state governments. When the new Federal Government tried to implement laws restoring rights over land for Aborigines, they found that they could act only in the territories controlled by the national government— that is, the Northern Territory and the Australian Capital Territory around Canberra and Jervis Bay. The complexities of defining and legislating land rights in the Northern Territory against trenchant pastoralist and mining opposition absorbed great attention from the Whitlam Aboriginal Affairs' machinery, but the Bill which was finally drafted had not been passed when the government fell in the chaos surrounding the Dismissal in 1975. Many Aboriginal activists in New South Wales were involved over the next year in applying pressure to the incoming and hostile conservative Fraser Government to save the Bill.

Although severely watered down, the Land Rights Act was eventually passed in 1976 and almost immediately Aborigines across the country began organising to pressure their state governments for land rights, at the least on the minimal Northern Territory model, but hopefully in more favourable terms relevant to each state's history and conditions. New South Wales Aborigines were in a difficult position: they had suffered intense colonisation for the longest, and so their traditional culture had undergone the most transformation. And New South Wales' land had been so intensively alienated that much of it was held by private owners in freehold. So its reacquisition without widespread public consent could occur only through the very costly and unpopular process of compulsory government resumption.

This was clearly going to be a difficult campaign, but there were older people in the state who were veterans of the 1920s' and 1930s' campaigns for land, and they were determined to pursue the goal. Particularly important were the coastal activists like Jacko Campbell, who had grown up in Kempsey but who had lived after his marriage in his wife's Jerringa community at Roseby Park, near Nowra. Jacko and other old south coast campaigners, like Guboo Ted Thomas, had strong links with Kevin Cook at Tranby, where Jacko sat on the Board. So with the Co-operative College's history of community-based but non-factionalised political activity, Tranby became the meeting place and resource centre for the network of land rights' campaigners in city and country.

The groups of black and white activists holding the meetings Isabel had been attending in support of the Embassy in 1972 had been re-forming around the land rights issue, as well as in defence of Aboriginal communities under pressure from police. The Black Defence Group had been meeting in this capacity through 1976. With strong input from Kevin Cook and Marcia Langton, who had recently moved from Queensland to Sydney, this group began reactivating the demands for land which had been such a hallmark of New South Wales Aboriginal politics. The state Government had set up a body called the Lands Trust, made up of Aboriginal members but with no power other than to fulfil government policy of quietly revoking or selling the remaining Aboriginal Reserves in the interest of 'assimiliation'. Jacko Campbell and many of the old activists hated the Lands Trust, and every one was angry with them making decisions without consulting communities, although Isabel regarded them as a necessary evil with whom she was to work when strategically necessary. But in mid-1977 came news that the Lands Trust was getting rid of yet another Reserve, and so the Black Defence Group planned a statewide community conference about land for the long weekend in October 1977. A big community football knockout was on then, bringing Aboriginal people to Sydney from over 100 communities. This seemed like a perfect opportunity to talk the land issues over with many rural people, as well as with those living in Sydney.

Isabel had been coming to Black Defence meetings occasionally, with her niece Barbara. As Isabel described it: 'Barbara was in and out like me. We were sort of doing a lot of washing on one side and then we'd come back and do a bit of ironing'.

Her involvement increased as the land issue gained prominence and she became one of the important community figures involved in organising for the 1977 Land Rights meeting, taking part in some of the trips to inform communities about the opportunity to get together on the issue:

> *Isabel:* We started getting involved in finding out about the land rights—how we could get land rights legislation into parliament. That meant we had to go right around, camping right around in all kinds of circumstances. The main thing was that we were going around to all the communities and letting them know. In the Black Defence Group, when we talked about setting up an organisation, we said if it's just going to be in the city, then you're going to lose it. What has to happen is that people from the city have to do the majority of work, because this is where the action is—in the city. But the meetings and the decision making should be taken back to the country area. And that was a good way of working it too, because all the resources were down

there in the city. And we had very little communications in the bush. We didn't have the faxes and mobiles they've got now. So when you consider that, you know, I think we did a good job in working with the communities.

The vulnerability of the western communities had been demonstrated by the big flood early in 1976, which followed on only two seasons after the huge 1974 flood. The floodwaters inundated low lying riverbank areas, and these were often Aboriginal reserves, like the Wollai, precisely because their flood-prone nature made them less desirable for white housing. The 1976 flood was so much worse than earlier ones because, in Isabel's view, the new built-up roads across the flood plain to service the cotton industry at Wee Waa had impeded the flow of water and banked it up across the Aboriginal community's housing. There were also reserves that were always cut off when floodwaters poured through the gullies between them and towns like Bogga-billa and West Brewarrina. This isolated large Aboriginal communities without food or access to medical services, yet there was never a planned or adequate response from the local Emergency Services groups because their priorities were saving white housing and graziers' stock. Aborigines' lack of control over the siting of their housing and their lack of access to normal, decent community services infuriated Isabel and was made very clear to her when her aged mother and Celia's sister, Aunty Maggie, were isolated and then had to be evacuated from Collarenebri to Sydney during the 1976 flood. Their situation had a very personal resonance for Isabel. Although Celia had been such a great traveller in her younger days, she had seldom left the north-western region. She and Maggie felt out of place and bewildered in the city, and their unease only emphasised their growing frailty as Isabel realised that age had caught them up during her years in the city.

Peter Thompson was back in the bush by then. He and Lynne Craigie had separated and Isabel remained close to them both, although Isabel saw Lynne only occasionally because she moved to Queensland. But Peter began work with the NSW Directorate of Aboriginal Affairs as Housing Project Officer, and assisted the community at Wilcannia as they developed an innovative plan for housing the whole community after the Reserve had been washed away, first in 1974 and then again in 1976. Peter Thompson's growing knowledge about the land laws and about how to make decent housing culturally appropriate as well as practical was of great interest to Isabel because it brought together the broad issue of land, with the detailed and practical questions of making houses work. She stayed in frequent touch with him for discussions about community organisations, as well as for his advice on archaeology and on his other long passion, linguistics.

Isabel as a witness at the wedding of Paul Torzillo and Heather Goodall in 1976. Faith Bandler is the celebrant and Peter Thompson, on right, is the other witness.

The pressures of home and political work were building for Isabel during 1976. She was our witness when Paul Torzillo and I were married in December of that year, in an event that showed some of the cross currents within which she was working. The night was a mixture of old and new friends: the celebrant was Faith Bandler, Peter Tobin rang from London, and there were friends there from unions and politics. Also attending were Isabel's old comrades from the western areas: Tombo Winters from Brewarrina, Julie Whitton from Boggabilla, and Mavis Rose and her family from Walgett. Our other witness was Peter Thompson, dressed like a bush lawyer in jeans, t-shirt and sandals, while Isabel, like Paul and I, was dressed up to the hilt as we celebrated in the back yard of Paul's parents' home. Isabel's family were all there, and we have some great photos of the long, hilarious night as jokes were told and good times shared. But it had been chaotic as Isabel had tried to get there, with the usual household confusions intensified while Isabel tried to concentrate on getting herself ready, with conflicts going on within the younger partnerships in the household, and an underlying tension simmering in the relationship between Isabel and Aub. Isabel had stormed out in exasperation and caught a cab on her own and left the rest to get themselves there, which they all did eventually to share a great night.

It had become clear to Isabel that the city was not a good place for her family. She was facing a rising conviction that the move to the city had been a mistake, that changes would be needed. But more urgent for her was the recognition that her relationship with Aub had broken down completely and she could not keep pretending that it was working. She grew more certain that before she even thought about how to get out of the city, she had to decide to get out of her partnership with Aub. This was becoming thinkable because she realised that her children were reaching an age where they could be independent, or at least where they could cope with her absence. She had to face the prospect of changing not just her situation, but herself. This would be a reinvention, as she took stock and gathered her strength to become a new person.

Isabel needed to work to maintain her financial independence and cover the mortgage payments, as well as to contribute to the family income; she saw a solution in a live-in job. This took her back to the domestic work of cleaning and cooking, but it offered a way out. Around the time she was the witness at our wedding, she had quietly begun searching the papers for likely jobs. The response was unexpected, but it served her purposes well and at the same time gave her a bemused glimpse at the 'upstairs and downstairs' of Sydney society life:

Isabel: I'd just left Aub then, and I thought: 'I don't want to live with other people'. And I didn't quite want to let everybody know about it, and I just saw the ad in the paper one day and so I made a phone call. And the next thing this big Rolls Royce pulls up outside Johnston Street. And someone said: 'Oh yeah, a big flash car out there'. And the chauffeur came in and he said: 'I'm supposed to make arrangements for you to come to Rosemont for an interview'. I said: 'What for?' And he said: 'For that position of cook with Lady Lloyd-Jones'. I hadn't realised where it was, you know. And I'm looking at the car and he's in his uniform, and I'm thinking: 'I wonder where the hell this is?' So I got the phone number and he said he'd make arrangements.

This is before I'd even moved out completely. I was back and forward, sort of thing. And anyhow, when I rang up and said: 'I got the message okay. So where would I have to go to keep this appointment?' So Lady Lloyd-Jones gave me the address, and said 'Just get a taxi and we'll fix the taxi up when it comes'. And for me to bring copies of my references. And she said: 'So you're really interested in coming out?' And it was just basic cooking, plain cooking. And when I saw the house I thought: 'Oh God. I couldn't cook here'. And the other maids were walking past with their little caps on and aprons and I said: 'Oh gee, I don't think I could fit into this'. But she said: 'Well, you could give it a try, if you wanted to. We decided we'd ask you to give it a try. And if you don't like it then . . . you know, no harm done'. And I said: 'Now, can I think about this for today?' 'Well, think about it over the next couple of days and just gives us a ring when you want to come out'. And I said: 'Okay'.

So they got the chauffeur to take me back to Annandale. And then I thought: 'Oh well, I need to get a place . . . I don't want to live with other people'. Because I was well and truly out of that relationship by then. Aud had made up his mind, he didn't want me back anyhow. And the kids didn't care much. So that's how come I got to go out there. And I think it was just an eye-opener to see how people could be real servants.

And those people didn't know what they were supposed to be doing or where they were going. Those servants had to say in the morning: 'Well, Sir Charles, you need to be at such and such a place at two o'clock and then somewhere at three o'clock'. So it was the staff that was arranging all their day for them. And their dogs had to be shampooed and whatever on the Wednesday morning.

It was interesting to me because they only had plain food, and didn't have any problem with that, you know. Oh, even when the people like Sir John Kerr and all them came, and John Laws and his wife, you know, they just had plain food. And I didn't mind. Because all I had to do was cook it and dish it up and . . . I thought it was interesting, you know. Just plain everyday stuff. But the night John Kerr was coming, they were having cutlets that night, grilled cutlets. And our gardener came in, he was an old Scott and he said to me: 'I suppose you're going to burn the bloody chops'. I said: 'No'. And he said, 'I thought you might burn the bloody chops . . . because I would!'

But you know, Lady Lloyd-Jones had a personal maid and her son Charles had a personal maid. And they laid their clothes out every morning. Even the dogs, you know, someone had to take the dogs for a walk. It was just unreal, you know, to realise how much they did for themselves—it was very little. I thought: 'Well, I don't think I could live this life'.

I used to come into the medical centre in Redfern for my check-ups . . . I was on blood pressure treatment. 'Oh no dear, you don't have to go in there, our personal doctor will come out'. But I said: 'Oh no thanks. I usually go to the one doctor and it'll be okay. I'll catch the bus in'. And she said: 'Oh no. Holmes can take you'. I said: 'Oh no, I go into Redfern'. 'Oh, you go into Redfern. All the way into Redfern from Woollarah'. And I said: 'Yeah, well they've been my doctors ever since I've been down here'. Oh, she said . . . 'Oh well, you know Holmes will take you there'.

And I thought: 'I can see me going in there with a bloody Rolls Royce!' And I used to feel terrible when I used to go into town, they wouldn't let me get a bus, they wanted the chauffeur to run me in. But in the end I'd just go: 'Oh all right'. And then riding along, I'm sitting in the front with the chauffeur. And I said: 'Holmes, you know I don't like this'. And he'd say: 'Why not? Just forget it, you know, we're just two people in a motorcar. Don't worry about what other people say'. I said: 'But look how everybody sort of . . . *looks*, you know!' He said: 'Well, we could get curtains, I suppose. Isabel, stop worrying about it'. He was a funny old man . . . he was an Englishman too. But see, her personal maid was an old Englishwoman, old Kath. She'd been with the family for a long time . . . I think she grew up in that role because she was the perfect servant. Everything she did was for Madam. Everything. She wouldn't go to bed until everybody else went to bed—that's how she was. But Madam had a nurse there too, a qualified sister there all the time. She was sick then, but she used to get out a bit when I first went there.

I think I had nine months there or so. And it gave me time to think about what I was doing. And it wasn't a lot of money or anything. But the worship, you know, to watch how they worshipped those people. If Charles came down and said good morning to [the servants], they'd think it was really extra, you know? He was a special man. And I used to just watch it, he might walk past sometimes and not even say anything to anybody. And there'd be other times when he'd pop his head in the kitchen and say hello. And they'd think that was really special.

The old gardener fellow, he was a bit militant, you know. And he might say something like: 'Oh that's not my cup of tea. I'm not into that kind of worship!' . . . And old Kath would get so upset. I'd say: 'Oh, don't worry about him Kath'. I used to worry about Kath. I'd think how's this woman going to get on if something happens to the old woman. Because I couldn't see her staying on as Charles' maid. And then when she was too old, they put old Kath out into that nursing home. It was a nice place, but she didn't know where she was when I went out to visit her. She was terrified because she didn't know what to do or how to get about, because she never had to go out of Rosemont. She never had to go out of that house. No sense of being able to look after herself out of that big mansion. So it was really sad to watch. She said, 'Oh, Isabel I don't know how I'm going to live here'. And I said: 'Well, haven't you got a family at home in England?'. 'Oh, my sister died and this one . . .' and so she'd go through the family history of who's left there at home and she'd say, 'Oh, no I couldn't go home to them'. And then she'd be talking about 'poor Madam' . . . And 'She's in a nursing home too, did you know?'

The people at the home were so impersonal and she was really going through a bad time. I spoke to the woman at the front desk and I said to her: 'Gee, she's very much out of her area. Even if she was somewhere close to Woollarah it might be okay for her'. And then the next time she wrote to me she said she'd moved back towards there. They'd got her a place closer. She said she was a bit happier, but when I went to see her again she still seemed really out of it. But she must've been a very old woman then. That was all she'd lived for—to look after that family. And when one of the grandkids got married, she got married there at Woollarah, and they had these big caterers come in and do all the big horseshoe things and, oh, Kath thought it was great, you know. And I'll say one thing, those kids did come out and make a fuss over her. And they brought her little presents and stuff like that, and she thought that was fine. But it was a marvellous experience just to see how they lived.

Isabel grew fond of Kath, Holmes and the old Scottish gardener, but her sympathy for them didn't mean she was compelled to become too deeply involved in their bizarre and alien environment. Instead, she was grateful for the peaceful time this gave her to collect her thoughts. But the burden of family illness and tragedy which she had been carrying was added to soon enough, when in May we had to tell her about the death of her good friend Peter Tobin, killed in a plane crash in Cuba just before he had planned to return to Australia.

For Isabel this sad shock was a signal that the hiatus at Rosemont had come to an end. It was time to face the new directions of her life. She resigned soon after from the Lloyd-Jones' and returned to Johnston Street, but the situation there was unhappy. Fearing another bout of depression, Isabel came to live for a few months with Judy and Jack Torzillo, Paul's parents, on the edge of Kuringai Chase at Terrey Hills. Isabel had become friends with the Torzillos over the years of knowing Paul, and had developed a strong friendship with Judy, based on their shared outlooks, despite their very different pasts. They were of similar ages, and as they compared their life courses they could each see clearly all the points at which Isabel had missed the education she wanted so keenly. But they shared an interest in active social change and a warm and supportive approach to family which gave them much in common.

The differences in their experiences became even more starkly obvious when Judy drove Isabel to a hypertension outpatients clinic at the Prince Alfred. Paul was doing specialist training at Dubbo Hospital so we were out of town, but Isabel hadn't been expecting any complications from this routine visit, so she just saw the young doctor who happened to be on duty. Judy sat with Isabel while he began to take a history, and when he asked how much she'd been drinking, Isabel carefully listed her glasses of water and cups of tea. The doctor snorted, 'Come on now. How much *grog* have you had today!' He refused to believe she didn't drink and continued to question her aggressively. Isabel was distressed and irritated, but not surprised by his abuse; Judy was shocked. Eventually, when the incident was reported to Paul and the Hospital Administration, the resident was shocked too by the disciplinary action he clearly hadn't been expecting. Such racist behaviour is usually hidden from the view of white, middle-class patients which means that it is still rarely reported and even more rarely punished.

The friendship which deepened between Isabel and the Torzillos allowed them to work out at last an assured way to save the house at Collarenebri. Jack and Judy took over part of the mortgage payments which lightened the burden on Isabel over the next five years. Jack, an architect, could give Isabel advice and assistance with building materials to repair and maintain the house so that it met the local government requirements which had also been an issue for her. With the financial pressure eased, her health stabilised and her spirits rising, Isabel began to make her arrangements to go back home.

She was being drawn back by the need to look after her mother and aunt. Her relationship with Celia had always been tense and difficult, so the decision was not easy, but it increasingly pulled Isabel towards going home:

Isabel: My Mum was starting to show that she was dependent a bit on me. And I could see that my old aunt needed us a lot. I knew I had to go home and look after her.

And sure enough Lindsay said: 'Well, look she doesn't want to live with me in Thallon, she wants to go home to the Block, she wants you to go home and just get things set-up for her. That'll be all you have to do and then she'll be right'. Now poor old Mum used to always rubbish me, and so I wasn't sure about it. But I went home then just to see what was happening, and I could see then that Mum wasn't very well at all. And that's how I made up my mind . . . We went home then. And oh what a mess! But she said: 'Isn't it funny, the black sheep always come back to you too, hey?' I said: 'Oh he's mad, Dad always said the black sheep is mad'. And she said: 'Yes, he used to always say that he wouldn't kill a black sheep because he reckoned he was a mad sheep'.

And it turned out to be important that I was there, because the others used to take her out too much . . . and gosh, some of the things that I went through in that little section of my life! I'd be saying: 'Don't give Mum any grog'. And they used to take her over there and get her drunk and they used to say: 'She's got to have some kind of life'. Then they'd bring her home to me, carry her inside and then she'd be real selfconscious about coming home to me, because she knew I didn't drink. And then I'd say: 'Oh here's my mother back again'. And she used to say: 'I shouldn't have went with them. I shouldn't have went'. And I'd say: 'Oh Mum you should've went because you had a nice day'.

I could see that what I thought about her having a day out mattered to her. And I could see what they were doing and they'd say: 'Oh, what else can we do? She likes to have a drink with us and stuff'. But it was hard times. I used to think: 'Oh just when she looked so well, they'd come over and get her over there and then when she'd come back she'd have to start all over again'.

Clare was having a terrible time then, too, with her bloke. And Rosie wasn't there. See, Jimmy Fernando never used to let her come home from Leeton. And that was a hard time too—watching Mum wanting her to come home and she never could.

Settling in to Collarenebri again in 1978 was both easy and hard for Isabel. In many ways it was a simple return home, but in other ways everything was unfamiliar.

She had come back to the often troubling relationship with her mother. It was unsettling for her to have to revise her reservations about Celia and sometimes heart-wrenching to cover the distance between them. Adding to the strains of living daily with her mother again after so many years was Isabel's almost comical frustration in watching Celia give up smoking, apparently effortlessly, while Isabel herself still struggled to do it. Isabel's daughter, Brenda, had followed her mother home with her own young children, and her cheerful support and attention to Celia made all of their lives much easier. Isabel found herself reaching a new understanding of the way her mother's difficult and unpredictable personality had been shaped by her troubled past. Eventually it brought her a new peace as she came to accept her mother fully for the first time:

Isabel: And it turned out that I was happy that I went back there and did that job. I went back there some time in September and it was in June the next year that we lost her. And I don't think I intended to settle down there again, but then I just did.

Isabel was different herself. In a demonstration of her new confidence, Isabel learnt to drive. Now single again, without young children to look after for the first time for years and with the financial burden of the house on the Block eased for her, she had a freedom and sense of independence which reinforced her newly developed assurance in politics.

Isabel had thought she was leaving Collarenebri behind when she headed for Sydney in 1972 looking for better educational opportunities for her children. But as it turned out, her son Tony came to feel that the real value of Sydney was in the learning opportunities it had given to Isabel herself:

> *Tony:* I think it was good for her, because when she was down there, all these housing companies were starting to be developed and she took that knowledge straight back to Colle and set up Mangankali. So I think that it furthered *her* education as far as getting funding and how to set up housing companies, and that sort of thing. She was the one who got the win out of it eventually.

Isabel's Sydney experience and widening knowledge of the networks of political power and lobbying gave her resources far beyond any she had previously had in her dealings with the power of the town.

And she had allies. Along with her old comrades in the town, like Doreen Hynch, Jessie Hall and Roy and Josie Thorne, Isabel found that Joe and Isobelle in Wee Waa didn't seem so far away now. Their youngest daughter Karen was living with them there and had matured into a strong and determined young activist in her own right. Barbara, too, was back in the bush, as the co-ordinator of the Western Aboriginal Legal Service (WALS) in Dubbo, and while it did not cover the Walgett–Collarenebri area, WALS' resources and its group of dedicated young lawyers were always available to back Isabel up.

Barbara was implementing innovative social initiatives in legal work to advance land and cultural rights and to protect women and young people. These goals were closely in line with, and had been inspired by, Isabel's own priorities. While they did not always work on the same issues, Barbara and Isabel were frequently in contact and acted to support each other. There were tensions between WALS and the leadership of the older, Sydney-based Aboriginal Legal Service (ALS), which still operated the Walgett office and so provided lawyers for Collarenebri courts. However, one of the ALS lawyers based in Walgett, John Terry, grew close to Isabel, becoming a stalwart defender for her against the continuing police harassment in the area, and a trusted friend.

Isabel, as always, insisted on working with everyone, negotiating her way through the minefield of difficult and sensitive egos involved on every side— black and white—and trying to ensure that the interests of Collarenebri Murris were met by all the legal services. Another friend, Peter Thompson, was living at Wilcannia with Edna Hunter, from a Paakantji family.

Old friends at Colle c. 1980: from left, Auntie Maggie, Clare, Pansy, Nanna Pearlie Mason and Josie Thorne (Nanna Pearlie's daughter).

Roy Thorne.

159

He continued to work creatively in nurturing strong community control of housing, the reassertion of cultural control over land and the development of language teaching programs, all areas which offered valuable experiences and resources for Isabel and her community as well.

As she settled back into Collarenebri with a deepening sense of assurance and direction, Isabel found herself exploring a relationship which was both new and old. She had been childhood playmates with Ted Thorne in the days of the Old Camp and they had shared a strong attraction as teenagers. Events had overtaken and separated them, and they had each gone on to other long-term relationships. But when Isabel returned to the town, Ted was back there as well, also single again and taking serious steps to control the drinking with which he had had to grapple for much of his life. He and Isabel came together in a relationship which built on the deep affection they had held for each other over the years. By 1979 they were living together and they wrote to each other constantly if they were separated when Ted went shearing. Few of Isabel's letters have survived, but she carefully kept a number of the letters Ted wrote to her when he was working in the sheds. His letters were short and affectionate, sharing day-to-day incidents and worries: concern over a workmate gone missing, notes about payments on household bills, stories about eccentric bosses. And each letter is threaded through with endearments and warmth.

At a dance in Collarenebri, 1979. From left, Ted Thorne, Amy, Isabel and her brother Lindsay.

Long weekend 1979
My Dear Bell,
So pleased to hear from you and to know you are all well at home. How
are Warren and Ray getting on? They were both a bit sick when I left . . .
How much do we owe on the mower? Next time I send some money you
might put a few dollars on it . . . The peach tree must be in full bloom by
now and the mulberry tree. Is it living? . . . My home is in Colly with my
Bell. Be waiting for me when I get home.
I will say Cheerio Darl.
Looking forward to seeing you again,
love,
Edward

This relationship allowed Isabel to be herself, an activist and a traveller, but
also a lover, a mother and grandmother. Each role was nurtured by the warm
and steadfast support which Ted gave unstintingly.

8
Changing Collarenebri, 1980s

If Isabel had changed, Collarenebri was different too. The sense of momentum in the struggle to gain decent washing facilities on the Wollai had raised everyone's expectations. Communities were starting to hope that Federal and State funds could be directed into effective local programs to make a real difference to life in the bush. And there was new structure in the Aboriginal community in Colle. The Mangankali housing company offered a formal organisation for managing the planning and implementation process for a project to really change the way people lived and related to each other and the town.

But Collarenebri remained a hard town, where petty segregation persisted and where the Aboriginal community was wracked by the effects of poverty, poor health and alcoholism. In some ways it was harder. The pastoral downturn had hit bottom now and jobs in the pastoral industry had all but disappeared except for a small amount of shearing and rouseabout work. The seasonal chipping work was about all that was around, apart from some work with the local government councils or with the few funded Aboriginal organisations. With no Aboriginal people employed on properties anymore, the land was now closed off behind fences and locked gates, so it was harder and harder to gain any access at all to places which had been important in the lives of Isabel and her generation, let alone to that of her parents and the older people in Collarenebri.

With less employment than before, there was a tense undercurrent of anxiety despite the new organisations and hopes for funding for community programs. Unemployment relief was ensuring some income into Aboriginal families, but as it was in the form of individual payments it was often being channelled into alcohol abuse. More young people and women were now drinking in the town and the burden of care for grandchildren fell onto grandmothers of Isabel's age. And alcohol, like poverty, worsened domestic disputes, increasing the violence which women and children were facing.

The potential for factional rivalries and jealousies based around family networks was always present and it often worsened as the new funding for Aboriginal organisations promised much but seldom delivered enough resources to really make changes for everyone. Too often, increasingly impoverished communities like Collarenebri saw their divisions deepening as they were made to fight over a single house or two, when everyone on the community was in real need of urgent housing improvements. The resulting frustration might cause people to collapse into apathy or boil over into conflict. So while Isabel came back into the community in some ways refreshed, she was not faced with an easier situation than when she had left.

The idea of building new houses was born during the ablution block campaign and Isabel seemed the obvious person to manage the process once she had returned home. But like her own children, the next generation had by now grown to adulthood and there were a number of young people in Collarenebri whom Isabel felt could be encouraged to take up active roles. She was insistent that her role in Mangankali was temporary and the goal must be to rapidly allow these young people to gain the experience she had learned in the tough town forums as a young mother. Graham Hynch, Roslyn McGregor and Keith Thorne were just a few of the young people she encouraged to take up active roles. She grabbed opportunities for them to learn by taking them into meetings, encouraging them to speak up and to take on formal roles in the local organisations. Tranby was committed to supporting rural communities and offered Aboriginals a chance for formal accreditation; so Isabel sent down a series of young people to take part in the college's flexibly-run Community Development, Literacy and Business Skills courses. Training, formal and informal, became the necessary central element for each of the programs she ushered into existence.

When Isabel returned to Collarenebri, the Federal government provided funding for Mangankali, but it was strictly for housing purchases in townships. The funding was trickling through with only enough for single houses at a time, or even less. The communities in the western area were organised into a region which met regularly at Bourke with the Aboriginal Development Corporation, the ADC, a Federal body which had been established by the Department of Aboriginal Affairs (DAA) to handle housing and enterprise funding. The facade of community participation was thin—in fact, the

ADC was allocating funds, rather than asking communities to decide on purposes and budgets. And they were making community representatives compete for the little amounts available. Although there were 10 communities in the region, only about five houses were being budgetted for each year. So the results were meagre: a community might receive the funds to purchase a house, but only if they spread their purchase over two financial years. As Isabel's son Tony remembers: 'We were going down there fighting for half houses!' Tony returned to Collarenebri in 1980, by which time Mangankali had gained two houses, each transported in modules and assembled on site, with a further house to be purchased during the year.

But Isabel had become concerned that this process wasn't achieving any training benefit for young people. She began to lobby ADC for a wider planning strategy, to secure funds to allow a number of houses to be built in sequence, using local apprentices, thus ensuring skills in the community were built up as well as houses. The outcome was an important concession. ADC housing allocation was to be linked with NSW State Aboriginal Employment strategy funding, to allow guaranteed wages to Collarenebri for two apprentices to be taken on over three years. Barry Murray and Tony Flick were accepted as the apprentices and the building program began. A local builder signed on the apprentices, tendering for the first building at a modest price; but his prices escalated alarmingly for the next house and even more so for the one after. But funding for houses became caught up in another issue.

Tony had returned to Collarenebri because of family tragedy. He and his wife, Peggy Peters, also from Collarenebri, had stayed working in Sydney when Isabel returned home. But in 1980 they had barely welcomed their second child, Sally Ann, when they lost her to Sudden Infant Death Syndrome. Grieving, they brought her to Collarenebri to be buried. Isabel and Aub put aside their own differences to stand with Tony during the funeral, supporting their son through this tragedy. Tony and Peggy decided that it was time for them to move back home where they would be close to Sally and to their families. With the housing funding slowly coming through, it looked at least as if there would be work for Tony.

There were other funerals that year and, like Sally's burial, they could be carried out only if the weather was dry, because otherwise the road to the cemetery was an impassable black soil bog. Many funerals had to be delayed in wet weather—increasing the bereaved family's distress—because just getting to the cemetery could take hours through the mud. It had been Isabel's priority to find resources to have the cemetery fenced and cared for but none of this mattered if people couldn't get to the graveside at all. As early as 1975, Mangankali had put in submissions to upgrade the three-kilometre track from the Mungindi road across a pastoral lease to the

Working on the cemetery: Isabel, her son Aub and his partner Pam, erecting Returned Servicemen's plaques, c. 1979.

cemetery, making it an all-weather road. This meant excavation, re-forming the road, dumping a significant amount of rock to stabilise it and then topping it with crushed rock to ensure a good surface in the wet. The shire council at Walgett was reluctant to take any responsibility for it, using the excuses that the track ran across private pastoral lease and that the cemetery was not regarded as the 'real' public one. Yet this road was the only access to an active cemetery which was used by around a third of the population of Collarenebri! The Mangankali call for an all-weather road was really a demand to respect the rights of the Aboriginal population to bury their dead with dignity and meaning.

Mangankali submissions had been bounced around from one section of the Federal and State governments to another: the cemetery road was not considered cultural enough for an Arts grant, but neither was it recognisable for 'housing' or 'enterprise' funding. None of the official Aboriginal Affairs departments could see why they should support the cost of bulldozing and surfacing a track that went out of town and across the scrub. The NSW National Parks Service had responded by registering the cemetery as an 'Aboriginal Place', based on its anthropologist Horrie Creamer's careful report in 1977.

But there was no other government response at all. The Mangankali committee was increasingly frustrated. Then in November, 1980, Linda Hall's young son, Howard, died suddenly and the tragedy of his death was deepened because heavy rains delayed the process of grave digging and of holding the funeral. But the distress pushed Isabel and the community into formulating a unique strategy. Tony and Isabel have both remembered aspects of this campaign:

> *Tony:* She'd always been chasing the funds to get that road fixed, but it was because of the close affinity she had with Linda Hall that it really got going. When we buried Linda's youngest son, Howard, he was 23 at the time. It was pouring rain and we basically had to carry him from the Mungindi road to the cemetery, it was just that boggy. And that really got under Mum's skin and it was the extra motivation she needed.

> *Isabel:* Now we really had to fight for that money to get the cemetery road done. I had meetings in everybody's house and said: 'This is what I think, but whatever you fellas say has got to go'. And the way we did it then, we said: 'Look it's not much use for us talking about building houses and planning anything else if we can't address that issue that affects all of us. So we're going to refuse to take any funding from the DAA until we get that rectified, because that's more important to us than the houses'. And everybody agreed to that. And I said: 'Well, you've got to know that when these people come over here to talk about this issue, we've all got to be as one'. And that's what happened.

> *Tony:* We used to go to the programming conferences in Bourke and they'd be offering everyone houses and half-houses and all that. And she just sat back on her haunches and said, 'No, we won't be taking no houses and no money for houses until we get money for the cemetery road'. And she kept that up for two rounds of meetings.

> *Isabel:* I wrote a letter to the Minister for Aboriginal Affairs telling him that that was our position. Then I rang and I said: 'So what's the big gossip on us then? Because we won't be getting any funding, will we?' And he said: 'Oh, it caused a bit of concern because they can't understand what you are on about. Because you can't put it under Enterprise . . . they can't find a category to put it under'. And I said: 'Well it's a *need* . . . a cultural need for us as a group of people. And we can't address anything else until we have that done'. And so they said: 'Well you can't put it under Housing, you can't put it under Enterprise . . .' And they were going through trying to find all the little loopholes that they could put it under.
>
> So I said: 'We have to make recommendations somewhere for changes'.

A familiar scene: Isabel in 1979 during a break in a meeting, having a card game with Debbie Rose (from Walgett, George and Mavis Rose's daughter) and Bob Bellear (with a winning card).

Tony: By the third programming conference, the other community reps had had a gutful too, and it was all decided before they even went into the meeting. Whether they'd decided it when they'd played cards before it or not I don't know, but that was more likely! So the third one, all the community reps refused to take their budgets or allocations too, until the cemetery road was done. They actually took a delegation to Canberra about it to get it all changed. There was Tombo Winters from Bre, Georgie Rose from Walgett, Yvonne Howath from Bourke, and the mob from Goodooga, Lightning Ridge, Weilmoringle ... all in that one group—it was basically all the communities.

The communities held firm and finally it was the State Government which backed down, at last taking seriously the fact that this community cared even more about their cemetery than they did about the houses they had been fighting for now for over a decade. The Wran Labor Government had just set up a new Ministry of Aboriginal Affairs. It was headed up by Aboriginal barrister Pat O'Shane, who knew Isabel and her family well from their period in Sydney and who, for the first time, brought an Aboriginal perspective to New South Wales decisions on funding priorities.

Opening of the all-weather road
to the Aboriginal Cemetery, 1983.
From left: Paul Torzillo (just out
of frame) whom Isabel invited to
make a speech, Isabel, Winkie
Orcher, Ted Thorne (holding
flag), Dezi Flick-Kennedy,
Georgette (Amy's daughter) and
Kylie Orcher.

But still the problems hadn't stopped, because Walgett Shire Council now insisted on a new, longer and more expensive route for the cemetery road, turning off the Mungindi road further away from the town. The Shire was being obstructive because, so Isabel believed, it wanted the contract to do the road work and hoped that if it held out long enough the community would give up. The Shire engineer confided to Isabel that he couldn't see any structural reason for the alteration in the route, and grudgingly conceded that his role was to inspect the Mangankali work, not to insist on a council contract. So over a weekend, a Murri contractor from Narromine was engaged, came in and did the work, soundly and efficiently. Before anyone could raise another objection, the road was ready to be opened!

The cemetery road was an extraordinary victory. Very few communities have seriously rejected funding to press their demand for recognition of cultural rights. So the opening celebration in August 1983 was a deeply moving demonstration of the community's commitment and solidarity. Isabel spoke powerfully of the community's sustained efforts since 1975 to take control of their circumstances and achieve the goals they had set for themselves. She put the road in a far wider perspective than any government had probably seen it: 'The cemetery is a place where Murris can feel at peace, as we are surrounded by our loved ones in spirit and we are able to strengthen our affinity with our land'.[1] For Isabel, the cemetery was not a lonely remnant of lost tribal lands. Instead, it was a symbol of the *continuing* presence of the whole of Gamilaraay land and of its *continuing* significance to its Murri owners. So she saw the decision by government to fund the road and recognise the importance of the cemetery as a major step towards recognising Aboriginal land and Aboriginal owners.

'New. Road'
Old. People!

Opening of the all-weather road
to the Aboriginal Cemetery, 1983.
Isabel annotated this picture of
herself and Ted: ' "New Road"
Old People!'

Once the funds for housing in Collarenebri had been freed up again in 1982, the question of where the next houses might go was again raised. Many people needed housing, far more than would be able to have one if the rate was one or even two houses a year. So the competition and jealousy over house allocation could be intense. Isabel made it clear to her family that she would not be seen to be favouring them. Tony remembers:

> *Tony:* I think that was probably the only unfair thing that Mum ever did to us kids. She'd always told us when she was in Mangankali and getting houses, she said, 'Don't you ever apply for a house, because I won't be giving you one. Because I don't ever want the community coming to me saying: "You housed your own people!"' That's why we never ever got a house off her! We weren't even allowed to put in an application. But that was her stance and she stood by it. So I got my house through mainstream Department of Housing and the rest had just to do what they could do.

Murris in Collarenebri needed houses both in town and on the Wollai, but the Federal government had been adamant that no ADC housing funds were to go to building houses on Reserve land. The basic policy was an assimilationist one, that ultimately Aboriginal people would be 'better off' forced out of the segregrated areas of Reserve living and into the general community, to live 'pepperpotted' among non-Aboriginal people. The major need in Collarenebri, however, was on the Wollai where every single family was living in inadequate houses without any infrastructure at all—without water, sewage or electricity.

Isabel realised that to develop a campaign to build enough houses on the Reserve, the key, just like the ablution block campaign, was going to be community confidence that the housing would meet people's needs and interests. So talking around was essential. Long hours of listening, sitting in the park or at a bingo game on the flat, or fishing on the riverbank, was crucial to working out what sort of housing would work for the people of the Wollai. Never having lived on the Reserve itself, despite her early years on the Old Camp, Isabel was careful not to presume to represent the Wollai unless she had been given authority to do so. And there continued to be families with whom she could not speak comfortably and she knew it was necessary to make sure they felt fully consulted as well. The sensitivities of small town life and long memories meant the consultations had to be, as they had been for the ablution block, carefully considered and planned, delegated and patiently repeated till it was certain everyone was happy.

What was clear was that the community had some important goals. One was a flexible approach to laying out the houses, so that kinship relationships and privacy were more important than the right-angled grid pattern that white planners favoured. Another was a high degree of community input into housing design, so that the houses met not only each family's needs, but also made sense in the local environment. And for Isabel as well as everyone else, there had to be a very high degree of Aboriginal employment and training during the building process to maximise long-term benefit for the community.

Isabel had been watching the early housing projects carefully at Wilcannia where Peter Thompson had been involved, at Roseby Park in Jacko Campbell's Jerrinja community and even earlier, at Bourke just down the Barwon River. The things people at Colle wanted were similar to the demands made by the other communities, but each of the others had found these goals hard to achieve. A big issue for all of them had been the refusal by governments to allow houses to be built on Reserves.

Bureaucrats and councils were determined to achieve grid-street patterns, arguing that it led to efficient service delivery, but really seeking to impose a very western form of discipline and order. Funding bodies argued that it was cheaper if everything was the same, which made it hard to plan individual differences between houses or to meet local conditions. And finally, the employment and training of Aboriginal people was always sacrificed to tight schedules and even tighter budgets. As Paul Torzillo's work has demonstrated, much of the building done by local white contractors for Aboriginal projects then and later was poorly supervised, shoddy or just plain negligent, leading to severe problems during normal family use; but bureaucrats still kept insisting that white builders would be more efficient and competent than Aboriginal ones.

So Isabel and the Mangankali committee found it tough going. They kept on fighting, just like they had for the ablution block, through a mixture of dogged stubbornness and unquenchable optimism. I remember ringing Isabel once after they had received another knockback. When I asked how she was, she joked with characteristic cheerfulness in the face of bad luck: 'Well, I'm stiff. If I was any stiffer I'd be dead!' She explained years later how obstructions had been thrown in their way:

> *Isabel:* See, they didn't want Aboriginal people to live on the Reserve, they didn't want us to build there. The Shire kept saying that it was a floodprone area, and so then I got the statistics about where the flood waters actually came into the town. And sure it cut the Reserve off, but if they built the houses four foot up they could deal with it. And then we showed another part where it came right up in the streets of the town itself; so if you declare the Reserve floodprone, then you've got to declare that town area floodprone as well.
>
> They didn't want to say who was stopping it on the Shire, so I said: 'I want to be at the next meeting because I want to determine whether we can build there or not!' So I wrote the letters to get permission to go to that meeting. When it came up it turned out that it was *our* councillor, the one representing *us*, who was saying that houses shouldn't go on the Reserve because of the floods. But I don't think that it was for that reason, he didn't care about that too much. I think he was afraid we were going to build our own shops over there. That *was* in my mind to do that, and maybe he'd heard about it because I'd said to the people: 'You can build your own shop here'.
>
> We built a big shed there that could have done that. But the people on the Wollai didn't plan to go that way anyhow, so what I thought didn't make any difference. I could only suggest something. When that confrontation came up again I wasn't feeling so bad about it, because I could say then, 'What's the argument now? Because this is what we plan to do'. And I still say that if we want to build a shop there we certainly should be able to. And then of course there was no further argument in that. So that was finalised. But it was only after two years of trying to negotiate with the Shire to build on there, because this is what they required and all that, that we found out what the real issues were. They could've said that straight out in the first place, but they were hoping that if they put us off long enough the people would decide to go uptown. I don't know whether that was a good thing or a bad thing. People wanted to live there, but all the younger ones will probably want to be uptown, I don't know.

But that confrontation over whether we could build on the Reserve at Colle in the early 1980s changed the whole thing in that DAA region. There were nine reserves there then, and after that everyone, like Bourke and Goodooga, was able to build on their Reserve.

The funding situation began to look up because the New South Wales Government, with Aboriginal direction in its Ministry, finally shifted its position on whether to fund houses on Reserves. Isabel had been in touch with Pat O'Shane and her officers about the community desires in Colle, and it was clear that the most urgent need was on the Wollai. The Ministry's pathfinding project was called the Five Communities Program and Collarenebri became one of these five. In this (shortlived) atmosphere of attention to community wishes, Mangankali was able to press its demands. Tony was involved on the committee at Mangankali and remembers the consultation with the community:

Tony: We had a fair bit to do with it, basically to design the houses and the locations of them, because every family wanted their own little turf and to be kept in their own family groups. It was a pretty new thing. The Ministry's architects came up there to Colle, and we went around. They

Isabel puts the case for new houses on the Wollai reserve to a New South Wales Parliamentary committee, including Barney French (ALP MLA) and Ron Mulock (ALP Deputy Premier), c. 1983. The existing Reserve tin house can be seen in the background.

had the basic design to start with and we'd go and sit down with people on the mission and say: 'What else do you need in this?' But because they wouldn't say anything, sometimes we'd have had more input than they would have had. That's how all them places got sleep-outs, just typical things that Mum saw might be wanted in them. And like the walls had to be strong, made of brick and made sure that inside was tough; she knew what they were going to be like and they had to stand the test of time. And they're still in good nick actually!

While they did not gain as much individual control over house planning as they had hoped, the community could make some of the fundamental decisions about house designs. The new streets on the Wollai were curved to allow the houses to be sited where each family chose, in proximity to relations but with enough distance for privacy. Perhaps the most important design decision to tailor the housing to the location was that each house was built up high on its own mound, making them all safe during even major floods.

But it was not without conflict within the community. The Reserve was dominated by one man whose relations made up the majority of Wollai residents. He was antagonistic to any homes being built for those residents who were not from his extended family, and resisted a planned layout which placed houses at any distance from the main group, as he knew they would be for the remaining families. As Tony remembers:

Tony: Well this fella ran the Reserve; he wanted all the houses down his family's end, the bottom end. But me and Mum stood and argued with him. And we actually bluffed him, cause we said: 'No, they said if they don't put one house up the top for the Lambs, they're not going to put none here, none on the Reserve at all'. So he said, 'Okay they can have one, but they're not getting no more'. And that's how come Keithie Lamb got his place up that end where he got it now. That was the only one that ever got built up there.

A key advantage in this project, as Isabel saw it, was that training was to be a central component from the start. The first two Mangankali apprentices had faced problems of isolation both in Colle itself and when they travelled to Dubbo to sit in on their trade classes. The Five Communities training was much better organised, linking the apprentices from each of the five communities in joint classes in a program managed by TAFE in Moree. Seven young Collarenebri Murris were employed as apprentices on the Wollai, and a number of them went on to gain advanced skills. Achieving this degree of

Six of the seven young Colle men in training on the building site of the new housing on
the Wollai 1987, including (from left): Michael and Frank Murray, Tony, Michael and
Peter Adams, and Noel Mason, Clare's youngest son and Isabel's nephew.

Aboriginal employment was a major win for the community and the work-
manship with which their jobs were done is evident in the houses' history
since their completion. In a 2002 review of the projects built in the Five
Communities program, the Collarenebri housing was found to be in need of
repair, but all the houses are still standing and holding up far better than
houses built in some of the other four towns.[2]

The process of managing the housing project had been weighing heavily
on Isabel. She had strong views about the importance of community
managers acting in transparent and principled ways to ensure that community wishes were carried out once funding had been achieved. Isabel had
hoped that younger Murris, who had been able to have more schooling than
she had, would be able to take up the administrative tasks, but this was not
happening as quickly as she needed. Tony remembers that in this period, the
accounting for Mangankali was 'basically Mum, and then just the accountant
in Walgett once a year'. So, with the help of Tranby College, Isabel laboriously taught herself bookkeeping, kept meticulous records of expenditure and
took careful minutes of meetings so she could implement decisions.

This was extraordinarily demanding work for a woman who had been excluded from basic education. Isabel had found that she preferred campaigning, planning and educating to the day-to-day detailed, monotonous work of administration. But as well, she was beginning to suspect that if she stayed in the active managerial role at Mangankali, other community members and particularly the younger ones, would hang back from taking leadership roles. She had put a huge amount of energy into both the housing project on the Wollai and the cemetery road upgrading, and the deaths and tragedy within her family had taken a great toll. She was recognising that she needed to measure out her energy, and she was by this time involved in a number of other activities. So she had decided that this was the time to retire from active involvement in Mangankali, making way for younger people to take up roles shaping their community. On the same day that the cemetery road was declared open in August 1983, Isabel announced her formal retirement, sketching out a future for herself as an occasional elder-statesperson, but no longer a day-to-day leader.

Of course, Isabel hardly settled into inactivity. At her busiest time at Mangankali in 1981, she had still been eager to support Joe and Isobelle as they tried to make a home in Wee Waa. They found themselves in growing conflict with the local government authorities there. Their long battle to get decent conditions for the seasonal influx of cotton chippers had continued, with only marginal and grudging improvements to the camps like Tulladunna and to workers' conditions in the fields. Joe felt strongly that the goals of both local government and cotton farmers were to do just enough to keep Murri organisations quiet, but not to make real changes to working and living conditions.

The final straw came when the local council decided to close Tulladunna to camping altogether in autumn of 1981, when the cotton season ended. The decision was claimed by Council as a great step towards improving Aboriginal conditions, because it was paired with the announcement of a new camping ground to be ready for the next summer, with well-serviced camp sites and good drinking water and washing facilities. The problem with the proudly announced new site, called 'The Piggery'—because it was next to an old pig farm—was that it was five miles out of town, and without any regular public transport. So for Joe, and many of the Aboriginal residents and incoming chippers, the new site looked like a very old strategy. They knew that the Council regarded the chippers' camping ground on Tulladunna as an eyesore because it was so close to town. They believed the Council had decided to act to keep the blacks out of town by forcing them to shift out to a distant Reserve and by restricting their practical access to the main streets and shops. They had seen this too many times in Collarenebri, in Walgett and in most other rural towns across the state, to be fooled into thinking that anyone had Aboriginal health and housing conditions at heart.

The Flick family in Wee Waa had stayed heavily involved with the cotton economy. Joe chipped and so did his middle daughter, Patsy, who often worked on the fields with her shearer husband Sonny Orcher to raise extra money at Christmas. They were all vulnerable to the continued questionable pesticide and herbicide spraying practices of the cotton growers. Joe's youngest daughter, Karen, had come back after her HSC at boarding school to become active in the community, as well as to take on the rearing up of her baby niece, Kulin. As a young mother, Karen was particularly worried by the issues of industrial contamination of the town's residents. And they were all acutely aware of the history of forced movements by which Aboriginal people had been shunted around the state at the convenience of white employers or the Welfare Board. Joe's wife Isobelle remembered, as a child of eight, the brutal dislocation from her home at Angledool when the community was forced at gunpoint onto semi-trailers to be trucked to Brewarrina in 1936. When the 'No Camping' signs went up at Tulladunna, the Flicks felt strongly that this was the time to take a stand.

They were supported by most of the other Aboriginal families in the township, apart from those who were going to be employed as caretakers at the Piggery site. Particularly reliable supporters were Arthur and Leila Murray, who had also come from Collarenebri, hoping to find a better, less racially segregated place to raise their young family. But like the Flicks, they had found that the rising conflict over cotton had soured the township's atmosphere. The family was troubled by the loss of stable employment in the area. The cotton industry appeared to be flourishing, but it offered only casual and short-term work. Alcohol abuse became a problem for the family, for younger as well as the older members, and their sense of frustration was intense. Arthur was outspoken and the family were eager to take a role in achieving reform and better conditions for the future. A number of people in the old Wee Waa Advancement Association began to think about a way to stop the forced closure of Tulladunna, and they decided on an occupation of the site. They would challenge the 'No Camping' signs, and re-open Tulladunna for Aborigines.

They were supported, too, by the networks in the region of people like Isabel, who had had so much experience now of their families and communities on the cotton fields, and were beginning to feel alarmed at what appeared to be a spread of the industry into other blacksoil areas like Collarenebri. And the organisations of the region also brought in supporters, notably the Western Aboriginal Legal Service, where Barbara Flick was now co-ordinator, and whose staff and lawyers were happy to be participants and legal observers.

Tranby too, which by now had a number of Collarenebri students, organised to send a bus with student and staff supporters for the occupation planned for June. Just as the organising process was accelerating, an industrial conflict within Telecom, the sole phone utility, began to severely disrupt communication, illustrating once again how isolated by distance the north-western rural areas were. And while the political activity around the planned occupation was well underway, it was during emergencies that the need for phones was acute.

That became clear with the tragic death of Eddie Murray on 12 June 1981. Just days before the occupation of Tulladunna was to go ahead, Arthur and Leila's 21-year-old son Eddie was arrested by a passing police car after being found heavily intoxicated in the main street. Instead of being taken home, which was an option open to the police—although they rarely used it—he was taken to Wee Waa police lockup. Within one hour he was dead, having died, according to the police, by hanging himself in the cell with torn bed blankets. His family was eventually informed after a considerable lapse of time. Shocked and in disbelief, Eddie's distraught father Arthur suffered a collapse thought to be a heart attack. Leila called on the Flick family to help to get out-of-town legal advice, but all the phones were dead.

Eventually, after waiting hours, a poor phone service was restored and Isobelle Flick managed to get one call away. It was to our number and I took the call, which was so faint and heavily distorted with static that it took me a while to work out who was speaking to me, let alone to make out the disturbing story Isobelle was trying to tell. I was asked to reach Arthur's sister in Sydney by car urgently, and to spread the news to any other relatives she suggested, and at the same time to try to get legal advice about how to take the crucial initial steps to organise an independent autopsy. It was distressing, but simple enough, to drive around to give the sad news to Eddie's relations. But with only an intermittent phone service operating, it was a nightmare trying to reach a lawyer in either Sydney or the bush, and to get an independent doctor to travel to Wee Waa to conduct the autopsy. I was eventually able to pass the message through to the ALS office in Moree which was supposed to manage the investigation, but problems within that office led to further delays and confused decisions. In this sad case, which developed to have so many complexities, the messy handling of Eddie's autopsy was to continue to cause many problems.

The occupation of Tulladunna went ahead, although now with a heavier sense of sombre urgency as the organisers decided they must highlight the question of police involvement with Eddie Murray's death as much as the issues around land, residential freedom and cotton contamination. The tents went up on a Friday night, just behind the 'No Camping By Order of the Council' signs, and soon the bright black, red and yellow of the Aboriginal

Tulladunna Occupation, Wee Waa, 1981. Breakfast in camp, including (fom left): Joe, Peter Thompson, Kevin Cook, Isobelle, Barbara, Neil Andrews (Aboriginal Legal Service), Julie Whitton, Stephen Fitzpatrick with newspaper (WALS), and Miriki (running), Kevin Cook's son.

flag obscured the signs themselves. Isabel came across from Collarenebri to take her place in the central core of the occupation camp. The weather was dry and sunny but the temperature was freezing and the nights frosty. Black families came out from town and the cars rolled in from Collarenebri, Walgett, Brewarrina, Dubbo and Boggabilla, as well as the Tranby bus from Sydney. There were often 30 or 40 people at any one time during the day, coming and going, but the core families camping in the tents on Tulladunna were the Flick families and the Murrays.

Even within the tents, the ground was hard and cold under the sleeping bags, and we were all icy stiff as we woke into the early morning brightness. But the fire was blazing. Old shearers like Joe were always up before dawn, and the billy was their first priority. Those early breakfasts around the fire were magic. Isabel, her sisters-in-law Isobelle and Doreen Hynch, Joe and the others, were easy together as only old friends are, joking, recalling ribald stories about each other and planning strategies over the hot steaming tea. They included their younger family members in the jokes, with more funny stories and lots of instructions about everything from getting a man to running a campaign. And the whitefellas there too, mostly old friends and trusted lawyers, were around the edges, warmly welcomed and enjoying the banter, even when they were sometimes the butt of the jokes. There was

Tulladunna Occupation 1981: Heather Goodall and Barbara Flick.

plenty to do, press releases to be drafted and issued, interviews to be given by phone to radio and newspapers.

Overnight, a wave of graffiti had appeared around town, sprayed not only on the bus shelters, the mayor's store windows and the County Council, but also on the town's war memorial, a red brick obelisque standing at the centre of the main intersection. This confrontational targeting was no accident. The lighthearted banter at the campsite was really a way of coping with the powerful anger felt by the campers. And the war service of their father and grandfather, Mick, and the dismissive treatment he had received on his return, was never far from the minds of the Flick family when they considered their position in the area. So the words spelled out the deepest issues of the decade for Wee Waa—land, police violence and cotton's poison.

The town map titled 'Your guide to Wee Waa' now said as well: 'Racism Kills'. The bus shelter walls read: 'The Cotton Industry is *Killing* Wee Waa' and 'Cotton Industry is destroying our environment'. The Post Office walls said: 'You walk on Aboriginal land'. The war memorial read on one side: 'What kills black babies? Napalm in Vietnam. Cotton Chemicals in Wee Waa', and on the other, 'Cops are the Murderers'.

The reaction from the town was muted, but with currents of strong hostility clearly evident. This was particularly after the graffiti appeared on the war memorial, commented on by local radio and in the paper, but apparently without awareness either that Aboriginal people in the area had made such a disproportionate contribution to the war enlistment in the region, or that the protesters were so closely related to war veterans. What the town response did show was a sense of bewilderment about how to respond to the strategy of occupying the campsite.

By Sunday afternoon, most of the people from out of town had to go back to work and many Aborigines from town had also gone home, feeling they had made their point. But the Flicks and the Murrays stayed, determined to hang on through the week to make it clear that they wanted the campsite re-opened permanently.

Isabel was there with Joe, Isobelle and their family. Barbara and Karen were doing most of the driving into and out of town, carrying press releases in to be sent, in these days before mobile phones, and bringing groceries out to the camp. On Tuesday afternoon, all the campers had left the camp for a few hours for the first time, to have a break and to catch up with other things in their lives. Just on dusk, Karen and Barbara drove the first car back, with Isabel and some other women. As they turned in off the bitumen and headed around a wide, smooth curving dirt road towards the camp, they saw movement as figures darted behind the tents. Isabel remembered what happened next: 'The girls were in the car, Karen was driving and Barbara just happened to catch a glimpse of metal and she was able to pull the steering wheel away. And there were these steel spikes stuck in the ground . . . just where you'd pick up speed. These great spikes were covered in sand, and they were specially made'.

Shaken, they got out to see what it was they had so narrowly missed, and found it was a set of roughly made sharp metal spikes, welded together to ensure that at least two of the car's tyres were punctured in a stretch of the road which most drivers traversed at some speed. They had narrowly avoided a deliberate and potentially lethal trap. The intruders in the camp could be seen watching from the shadows of the tents, and the women decided it would be unwise to try to go into the camp now. Isabel said: 'And they came straight back uptown and got some boys to go back with them, and when they went back, on both sides of the road there was these two boxes of 42s and, you know, that's where the massacre would've happened. And that's when we decided it wasn't safe to camp down there'.

So they retreated back into town, spending an uneasy night until they could go out in safety in the early morning. When they did, they found the camp sacked, food stores stripped, tents pulled down, belongings stolen. 'So we'd go down every morning and set up the flag and the camp every morning. You know, we were closely watched all the time, if we were driving around someone was behind us all the time. And it was spooky but we knew they weren't playing games with us. And it took all that to be able to highlight the fact that something needed to be done about the Deaths in Custody'.

The town, stung by the challenge to its symbols of law and order and nationhood, had shown its ugly face. Would the townspeople have been surprised to know the campers were the children and grandchildren of war veterans? Would they have understood that the graffiti was a statement that the town, its police and its cotton growers had dishonoured the veterans' sacrifices?

Isabel, like the others, was shaken by the deliberate attempt to harm them. A young Murri in Moree, Cheeky Macintosh, had just recently been shot dead in an unprovoked attack by white vigilantes, waiting in ambush behind a tin fence, so the threat at Tulladunna felt very real. Isabel frequently said about these events in later years: 'We've all endangered our lives and the lives of our families and this shouldn't have happened in this country'.[3] They continued to speak out against both the forced closure of the Tulladunna site and the cotton industry's impact. But the immediate priority for the Flick family, particularly Karen and her aunt Isabel, now became the support of the Murray family as they prepared for the inquest into Eddie's death.

Isabel took a strong role during the inquest, despite, or perhaps because of, the fact that for all the Flick family the case had disturbing overtones of the inquest into Lubby's death. Isabel accompanied the Murray family on their many trips from Wee Waa to Sydney to see barristers. Then she was

Isabel with Leila and Arthur Murray and others at the Coroner's Court, during the inquest into the death in police custody of their son, Eddie.

with them at the inquest, held partly in Narrabri and partly in Sydney. Isabel testified in support of the family in their belief that Eddie had not given any indication of depression or intentions to harm himself, and that suicide, in their long collective experience of their communities, was extremely uncommon among Aboriginal people.

The Coroner's inquiry revealed many discrepancies in the police testimony. The mode of Eddie's death involved complex knotting in thick fabric and this raised suspicions because it seemed beyond the capacity of anyone in his very severe state of intoxication. His clothes had been taken from his body at the hospital morgue and burnt, rather than being handed over to his family. And the Murray family lawyers demonstrated that one policeman had lied about his whereabouts at the time of Eddie's death, that this officer had developed an elaborate story to place himself away from the lockup at the time by giving a detailed description of picking up his wife when she was discharged from hospital. When the family lawyers subpoenaed hospital records, however, it became clear that the discharge had occurred on another day altogether. The Murray and Flick families were convinced these matters would be enough to bring in a strong finding of foul play, but the Coroner's verdict was simply an 'open finding', indicating that the Coroner could find no evidence of either suicide or murder, and thereby closing the door on further police investigations.

They returned home to Wee Waa only to be met with intimidation and violence, as cars prowled around their home at night, threats were shouted at these 'troublemakers' and eventually Arthur and his nephew, Donny, were attacked in the street and left injured. 'Whites will not drive us out', a distressed Arthur declared. 'My son is buried here and I'll stay here too!'[4]

Isabel was deeply suspicious of the Coroner's finding. She could see the Murray family was fragile and she remembered her own collapse into severe depression after Lubby's unresolved inquest. She committed herself to supporting them at any cost and she did so faithfully over the years. Karen Flick also took on the heavy family responsibility and became a consistent advocate for continued investigation of Eddie Murray's death. His was only one of a cluster of suspicious deaths in police custody or in gaol. The Murray family's call for their questions to be answered met with immediate empathy from the family of John Pat, recently found dead in custody in Perth, and from the families of other young men and women whose deaths in custody had never been adequately explained.

The momentum was building for a national campaign demanding full, independent investigations into all these suspicious deaths and an end to Aboriginal deaths in custody. Isabel turned to her long established source of support in Sydney, Kevin Cook and Tranby.

Isabel: We'd built up a good sort of communication thing, and if I ran into some kind of problem out there I could always ring Kevin and he'd be running around like scalded chook too. But he'd always find some way to handle my stuff as well and then we'd analyse it a bit later. So I reckon we had a really good little unit to keep us going, sort of thing. And I suppose when you look back that's probably what Pearl Gibbs and all that little group had—just that little unit among themselves that you can trust and so you can get on with the job. It's all about who you can trust with some of the stuff, you know, that you're actually doing, because you could be making a decision and then it gets out and it gets blown away a bit. And then everybody is rowing with everybody.

We had to be always mindful of stuff like that. But especially the push for a Royal Commission into the Deaths in Custody was a pretty full-on cause with us. And I think the person that did so much in that was Karen. Karen was the real mover in that. She's a no-fuss person and she'd hate me for saying it. But she played a heavy role in that. And we knew we had that support here in Sydney from Kevin. And when we were talking to the lawyers, well, it just automatically happened, eh? Kevin did all the lawyer stuff, and getting them together, and we could just come down and it happened.

Karen became a key organiser, along with other Aboriginal women, in a campaign which built up, until in 1988 the Government was forced by public outcry to establish a nation-wide Royal Commission into Aboriginal Deaths in Custody.

When the Royal Commission hearings occurred for Eddie Murray's death, Isabel was there again. She repeated her conviction that suicide was rare among Aborigines, and supported the family's account of a happy young man whose problems with alcohol must not be used to allow the Wee Waa police to avoid serious investigation of the many questionable aspects of their case. Yet, once again, the conclusion of the Royal Commission was an open finding. Although recognising the glaring contradictions in the police case, the Commissioner found no firm evidence indicating murder or accidental death. And by this time, a bleak picture had emerged of the tensions in Wee Waa and more was known about the depressive effects of high alcohol intake, both of which offered at least some explanation of why suicide could not be ruled out. Like so many of the Royal Commission reports, in this one the police were scathingly criticised for their negligence, their contemptuous treatment of Aboriginal prisoners and for their shoddy record keeping. But without an attribution of blame, the families of the dead were deeply unsatisfied. The Murray family never abandoned the search for a more just outcome. They moved to Sydney, contributed to the monitoring of the Royal Commission recommendations to try to ensure less detention and safer conditions, and went on collecting evidence to call for a reopening of the inquest into their son's death.

Isabel continued to support the Murray family strongly. But over the years, this struggle had taken on a new poignancy for Isabel. When Lubby died in 1973, and even when Eddie Murray died in 1981, suicide was indeed very, very rare in Aboriginal communities in rural New South Wales. But there were extremely high rates of trauma and accidental death for young Aboriginal men, many of which, like car crashes in circumstances of severe alcohol abuse, could be interpreted as expressions of reckless despair, perhaps in response to years of deteriorating social conditions. But Eddie Murray's death in 1981 initiated a period of high publicity surrounding the apparent suicide of young Aboriginal people by hanging. More and more cases of Aboriginal suicide by this means did begin to occur, some in custody but many in family and community settings. Perhaps because of a widespread sense of frustration and despair, along with an element of copycat bravado, more and more young Aboriginal people tried to take their own lives, until by the late 1980s it was an undeniable and tragic public cry for help. In May 1988, the tragedy hit Isabel's family too, when her young nephew Noel Mason suicided in Collarenebri.

Isabel's anger at the treatment of Aboriginal people by police and gaolers never diminished and she was always suspicious of the police, knowing how they could abuse their power over Aborigines without fear of punishment. She deeply wanted a situation where such abuse would be punished and where there really would be justice for all. But from as early as 1984, Isabel had begun to call for recognition of the crises in which young Aboriginal people were finding themselves. She became more vocal in her defence of the children of alcoholic parents. She came to see these children as the innocent victims of the plague of alcoholism. When alcohol programs began to be established in the towns along the river, Isabel supported them strongly. She became a director of the Orana Haven Centre, which offered a place to live out of towns for alcoholics. She invited the Alcoholics Anonymous caravan to be parked on the Block in Collarenebri, and she encouraged her old friend Roy Thorne towards his eventually successful victory over grog.

But she was troubled to see that most of the rehabilitation programs concentrated on offering shelter and treatment for the alcoholics, but nothing in support for their families. She saw many children who were, to all practical intents, orphaned by alcohol abuse. Both alcoholic parents might be taken out of town to alcohol rehabilitation residences, but their children were left to roam the streets or to camp with relations as best they could.

She became much more outspoken, too, in her calls for the recognition of the damage which domestic violence did to women and children, and the urgent need for Aboriginal communities to address these problems themselves. Isabel had taken practical, personal actions so often in the 1950s and beyond, when she opened her house as a refuge for women in violent relationships.

But from the mid-1980s she was calling for a community-wide approach, and one driven by the women who were both the victims of family violence, but also the ones who could bring the sense of urgency to make changes. During an important women's gathering at Winbar in 1985, Isabel said:

> What makes us angry is what happens to the children while alcoholics are being tended to . . . too often it is the grandmothers, aunties, sisters and other women in the community, who end up with the responsibility of caring for these children. They are at risk, they are the victims of our communities . . . We need funds to organise holiday camps as a matter of urgency, to be organised by us for the kids . . . There is too much money spent on alcoholic rehabilitation and proclaimed places, but not enough on kids. The only time there's real interest is when the kids are starting to lag behind in school and they bring the Welfare in, and the kids get charged with something. And we need to organise refuges for kids, and places for families to go in crisis.[5]

Late in 1999, a book was launched outlining the Murray family's case for a reopening of the inquest into their son Eddie's death. The Murrays asked Isabel to launch it. Her simple speech resonated with the deep echoes of all these concerns:

> Once again, we have to petition the justice system for justice!
>
> Leila and Arthur are to be commended on their determination to continue to fight for this—not only for their son, but for all Aboriginal people. I know the heartache and trauma this family has suffered. I am honoured to have been able to share this struggle from 12 June 1981, in Wee Waa. We've all endangered our lives and the lives of our families over those years and this shouldn't have happened in this country. This family, as do all of our families and communities, has a right to the basic human right of justice.
>
> Money is not the issue—justice is the issue!

9
Land Rights on the Ground, 1983–1993

There might have been enough things to keep Isabel busy after she retired from Mangankali, between the continuing campaign against Black Deaths in Custody and her growing role in the regional women's movement. But there was another process gathering momentum: the land rights movement.

Land rights as a political idea in the 1970s drew its meanings from a mixture of traditional Aboriginal land relations, western land law, utopian socialist ideas, and from contemporary Aboriginal aspirations. So it was a complicated idea which meant different things to different people even before it was translated into legislation in 1983. What did it end up meaning in the day-to-day lives of Aboriginal people in rural New South Wales? Isabel's life had been entangled with issues about land, along with those of cultural heritage and people's relationship with their country, for as long as she could remember. So her story in the 1980s gives some answers to that question.

From the tabling of the Select Committee Report in 1981, it had been clear that there would be land rights legislation in New South Wales. The question was what sort of process would bring justice to people whose country had been invaded over the longest period of time and whose cultural expressions had undergone the greatest changes under colonialism. The land campaigners in 1977, including Isabel, had set up the New South Wales Aboriginal Land Council, a non-government body not to be confused with the later official body which took its name.

This original Land Council aimed to carry the struggle for land from rhetoric to reality. This body made a major input into the hearings of the

Select Committee, during 1978 and 1979, as it took evidence from Aboriginal people both in Sydney and in rural centres. The Land Council members travelled far more widely than the Select Committee did to ensure that Aboriginal communities in the most remote areas were well informed about the issues being discussed and that they had a chance to organise their own thoughts and priorities before speaking with the Committee. Isabel laughed about the travelling: 'Yeah, I'm a funny sort of a person. I spent my life on the road really, eh, when you look at it. Ted describes me as an "Old Man Kangaroo"—he just looks around and away he goes. But we had a lot of meetings all over the place that time'.

Isabel delighted in telling young people in later years the true stories of how the Land Council members got around by hitching rides, sleeping on floors, borrowing money to pay for petrol or a train ticket, playing cards while they talked strategies and camping out wherever possible so they could enjoy yarning long into the night with old and new friends. There were no travel allowances, no sitting fees and no expense accounts. These organising trips depended partially on the resources of Aboriginal-controlled organisations like Tranby, WALS and ALS. But they depended just as much on the generosity of community members who offered meals and floors and on the frugality and tireless enthusiasm of the Land Council members. Isabel, along with old friends like Jacko Campbell, Julie Whitton and Tombo Winters, would look back in later years on that period and wonder at how much they had accomplished on a shoestring, but also on the great enjoyment they had gained from each others' company and the excitement as well as the exhaustion of the job. Isabel recalled those meetings:

> *Isabel*: I remember Jacko saying he was going to put a sign up on the Jerrinja Lands saying: 'This is Jerrinja Land . . .' and you could have thought he was going to say 'Keep out'. But what he wanted to say was: 'We hope you enjoy yourselves'. He just wanted acknowledgement for his family. And I think that's what all of us wanted really. It's just the basic rights, you know.
>
> And see, when Jacko used to come down and meet up with the rest of us, he might be worried about something happening out there, say he was having some problems with another one of the old fellas . . . well, we'd still have to work with them, but we'd have to rethink how we'd be working. So developing strategies about how to cope with our community members too was no easy task.
>
> There was a lot of goodwill there among us, you never heard people swearing and going on. And we'd sit for days and talk about issues and we used to give each other a hard time and all that. But on the final day

it was the crunch time, you know, we just sat down and said: 'Okay. Who's doing this? Who's doing that?' And that's where we developed that idea that nothing happens unless it comes through a meeting, and we were pretty strict on that because it was working so well.

The communication was really good so that you could get a message to the members from the city to all the country areas. Within a couple of days you'd have everybody notified of a meeting or of a decision that had been made. So it was really good in that way.

And it was good, too, because we were all organised at the one time, and all aware of what was going on. And you know, if you didn't agree with something, well, you still had time to let people know that. When I look at it, it's amazing you know, the communication that we had right through—right down to Dareton and everywhere.

As a result of all this talking, the Land Council influenced the Committee's recommendations on some important principles. The basic premise was that Aborigines deserved and needed a land base for economic, social and cultural reasons. The Report then set about suggesting a mechanism to achieve this end. It recommended a system by which Aborigines could claim land which had not been alienated by freehold or leasehold. The bases for their claims could be an economic or social need, an historical association or a traditional affiliation. This approach recognised the massive damage as well as change which had occurred as indigenous cultures developed over the two centuries of colonisation. It did not demand that people prove that they still had an improbably 'traditional' lifestyle or relationship as the only way to demonstrate an affiliation to land. As most land had already been alienated in New South Wales, however, claims were never going to transfer a significant amount of land, so the Select Committee recommended establishing a substantial fund to purchase land.

The structures to allow Aboriginal people to organise to make claims and purchases and then to manage their land were to be a series of land councils, an idea derived from the Northern Territory but with distinctly local aspects. There were to be three 'tiers', the first and most important being the Local Land Council, which would hold what was to be the communal, inalienable title to each piece of land successfully claimed or purchased. Every Aboriginal person in the state was eligible to be a member of at least one Local Land Council. These remain the most inclusive and democratic of any body operating in Aboriginal communities. The Local Land Councils would meet regularly in Regional Land Councils, which would allow regional planning, economies of scale in purchase and management of land, and sharing of information.

The Regional Council boundaries reflected the pre-existing, long established and very practical networks of kinship, support and communication which in rural areas arose as much from traditional language and cultural affinities as from geography and recent economy. The region was the way Isabel had experienced the on-the-ground organising networks which supported the cotton strike in 1973, for example, and the campaign to get the cemetery road upgraded in 1983. The Regional Councils would elect a delegate to attend a State Land Council, to which Regional decisions would be reported. Power was to rest with Regionals and Locals, rather than the distant State Land Council, to avoid the alienation which local Aboriginal communities had felt towards government initiated, Sydney-based and centralised bodies in the past.

The Select Committee report was generally favourably received by Aboriginal communities. After a discussion period, the State government introduced a Land Rights Bill which incorporated most of the popular recommendations, and so received fairly strong Aboriginal support. But there were some very big stumbling blocks along the way to having the bill enacted. A backlash had been building among rural white residents, fuelled by the misleading mining industry campaigns against the Northern Territory Land

Barbara Flick and Kevin Cook at a demonstration demanding Land Rights, c. 1981. The sign behind them is in Paakantji, from the Wilcannia people, and it reads 'We are in OUR OWN country'.

189

Rights Act, and fanned by scare-mongering from New South Wales farming industry groups, like the Farmers' Federation, which pretended that white people would 'lose their back yards' if land rights became law. Not only did the conservative opposition parties in New South Wales oppose the bill, but the right wing members within the Labor Government also opposed it, especially those with links to white rural pressure groups.

Like most legislation, the 1983 Land Rights Act eventually ended up as a patchwork of compromises and concessions. Several government members moved last minute amendments which severely hampered the Act's implementation. The most damaging of these clauses, pushed through by the Labor Minister for Lands, blocked any claims over vacant Crown land if it could be shown to be needed for any undefined 'future essential public purpose'. The proof of such a need could not be tested by any judicial review. This and other amendments were to have a destructive effect on the new Act's effectiveness, allowing local governments to block legitimate claims on flimsy grounds. Just as seriously, the amendments undermined Aboriginal confidence in the Act itself.

The other major stumbling block was the decision by the Wran Government to use the opportunity of the Act's passing to insist on a linked Bill being accepted, which would retrospectively validate all previous revocations of Aboriginal reserve land in the twentieth century. Over 20 000 acres of Aboriginal reserves, many of them independently-run Aboriginal farms or places of deep traditional significance, had been revoked since 1913, including that at Collarenebri in 1924. Aboriginal protests had been intense, particularly in the 1920s, but the lands were still revoked to make way for soldier settlers, none of them Aboriginal, or for closer settlement.

Only in the mid 1970s did it become clear that these revocations, and the subsequent sale of these lands as freehold, had all been done on a faulty legal basis because of confusion over which department 'owned' the land. So all the subsequent titles over these 'freehold' lands were invalid. Instead of reaching a negotiated compromise, in which Aboriginal people received some compensation, Premier Wran insisted that if Aborigines wanted a Lands Rights Act at all, they were going to have to accept this retrospective validation of the illegal appropriation of a very large amount of their land. This left many Aborigines with a sour taste about the Government's sincerity on the whole issue.

Once passed, however, the Act needed Aboriginal involvement in the process of creating the land council structure, defining the boundaries of the various land councils and clarifying exactly how they were going to work. After thinking it over, Isabel's niece Barbara and some of Isabel's closest friends, like Kevin Cook, decided that the Act, despite its failings and compromises, was the best they were likely to get and so they should work

*Tony Flick at a Land Rights rally,
c. 1982.*

with it. They sat on the Interim Land Council on which they spent months visiting communities to discuss the possible Local Land Council boundaries and suggesting strategies to make this new structure actually work. One important step was to ensure that Regional Land Councils could support Locals to consolidate their annual allocations of funds to make more substantial purchases of land.

Isabel was an active adviser during this process, endorsing Barbara's and Kevin's position on the Interim Land Council and encouraging Collarenebri people to get to know the Land Rights Act and see how it might work out best for them. The Government intention was that once the Land Councils were set up, each Local Land Council was to begin to receive its annual share of the land fund and could then make its decisions about how to spend the money. What became clear to everyone very quickly was that the money going to each of the 113 Local Land Councils annually was both too small and too large. Each disbursement to a Local was too little to buy much more than a house block, even in Colle, and not even that in the larger towns, because of high New South Wales land prices.

The only way substantial amounts of land could be bought was if the Regionals were able to function effectively to pool Local Land Council payments and to purchase properties on a rotating basis on behalf of Locals. So only one or two Locals might gain a piece of land in any one year, but eventually they would all have one, and the process could start all over again. This asked a great deal of impoverished communities: they had to control their desires to call for land in their own area first, trusting their representatives on the regional organisation to ensure that it dealt fairly so that eventually each Local Land Council would gain a piece of land.

This worked well in the far western region, where funds were pooled and large properties were purchased in sequence so that eventually each Local had a substantial property for which they held title and which they controlled. A more divided Regional Land Council in the northwest shared this goal, but was not able to start to put it into effect for some years. Then a change of government in 1988 severely undermined the land acquisition process, disbanding the Regional Land Councils and transferring their role to a centralised State Land Council. The upshot was that the three or four large properties finally purchased in the north-western region never passed into Local Land Council or local community control.

But if the annual allocation to each Local was too small to purchase much land, this amount of money was still large compared to most of the local organisation budgets, and it would certainly accumulate to a much larger resource over time. This scale meant that the demands for reporting financial management were complex and at first confused. In most rural townships, and certainly in Collarenebri, the middle-aged people managing these new funds had, like Isabel, been excluded from formal education and later training. Only a few had had Isabel's tenacious determination to educate themselves in the skills of literacy and numeracy which were essential to fulfilling the paperwork needed for acquitting the land rights grants. So for the older, established community leaders, the new responsibilities were intimidating and burdensome. In the worst cases, confusion about the processes gave dishonest individuals the opportunities to move in and practise outright fraud. More often, the complicated paperwork invited slipshod ways and shortcuts as poorly equipped communities tried to take on Local Land Council administration.

Another rapidly emerging problem was that the goals of the Locals were ambiguous. Long time activists like Isabel expected that the funds would be used only on the purchases of land and that the land councils themselves would be involved only in the claim and acquisition of land and then in its cultural development. But for many people, land and housing were part of the same thing, and from the very beginning the Local Land Councils were called on by community members to take up a role acquiring houses and managing them. The Land Councils were a new idea and, for sceptical community members, they needed to show results, to have tangible, immediate outcomes, not just abstract or long delayed benefits.

Housing fitted this desire for short-term and tangible outcomes and this increased the community pressure for the Locals to become housing managers. Moreover, the Land Rights Act authorised immediate transfer of all existing Reserves to the relevant Local Land Councils, which meant that the locals inherited the housing stock already in existence on these reserves, and were drawn into a role in its management, even where a local housing company was already acting as manager. Government agencies, too, saw the land council network as a convenient structure onto which to offload many difficult and long-term administrative problems, and housing was one of them.

Isabel was on the pension after her retirement from Mangankali and her health was fragile. A severe case of pneumonia and another bout of depression brought her to Sydney, where she was nursed back to health by Cathy Bannister and Brian Doolan, close friends who were involved with Tranby. Once Isabel returned to Collarenebri she took an active role in the Local Land Council, encouraging younger people to take on the formal positions and contributing to the council's discussions on its goals and strategies.

The first expectation everyone held was that the Land Rights Act would allow Murris to claim some of their land back, but in the Western Division around Collarenebri there was little land which was not alienated as pastoral lease. The few remaining pieces of Crown land were rapidly under claim, like the town common at Engonnia to the northwest of Collarenebri, but local government and the State Minister of Lands acted to obstruct them. It seemed clear to everyone in the region that land claims were not going to deliver much.

Isabel didn't give up so easily, particularly when it came to the Aboriginal cemetery, which held intense cultural significance for Collarenebri Murris, with its deep connections to their present and their past. As Isabel had said at the road dedication in 1983, this land represented the whole wider expanse of Gamilaraay lands and it was a testament to the sustained relationship between the Collarenebri Murris and their land. Isabel reflected on the bitter-sweet implications of the cemetery in later years:

> *Isabel*: I remember the older women when I was a kid, worrying about 'no-one's going to look after it' and maybe that was implanted in my mind, but I realised how important that was as years went on. It makes me realise what we really did lose. Because it proves that that particular area was set aside by the king at the time, there was 100 acres there, revoked in 1924— just a little piece of land in all those big leases, it makes you feel deprived. And yet you're still aware of the fact that it's part of that land that's been put under lease, that our history is a part of that wider leased land.

Since the 1924 revocation of the Crown land reserve, the current cemetery, the very old cemetery behind it and the lagoon from which people had brought water to burn bottles, had all been part of a western lands pastoral lease held by the Copeman family. While she had still been at Mangankali and trying to scrape up funds for the cemetery road upgrade, Isabel had been talking to the lessee, Clara Copeman. This was another example of Isabel's ability to reach out across the deep gap between black and white Collarenebri residents to develop real communication about crucial issues.

Isabel had achieved a first step towards bringing the cemetery back into Aboriginal ownership when, in 1982, acting with the NSW Lands Trust, she reached an agreement with Mrs Copeman which protected the cemetery lands and guaranteed Aboriginal people's access to them. The Land Rights Act in the following year seemed to offer a way to achieve greater security over the cemetery by bringing the actual title of the land, communal and inalienable, back into Aboriginal hands. But a land claim was impossible because of the existing western lands lease. So Isabel, this time on behalf of the Local Land Council, went back to Mrs Copeman and began talking again. Doreen Hynch remembers that Isabel would meet Clara in the sandwich shop in town, chatting over how they could take the arrangement just a little bit further.

The upshot was extraordinary. Between them, Isabel Flick and Clara Copeman organised a complicated sequence of steps. First, Mrs Copeman would voluntarily relinquish the western lands lease around those sections which were of great significance to Murris, as agreed on in 1982. Once this was finally accepted by government and gazetted in 1988, Isabel immediately initiated the steps for the Land Council to lodge a claim, in January 1989, over what was now vacant Crown land. With assistance from Colin Clague in the NSW Lands Department, the claim was formally accepted in 1990. And at long last, after the slow process of claims investigation had dragged agonisingly along, the land claim was finally granted and communal freehold title to the land passed to the Aboriginal community in 1996. The process had been so slow and bureaucratic that many Murris in Collarenebri lost track of it, but Isabel was dogged in her pursuit of the goal and simply refused to let it slip. She and Clara Copeman demonstrated that communication and patience could achieve outcomes of deep significance to all sides, an early and very real example of lived reconciliation.

There appeared to be no other areas of land able to be claimed, nor other opportunities for the productive negotiating strategies which Isabel conducted so well. And other land holders were much less sympathetic and co-operative. Tension had mounted over land rights after a long period of loss of Aboriginal jobs, leaving few Aboriginal people with access to properties as workers anymore. So it was easy for anxious and misled graziers simply to lock the gates, as did the lessees of the land on which the Old Camp lay, between the cemetery and Isabel's Block on the edge of town. The denial of access to the Old Camp site was one issue which still made Isabel tremble with anger when she spoke about it years later in 1999. The locks meant that Murris had to ask permission to get onto what had been their home for so many years and the anticipation of humiliating knockbacks kept most people from asking. 'Because when they put the locks on the gate, you didn't know whether you were going to get in or not, and so we didn't want to argue the point about things like that.' So in the mid-1980s, far from gaining more access to land for cultural and social purposes, Isabel and her community seemed to be losing the little access they had had in the past.

As the North-Western Regional Land Council was so slow in its collective land purchase program, the pressures on the Locals in the area to turn to housing management increased. There were many families living in the town who needed housing, not just those on the Wollai, and the Land Council members increasingly saw the purchase of housing blocks and the building of houses as the LALC's legitimate function. Isabel's voice on the Local Council was consistently to seek sensible ways to do this, if it was the direction the Land Council wanted to go in. Although it didn't always win her friends, Isabel maintained that a housing priority list was essential, because it would allow housing to be planned and allocated fairly to those in most need—either because of family size or poverty—and to those who had been accepted onto the queue first. Only this type of process, she argued, would allow housing to be allocated in such a way as to strengthen community relations, rather than destructively set family against family in attempts to shortcut the queue.

But Isabel also stressed the Land Council's need to support the other town organisations, like Mangankali, in gaining better infrastructure for the whole Aboriginal—and indeed, for the whole town—population. The water supply, particularly, was a glaring problem. Despite the housing program nearing completion on the Wollai by the late 1980s, the water supply was still inadequate and, like the town's water supply, it was drawn directly from the Barwon River. Isabel argued that urgent infrastructure needed to be installed to upgrade the whole water supply for everyone.

But there were wider dimensions to land rights than water supplies or even gaining tenure over land. Isabel felt herself strongly connected to the whole region now. Her relationship to the north-western Gamilaraay/Yuwalaraay area from Boggabilla and Moree across to Walgett, was built on family and friends, as were her links up into Queensland through Mungindi, Thallon and St George. But she had also built up a network of relationships through the Legal

Service network and then her friendships with the WALS activists in Brewarrina, Bourke, Wilcannnia, Broken Hill and beyond. The land rights campaigns had cemented those comradeships, and when the opportunities came, Isabel was eager to get to meetings where she could catch up with those old friends.

One important meeting like this was the blockade of 'Mootwingee' National Park in 1983 by the communities of Wilcannia, Broken Hill and Menindee. These were people with a strong affiliation to Mutawintji, a wonderful and mysterious site of rich art galleries and powerful stories, hidden in the navel of the hills. This site had been taken over by a grazing lease, its name anglicised to Mootwingee, and then purchased by National Parks in the late 1960s and exhibited as a natural and historic site, with little consultation with Aboriginal people about its continuing cultural meanings. But Aboriginal people in the surrounding area knew the site well and continued to visit it and teach their children about it. They were angry and offended over many years by The National Parks and Wildlife Service allowing unrestrained visitor access to areas which Aboriginal people knew to be only for initiated men.

Finally they had had enough of not being consulted. So tourist buses from Broken Hill were met with the bright signs in red, black and gold on the long weekend in October 1983: 'Mutawintji: Closed by the Owners'.

I was with Isabel that weekend, driving her down with a group of Tranby students. As we drove in, we could feel the intense excitement and see the energy in the noisy crowd. The blockade camp was two hundred strong, with elders like Alice Bugmy, Jim James Bates, Tibby Brier, Dorrie Hunter and May Barlow, along with the younger leaders like William Bates, Maureen O'Donnell and Badger Bates. All around were kids, eager to muck around as they set up the campsite or to help hunt bush tucker. A group of Aboriginal people were always at the gates, stopping tourist buses and patiently explaining to the tourists the importance of the site, before courteously asking the bus driver to turn the bus around and head back to Broken Hill. The Regional Land Council had invited friends from across the region, and Tombo Winters was there, along with Barbara Flick with the WALS mob.

When Isabel arrived around midday Saturday there was already bush tucker in abundance, with emus being cooked in the holes as we drove into the camp, kangaroos being griddled on the fire and the dough for johnny cakes being mixed and thrown high in the air, stretching it out to its proper round flat shape. This bush camp was a new way of doing politics in New South Wales, exciting and very, very different from the formal meetings in halls with motions and 'Chairs', which so many local organisations like housing companies had come to feel was expected of them all the time.

This blockade involved direct action with powerful symbolic effect, just like the Tulladunna occupation in 1981. But as a bush meeting, it drew on the confidence of the far western communities to hunt and occupy their land, to *live* on it and *from* it with an assurance which had become harder for the Murris from further east, where pastoral leasees had locked their gates so much earlier, and where women, in particular, had been separated from real contact with their country except on the riverbanks close to camps and towns.

A big element at Mutawintji was teaching and learning: teaching about the beautiful stencil galleries in the hills, teaching about the areas where only men could go, learning strategies for getting their message across as they talked to tourists at the gates or screenprinted t-shirts back at the main camp. Isabel revelled in this blockade and talked about it for years afterwards, seeing it as the model for the way she wanted land rights and community life to be developed:

> *Isabel:* The good thing about the blockade at Mutawintji was we had the older people more or less guiding us and the younger ones were learning, and it was a good time. We were all together, camping. There was no five-star accommodation, but plenty of unity, we had real unity. In one end of where we camped, we set that aside for people if they wanted to have a drink or a singsong. After a meeting, well the young ones went down there, but it was a very well disciplined blockade. Because I think everyone recognised the importance of being able to talk to all the people who came in buses from everywhere and to get their reaction to being turned back. It was really good and everyone supported each other. It was the men's job to provide the bush tucker and to teach the younger ones how to do that; so there was a lot of men and boys' stuff going on there, and women and girls' stuff. And us older ones, while we were having a game of cards we were still planning what we could do to bring about the changes.

The Mutawintji Blockade had a powerful effect on Isabel, intensifying her desire to restore the symbols of cultural links between her community and the land. The reality of land rights was much more to her than the small patches of land which would be the most any claim and purchase process could acquire. As she had said about the cemetery, its boundaries spoke not only of the people buried within it, but of the limitless expanse of Murri land of which it was the remaining visible symbol. For Isabel, land rights meant a new set of relationships between a whole people and their land, no matter who held the particular title deeds. Isabel wanted a real reoccupation of her country.

At times, that was easier to see from outside of town. The perspectives of the region and her comradeship with the women of the far west as well as the northwest gave Isabel the refreshing sense of expansiveness which made small-town life, with its petty tensions and jealousies, much more manageable. So Isabel was eager to support the Western Women's Council when Barbara Flick and Maureen O'Donnell from WALS proposed it at a meeting in 1984. The resources of the community organisations seemed too often to be absorbed in meetings at which men dominated the numbers and the style. There wasn't often a place in the car for women with kids or for older women to travel to these meetings, which cut them off from the important social networks as well as the political decision making.

The Western Women's Council, based on the Land Council model, would grab some of those resources and focus them just on women, giving them a chance to spend some time with each other, and exchange experiences and ideas. A key goal was to bring women together outside of towns, to have their own bush meetings so they could get back in touch with country and to get to know each other outside the white town context. As pastoral jobs for women had been cut back, many had become confined to the townships and so their knowledge of and confidence in being in the bush was ebbing away. The promises of land rights meant little for these women if they weren't able to get back into the bush and feel competent and at home enough to make it their own again. The new bush meeting style, and particularly the Mutawin-tji Blockade, had been so exciting and satisfying that everyone was eager to repeat the experience but to concentrate its impact on women.

The main bush meeting of the Women's Council which Isabel was able to attend was over Easter in 1985 at Winbar, the large back block of what had been a massive river-frontage pastoral property on the Darling River between Wilcannia and Louth. Winbar was the subject of an intensely fought land claim. This was one of the few claimable places with a pastoral history, which meant that Aboriginal people had been able to live on traditional country at the same time as they worked in the new economy. The Western Lands Lease over it had lapsed when the property was broken up in the mid-1970s and the river-front blocks sold, leaving this section idle as vacant Crown land and making it immediately claimable.[1] Isabel's friend, John Terry, acting for the Western Regional Land Council, was conducting a tenacious pursuit of this land against vigorous opposition from the State Government. The Women's Council decided to hold their bush camp there to emphasise the wide and sustained Aboriginal demand for the rights to this country.[2]

But this was a tough camp. Winbar is far more isolated than Mutawintji or the site of the first camp the Women's Council had held at Mt Grenfell at the end of 1984. The black soil Winbar roads were boggy with intermittent rain limiting the amount of food collection the women could do, as well as frustrating the kids who were there. But for Isabel, and for Barbara Flick too, this camp left warm memories of the deepening relationships among the women of the region. In her later recollections, Isabel pointed out that much effort went into getting to this camp at Winbar. She explained how comparing the differences between experiences in the two regions was important for her in understanding how much her community had lost, as well as how much the common experiences of women under mission life and 'apprenticeship' had shaped their lives:

> *Isabel:* When we set up the Women's Council, we knew that one of the important things was to get back into the community, not just meetings in Sydney. The message got around better that way and more people got involved in community things. From Menindee to Bourke, and Engonnia, and to Toomelah and Walgett, it was good for us to get together and talk about land and what we could do.
>
> And there was no money . . . no TA, we just linked up with each other by going down to the phone box and seeing who's going through our way. Sometimes we had to wait for pension days or social days to even start travelling. It might take us two or three days to even get to the places we were meeting. Now Winbar was pretty far out and I can remember we did a lot of hitchhiking to get there . . . I think Julie [Whitton] and I met up with someone going down that way. It was more or less who was going our way . . . and we just ended up out there!
>
> See it was harder for women to get money for travel. Then it started to get really impossible, because we needed to do a lot more working in the community once the Land Councils were up and we'd have local meetings organised. So you couldn't just break off a meeting in town and go to Wilcannia because there was a meeting for women on.
>
> We found a lot in common, even though I think we've lost more of the language than the people down Wilcannia way, where they were still able to practise theirs, while we are trying to retrieve stuff. So that was something that we all felt they had an advantage in that. But we had lots of common work experiences on stations and for some of us in 'apprenticeships'. And the thing was, even though some of the stories were sad, we were able to laugh at some of the things our people endured to sort of become educated.
>
> The bush foods were a really important part of the camp at Winbar. And the women did that, that was all women. It was a learning thing for me too, because even though as a kid I was taught how to fish and look for bait and stuff like that, but to see the younger ones bringing back a kangaroo or an emu and actually cleaning it and stuffing it and cooking it, it was a real educational time for all of us.

Barbara has pointed out how important it was for the women who had been 'apprenticed', and who were feeling that their experiences were irrelevant to many younger people, to be able to find this common ground across the region and to be recognised and celebrated for the strength they had shown.

Isabel's memories of this camp stressed its valuable outcomes. But the audio recordings made by the Women's Council during their meetings at this bush camp have a tense, sharp edge which reflected the difficulties these women were facing in their community lives and in regaining confidence on their country. Isabel was outspoken as the motions were discussed, stressing the importance of supporting children in crisis and protecting women and children from the violence caused by alcohol abuse from within the Aboriginal community and by police attacks and educational indifference from outside. But another issue for all of them was that the poor weather and bad roads had demonstrated how fragile their hold on their independence was in this remote and poorly serviced area. Particularly for women responsible for elderly people and young children, their need for access to medical facilities frustratingly underscored the degree to which they could no longer be wholly independent on their land. This was demonstrated when a car which went out to shoot emu had become bogged for hours, and those left in camp worried about how they would find them and then how they would cope if someone had been injured.

Even more difficult was a challenge by some of the younger women to the general agreement that there should be no alcohol at the camp. These young women disappeared from camp early Sunday morning without telling anyone, then eventually turned up hours later, bringing grog back into the camp. By the time they returned, their families were relieved that they were safe but furious that they had flouted the desires of the majority of the women in the camp, showing no respect for themselves and their elders. One mother seized her daughter's carton of beer and hurled it, unopened into the scrub. And there it stayed. Her sister is said to have found it years later, label faded but still unopened, a silent monument to a mother's fierce determination to stop grog from destroying a time that was deeply important to her and her family.

And finally there was the frustration which many women were feeling about their marginalisation by men in the decision making in their own communities, in organisations like the Land Councils and the legal services. Isabel summed up many of these strands of tension, about women, communities and land, when she said to the women at the close of the meeting:

> Isabel: I think we learnt a lot from this trip here ... It frightens you to think how dangerous the country is. And the responsibility is there, and it's not only for Maureen and Barbara, but for all of us. We have a

responsibility for each other and that'd be the same if it was in a town, even if we had the meeting right in the town hall, we still have the responsibility to each other because we've travelled a long way. Collarenebri and Menindee is not just a stone's throw apart . . .

But I wouldn't like to see us get disheartened by this. Here was I saying yesterday after that car got bogged, 'This is the last meeting for me'. What sort of women are we to say that? We'd be gutless, eh!

Men have been laughing about this women's council, you know . . . But you've got the best land council structure of anywhere. Every other land council are all governed by men, or women who are only there to line their own pockets . . . Those men laughed about this women's council and made snide remarks . . . but if we stay solid, even though we are a small number, we can change those land councils.

Although she had formally retired, Isabel's relationships across the region kept her busy over the next year or so, travelling to meetings at the same time as she continued to actively involve herself in Collarenebri affairs. Her contributions to Collarenebri and to the wider Aboriginal community were recognised in April 1986 with a Medal of the Order of Australia, an honour of which she was quietly proud. It allowed her a sense of justification after all these years of battling with the local authorities to have her work, so often labelled 'making trouble', finally acknowledged as a valued contribution to the community. And it also gave her a new lever to add to her arsenal when she was trying to exert pressure on some official. She could now sign her most challenging letters to authorities with 'Isabel Flick, OAM'. Yet she never took it too seriously. Whenever anyone asked her what OAM stood for, she would laugh as she answered: 'Oh, that stands for Old Aboriginal Moll!'

Despite being busy, Isabel had more time for her grandchildren in those years, many of whom were living in Collarenebri or close by. She had been saddened for a long time by her estrangement from Ben's wife, but she kept in touch with Ben and his children in Bathurst whenever she could. She enjoyed all her grandchildren, but the housing shortages in the town in Collarenebri had begun to have a severe impact on her own family. Because of Isabel's refusal to allow her children to apply for houses from the Aboriginal organisations, some of them waited longer for housing than they might otherwise have done. Tony and Peggy with their six children had finally got a comfortable Housing Department house not too far from the Block and a bit later on in 1988 their son Mark was born. But Larry's family and Brenda's family, as well as Amy and young Aub, were all living with Isabel and Ted at the Block itself, making the small two bedroom house unbearably crowded. Amy had been on the Department of Housing accommodation list for a long time and so when she was finally allocated a house she took it even though it was in Moree. Then Brenda and her family moved to a double-decker bus which they parked on the Block behind Isabel's house, relieving the pressure but falling outside any regulations about habitable dwellings.

The house itself continued to reflect the economic difficulties Murris faced in the region, and Isabel had not ever had enough spare cash to upgrade the services to it. Like many older houses in Collarenebri it had never had electric hot water. Instead, water was heated in a drum over a partially open fire. Later in 1986, fire once again claimed a terrible price from the family. Brenda had travelled to Sydney to accompany Isabel to a doctor's appointment. Amy was on the Block minding the kids and was occupied with Brenda's baby, Isabella. Brenda's two elder daughters, Bernadette aged nine and her younger sister, Chantelle, happened to be near the water heater when some young boys on the far side of the fire, unaware of the girls' presence, threw an aerosol can into the flames in imitation of a recent TV show. The explosion was directed entirely towards the two girls, and Bernadette particularly was terribly burnt. Amy had the presence of mind to stand both of the girls in the cold water shower, but she could do little to relieve their pain. The girls went through months of agony and lonely hospitalisation, and then for many years after had to wear pressure bandages and masks to reduce their scarring.

This terrible accident, with its echoes of Barbara's burns on the Block, was to draw much of Isabel's energy over the next years as she tried to support her granddaughters and their mother. But then in November 1989 another tragedy hit them all. A flapping curtain ignited on a fan, and Tony's house went up in flames. Isabel tried to explain later how their loss had changed her life:

Isabel: When people get unhappy, I think what a waste of time. And that's why I can't grieve anymore. At first I could. I could stop and let myself grieve, like when Dad died, and Mum . . . I used to do that. But then when I lost the little grandson in that fire, I don't think I ever got away from that scene, you know, and that day. We were having this big meeting in the hall about the Aboriginal Legal Service, and we were really into it and people were having shots at me because I was being very adamant about moving away from the city office. And then all of a sudden we heard the fire engine. And then someone said: 'Oh it's up from your way'.

And then when I looked and I saw the fire engines going that way, and then I thought: 'Oh gee, what could've happened at home?' So I was just going to get in the car and Amy comes past and she said: 'Well, quick Mum we have to go up to Tony's place'. So, standing there and watching everyone trying to put the fire out and everything. And then I'm looking around and counting all the kids and I'm thinking about everybody and I said: 'As long as all my kids are out'. But the baby . . . Then when they told me, of course, I just couldn't handle it. I could see all my grandkids expecting me to fix it. Because I think they had this idea that I could fix anything.

That was the hardest part for me to deal with—my grandkids grieving. I realised then I had to not worry about how I feel. I've got to worry about how they feel. And that took . . . oh, many many months of just making sure that I was there whenever they wanted to come there and cry. And I think then all those deaths . . . the loss of my young sister and our little granddaughter, and then the first young grandson, and then . . . I think all those deaths came back on me then. And I realised from there on that I couldn't grieve the way I used to, I had to change my ways of dealing with death because these kids were expecting so much from me and I knew I had to be alert all the time to give them whatever comfort I could. And I think it was from there on that I realised that I can't stop now and grieve. That's how I've got to be doing something all the time.

The accident shattered many lives. Its burden separated Tony and Peggy not long after, and Tony moved away from Collarenebri, leaving a painful gap for Isabel and the rest of the family.

Isabel's own grieving took the form of furious activity. She decided she would go back to work, taking up the job as co-ordinator of the Local Land Council, even though by now she was troubled like everyone was by the feuding which had grown up about housing priorities and the tensions arising from the slowness of the region to deliver land purchases.

There were a number of frustrating problems which she inherited with this job. One was the intractable issue of the rents on the Wollai, which underneath was an example of a thorny problem in any small community, where people are reluctant to take action against relations. The land had come under the control of the Land Council in 1983 as it had been Reserve land, which meant the Local Land Council was responsible for collecting the rents which were needed to pay for maintenance of the housing stock which Mangankali had built. One Wollai resident had taken on himself the role of rent collector, but had allegedly never passed the rents onto either Mangankali or the Land Council nor, seemingly, was any maintenance carried out. Too many of the Wollai and town community were related to this man to challenge the situation, but the problem only became worse as regular maintenance on the houses could not be undertaken for lack of rent money.

A wider problem was the bitter opposition of the conservative State Government, elected in 1988 and, particularly from the National Party side of the coalition, deeply opposed to the previous Labor Government's Land Rights laws. The incoming Premier had tried to seize the whole Land Council's land purchase funds outright, but this was such a flagrant breach of common law that the government was forced to retreat. Instead, it pushed through amendments to the Land Rights Act which severely disabled it. One major legal change with long term consequences and with intense symbolic significance was the abolition of inalienable title, making communal inalienable Aboriginal land simply saleable freehold and therefore much more vulnerable.

Another major change removed all effective power from the Regional Land Councils and handed real decision making over to the State Land Council, which was thereafter to have directly elected and paid members. Dismantling the Regionals meant that each Local Land Council would now be on its own: its buying power could not be enhanced by pooling with other Locals within the region and so the regular payments from the land purchase fund, never enough to buy much on their own, would be more likely to go towards an office, a house block, a salary or a vehicle. These might all be for legitimate Land Council purposes, but they meant that there could never be a significant land acquisition program. And it was clear to everyone at community level that the new State body would entrench a centralised decision-making body very similar to the old Lands Trust with Councillors, cut adrift from the communities which elected them, who would find it hard to stay in touch with individual community needs.

Isabel had been deeply committed to the ideas of the early Land Rights Act. The inalienability of communal title and the strength of the Regions were central principles to her, as they were to many Aboriginal community members across the state. There was a groundswell of opposition to the amendments and Isabel along with many others travelled to Sydney to register their dismay and anger at the way the government was heading. Liberal Premier Greiner tried to confuse the issue by calling in Charlie Perkins—who had had little previous involvement in New South Wales politics—to 'report' on the proposed amendments. His consultation with communities was rushed and inadequate in Isabel's view. She argued that Perkins was unashamedly supporting the establishment of a centralised State Land Council. She saw this as a form of organisation in which Perkins, with his long career as a Federal public servant, was now most comfortable and which would give a small group of Perkins' allies a chance of controlling, more readily than they could othewise have done, the network of locally-grounded Regional Councils. With the Perkins' report coming in, as predicted, in support of the Greiner proposals, the State Land Council members were the last obstacle to the amendments which promised them a five-year job, a car and a substantial salary. Although they couldn't stop the legislation being introduced to Parliament, they carried the symbolic and strategic burden of the decision to oppose or endorse the amendments. With a number of independents opposed to the bill, the Labor opposition votes were crucial in defending or undermining their own Land Rights law. But divisions had always been deep within the Labor party on the Land Rights Act and the Aboriginal Land Council members needed to demonstrate united opposition to the amendments if the Labor opposition was to be swayed to vote against the amendments.

Many people from all over city and country New South Wales again came to Sydney to reinforce their concerns when the State Land Council met for the last time to consider their position on the amendments before the legislation went to Parliament. Isabel was there with her son Aub, and her nephews Deakin [Lubby's son] and Gavin [Lindsay's and Rosie's son], her brother Joe and many others who were familiar faces from the land rights campaigns of the 1970s and 1980s. Isabel's niece, Karen, along with Judy Chester, Kevin Cook's partner, had been working at the State Land Council and they too were deeply opposed to the amendments, so they were there alongside the Local Land Council members. They all rallied at the Liverpool offices of the State Land Council to plead with Council members to consider the community before they considered their own personal futures. When it was clear that some of the State Land Council members were already nego-tiating with the Greiner ministry, the demonstrating Local members occupied the building, set up camp and refused to leave.

The sit-in lasted three days, with a series of confrontations within the building between the Local Land Council members and the State Land Council members. But it had become clear by then that a number of State councillors were wavering in their opposition to the Greiner changes. The Bill went into Parliament, but the Labor Party opposition was too divided to vote against the amendments. A sombre crowd of around 1000 Aboriginal community members from all over the state stood silently in the streets outside the locked gates of Parliament, confronted by police and security guards. The crowd was grimly standing watch as the Land Rights Act was torn apart. Isabel stood with Joe, each silently frustrated by their inability to save the structures they had fought so hard to create.

Then, off to the right, there was a brief disturbance and Karen, Deakin and Amy were over the side fence. The pressure from the supporting crowd pushed the fence over after them, and the demonstrators flooded in to the forecourt. Karen and Deakin were by this time up on the verandah of the House, heading through the doors to make their case face to face with the Government. Joe was close behind, up the main steps to the door to follow Karen and Deakin into Parliament, but the police grabbed the grey-headed old man, turning him and forcing him back down the stairs, only to find themselves confronted by Gavin,

Joe Flick is, amid a shower of water thrown by demonstrators, forced down the stairs of the New South Wales Parliament after attempting to enter during a 1991 demonstration to protest against the Greiner Government's amendments to the 1983 Land Rights Act.

protecting his uncle. In the confusion, Joe turned and headed up the stairs again, his agility taking the police by surprise, but he was grabbed at the top and shuffled down again into the forecourt. Within minutes, Karen, Deakin, Amy and Gavin were each sitting in a van in custody, and Joe had been roughly escorted down the stairs yet again. The crowd had burst into life, now shouting their anger and frustration in the forecourt, at least able to make it clear that the State Land Council did not speak for them.

The Greiner amendments to the Land Rights Act became law, and they drastically changed the conditions for Local Land Councils all over the state. Land acquisition virtually ceased. Figures were notoriously difficult to extract from the new State Land Council for years after these changes in 1991, but the few figures which did leak out told the same story: no new land purchases and the only claims granted were those lodged before the amendments. For Collarenebri, the dismantling of the North Western Regional Land Council meant that there would never be the scope to purchase significantly sized properties and have them under local control. The three or four grazing properties the North Western Region had finally purchased, just as the amendments became law, stayed under the control of the State Land Council and their ownership and management have never passed into local hands. Pressure from the conservative state government and a hounding press encouraged a commercial approach to land management in the State Land Council, where the need to demonstrate a competence in profit-making overtook the hopes for cultural and social access to land which had been so important for many communities. Isabel discussed her frustration at this direction:

> *Isabel:* They just haven't got the right kind of management in place in lots of places. See, I think out in the northwest the State Land Council have now got a lot of land. That Kaluma Station is a big property. But it's hard country. It mainly ran cattle and certain types of sheep. There wasn't much else going. But there could be other things developing there. And that's where we wanted to really develop initiative programs for kids, for some of these kids going before the courts. And then there's still room to go and work another side where you're working with kids . . . not just the ones before the courts.
>
> We had a really good proposal we put up to the New South Wales Ministers Pickering and Virginia Chadwick, when we had a meeting with them at Lightning Ridge. And because it was going to cost a little bit of money they watered it down, right down to where they just gave them a bus and a little shelter in Bourke, where they can just pick up kids who are on the streets, so they are more or less treating them just like drunks. So it did away with the plans that we had for incentive programs—to set up our own small courses . . . do up old motor cars, make them roadworthy and sort of give the kids incentives by giving them those cars to take responsibilities with them. And woodworking . . . we were going to set up our own furniture factory out there. Oh, I just forget how many different programs we had planned to set up there for the girls and boys through the Regional Land Council level. But it was after that that the amendments took out the Region. And then of course we lost all that direction then.
>
> I hoped that if we could get these women's organisations up and going we could just be putting up those proposals over and over till they get up. With all this law and order stuff about, as soon as there's a problem in a town they want more cops, so that's what happens. But we wanted to say: 'Well, that's not the way we want to go about it'. I think they're doing great things out at Goodooga now with the kids, because they've got that big property at Mogilla and I think they're starting to run programs for kids there. But that's the Indigenous Land Corporation, the Federal one, not the State Land Council, and it's not under our control.

In the wake of the Greiner amendments, the management of housing—its construction, allocation and maintenance—became the major role of the Local at Collarenebri. Reluctantly, Isabel was drawn into a relentless sequence of community conflicts about who should have priority on the housing list and how rents should be extracted from reluctant tenants. In the meantime, she managed a major building program through the Land Council, in which substantial brick houses began to be built in the township for Aboriginal families. Not only were these houses important in improving the living conditions of Murris, they were the only new building occurring at all in the little town. Isabel and her community were literally changing the face of Collarenebri, the town which had tried for so long to keep them segregated, confined and out of sight.

Isabel still refused to accept applications from her own children for the local housing lists, and the Department of Housing did not have houses to offer in Collarenebri. Larry had lived in Collarenebri all his life and neither he nor Brenda wanted to move away, but their position was becoming desperate. Walgett Shire Council made an inspection of the house on the Block, issuing a severe warning. The bus and tin room attached to it which were housing Brenda's family was completely unacceptable to Council, and this still left Larry's family, with 11 people, sharing the house with Isabel and Ted. The council was adamant that although each of the dwellings and surrounds was clean and well kept, the property's gross overcrowding demanded the immediate rehousing of at least 14 of the 18 people on the Block.[3] Isabel was left with no alternative but to agree that her children would apply for Land Council housing, entangling them all, as Isabel had predicted, in the dispiriting local grumbling about housing allocation.

But Isabel sustained a determination to make the Land Council do more than manage houses. Living on the Wollai, like living on most Aboriginal reserves in New South Wales, had always been made more difficult by the refusal of local authorities to ensure that road access was safe and that services like water and electricity were available. Reserve communities all over the state have horror stories of being isolated in floods because of dirt roads and of summer epidemics traced to poor water supplies. But the essentials which councils insisted on for any residential housing development turned out not to be so essential when the residents were Aboriginal. These problems had rankled Murris in Collarenebri for many years and Isabel was determined to get them solved. But as she had found so often, the attempts to achieve sensible and modest outcomes met with delays and obstruction as local government tried to manipulate the outcomes or just make a bit of money from the Federal funding which had begun to flow to address infrastructure problems in remote areas.

It took ten years after the cemetery road was upgraded before Isabel could get the Wollai road sealed. By this time, a new Federal administrative structure, Aboriginal and Torres Strait Islander Commission (ATSIC), was in place, with elected Aboriginal commissioners and regional councils. In western New South Wales, the Murdi-Paaki Regional ATSIC Council covered both the north-western and far western Land Council areas. Isabel was elected to the first regional council, where her long experience meant she was a respected voice. The endorsement of the ATSIC Regional Council for the sealing of the road did not remove the local government obstacles, although it gave Isabel a bargaining tool. The actual implementation of the project needed sustained negotiation and intervention at the local level, and Isabel took that on in meeting after meeting. She could now confidently orchestrate such meetings, like one in which she had to mediate between white shire officials and a white contractor. She had travelled a long road since her first shy attendance at town committee meetings in Collarenebri with Harry Denyer in the 1960s. She reflected: 'And so we had to have a confrontation just to get that road done. But we won. I can look back and say: "Yes, I've done a bit there"'.

The other critical infrastructure problem took Isabel back to her early campaign for an ablution block on the Wollai, but it also expanded to have implications for the whole town. The water to the Wollai was still drawn directly from the river, but so too was the town water supply. Isabel had been campaigning on this for some time as an urgent matter, but there was very direct resistance this time from white townspeople who were worried about their water rates going up:

> *Isabel:* When I took up the issue of the water supply in Colle and the sewage, we started to talk at a regional level at ATSIC about those issues. So then it was put up national for those areas to be addressed. And, of course, in a town like Colle you're not only talking about a Reserve, you're talking about the town. The first thing they said was: 'Oh Isabel you know that can't happen. Who's going to pay rates? We're going to have higher rates . . .' So, there was a bit of an outcry there.
>
> And I said: 'The issue is that Aboriginal people have a right to have clean water. I pay $500 a year for my water. I'm a taxpayer too, in that sense I pay my rates the same as anyone else. And I'm going to have clean water. I'd rather have clean water than what we've got'. And they said: 'Yes, and you know what's going to happen? Our rates are going to up and . . .' And I said: 'Well that's understandable, everybody is going to be concerned about that. But the sewage that's right next door to our older people that we've got down there, that's not good. We shouldn't have it. We're entitled to have the proper kind of ponds'.
>
> And one day one old fella came in the office and he started going crook on me. And he said: 'Look, it's all right for you blacks, you get

every bloody thing paid for you'. And I said: 'Let me tell you this, I pay for my own. Just a minute I'll get my rates notice'. I threw it on the table, and then I threw the Land Council's rates on the table. And I said: 'We pay our rates the same as you do. You shouldn't go on like this'. And he said: 'Oh nobody can tell me what to do . . .' I said: 'Okay'. And when I went into the shop next door everybody is saying: 'Oh God, there's going to be a row now'. And I said: 'No, I just showed him that we pay rates too. He thought we didn't pay rates. But once he understood that, what else could he say'.

Then in the summer of 1991, the Darling River died. A massive bloom of vividly-coloured blue–green algae stained the river for a thousand kilometres from Mungindi to Menindee. Stock and people could not bathe in or drink from the poisoned river, and for most towns that meant reliance on their rainwater tanks and filtered water systems. But for Collarenebri and the Walgett Shire Council, it publicised the shameful fact that it was the *only* town on the whole river which had no filtration system at all for its drinking water. Isabel's campaign suddenly looked prophetic. Her contacts with Aboriginal public servants and her familiarity with the issues made her an important member of the town's negotiating team to ensure an upgraded water supply for the whole town. The 'troublemaker' was now a valued citizen!

Isabel: So when that blue–green algae issue came up, Pat Dixon was very good in supporting me there. She's a Murri from up this way and she was in the Public Works Office in Canberra then. When she said she'd be up there, she'd be there. It started to develop into the local people turning against the Shire, which should've done it anyhow, for everyone. And at last they had this big meeting and they invited people to go along to it, and a fellow from Canberra said: 'Look, this should've happened 13 years ago. So what are you all on about? It's twice the price now. In another 10 years it's going to be twice the price again'. Yes, so that was a big issue that brought about changes. But in the end it didn't take much arguing the point once Pat and a few others got involved in Canberra, and they more or less said, 'Come on, this is what's got to happen here'.

So they decided that it had to go ahead. And oh God, when it happened! When they got that sewage pond and the filtered water then they did have a big do: the Shire did this and the Shire did that!

The big issues of housing and infrastructure were major preoccupations for Isabel, but the issues closest to her heart were still the questions about how to make the relationships between land, people and culture stronger. The cemetery remained at the forefront of her attention. In 1988 she had organised for a group of researchers to come up and follow up the earlier National Parks and Wildlife Service work with a proper survey of the graveyard and an attempt to identify and document the burials.[4] Working from her small office in the Land Council building, she used the results from that survey to gain small packets of funding here and there for better protection, like new fencing. And she persisted with the land claim over the cemetery area, repeatedly writing to the Lands Department which seemed at that stage to have lost the claim in its endless corridors.

But another project had lain uneasily on her conscience for many years. She had always worried that they had let Mick down when he alone tried to stop the removal of the carved trees from Collymongle station in 1956. Most of the few remaining trees had been cut down too, but were taken to the enclosed garden of the Collymongle homestead. Isabel had become more and more angry over the years, but was in an awkward position because as a woman she felt unable to take the major responsibility for taking steps to retrieve objects believed to be restricted to men's view.

Demanding the repatriation of the Collymongle carved trees, shown here in the private garden of the Collymongle homestead, c. 1987. Isabel stands with her sister-in-law Isobelle, and Melva Nicholls from Walgett and Collarenebri. The three women, supported by Tony Flick and Karen Flick (who took the photo), had just confronted the manager of Collymongle, which had by then become a large cotton company.

Isabel: They put those 11 trees in the homestead garden as ornaments, and I guess the fact that Dad was so concerned about the cutting down of those trees in the first place, stuck in my mind. I kept talking to Parks and Wildlife officers and saying: 'These carved trees in the garden out there don't belong there really. And I feel insulted that they're just being used for their little ornaments with water spraying over them and they're all covered in green slime'. And I could see them deteriorating and so I began trying to get some kind of action there.

Different Boards of Directors of Collymongle would say: 'Look, when we bought this property we bought everything on it'. And I kept maintaining that they were our property. And it really wasn't nice to get into that, because here I was, on my own, and I was a woman, I didn't have that right really—according to our law—but I knew that someone had to do it.

They finally said, 'Get them out of the garden, take them where you want to take them'. Then I didn't know where to take them! We didn't have a keeping place in town, and so when we finally got them out of there, we just had a little gazebo built and placed a little bit away from the property house itself. That is just until we can get some place of our own where we can take them and preserve them for the future generation. So we still need to do a lot of work there, just on that.

At least we got the freedom now to be able to just take them wherever we want to take them. And it seemed silly at the time, that we couldn't do that. Because I maintain too that they were always ours. There were 98 trees, I think, on that Bora Ground, carved trees. And now there's one still standing. There is a video of them actually being cut down and taken away. The bulk of them are in Adelaide, in a museum in Adelaide which seems so stupid. Then there's some in Brisbane. So they're scattered all over the country. And then recently, two of the ones that we had in the gazebo were stolen. And I suppose that's likely to happen again, who can tell?

They were stolen very carefully. Oh, it was a well planned operation, because they cut the wire mesh around the gate and levered them out through there and just stood it all up again. It was done on the weekend. So they're in someone's private collection I guess. And there's all kinds of little backyard museums happening everywhere, so I suppose if we could we'd find those two carved trees in one of those.

That was another assault on us, you can say it's another form of abuse. Because it's just abusing the things that mean so much to people. And, even though the people don't talk about it a lot, it does mean a lot to people. I think people don't talk about it because they lack the confidence to come out openly and say that.

Finding a way to bring the rest of the trees home required a proper place to house them and a team of custodians who must be male. There were very few older men in Collarenebri: the reality of Aboriginal mortality statistics is the tragic early deaths of men, many in their fifties. By the early 1990s, Isabel's generation of strong older people in Collarenebri had few surviving men. She worried over how the process could be undertaken, but was confident it would progress in the hands of Roy and Ted Thorne and her brother Joe and his son, Joey. In the meantime, with the Land Council members, Isabel worked towards organising occasional small bush trips, just for the day, taking out older members of the community, as she talked around the idea of a cultural centre which might one day serve the many purposes which were still needed.

In 1993, Isabel's work was warmly honoured by two communities, her own at Collarenebri, and also at Brewarrina, who each presented her with their Community Awards. Isabel appreciated these awards deeply and was moved that the years she had spent trying to make changes had been valued by her own mob. Then later in the year Tranby Aboriginal Co-operative College awarded her its first honorary doctorate. She wrote later that while the OAM was a strategically important acknowledgment from government of her role, the Tranby award meant far more to her—she had watched the College mature over the years under Kevin Cook's management to its flourishing as a rich source of inspiration and support for so many activists like herself. The award was so valuable to her that she felt it would also be worthy recognition for the lifelong work of her brother Joe and one of the first things she did was to write to Tranby to nominate him for the award, which was bestowed in the following year. For herself, she was proud to have been honoured by the organisation she admired so much. Not bad, she thought, for an Old Aboriginal Moll!

10
Sisters, 1993 on

Early in 1993, Isabel's sister Rose finally came home to Collarenebri, bringing another change into Isabel's life. Rose moved into the bus on the Block, just as Brenda and her family shifted nearby into a caravan for a while. Rose and Isabel had always shared their father's trait of being tightlipped about their private lives. Ironically, in this small community where everyone knew most things about almost everyone else, neither of the sisters had ever talked easily about their personal relationships or their deepest feelings. Rose's time in Leeton had been difficult and in order to cope with that she had built up a steely defensive wall around herself while she was down there. It was only when she returned home that Isabel began to learn more about Rose's life there. By the same token, because Rose had had to cut herself off from her family, she knew very little about Isabel's life till she came back to Collaren-ebri. Rose has remembered the way they slipped easily into their childhood nicknames as they slowly got to know each other again—Charlie for Rose, Georgie for Isabel:

> *Rose:* I went down to Leeton and reared my family. And when my marriage broke up I came home. I'd come home before and I'd gone back again, 'cause I'd used kids as an excuse. But this time I had no kids, I only had a dog. When I first come home to stay, I said I wanted to be brought up to date. She and I used to go for drives up the road there, the Mungindi road or Moree road. I asked about her. And she asked about me. She said, 'Look, all you ever done, Charlie, was work! You done

nothing interesting!' I said, 'Never done nothing interesting!' I was always making sure that kids went through to year 12, I had to get kids to uni, do all those things, that was part of that way of thinking. Then work to pay off a place. I used to write stories, but I always used to plant my stories 'cause I wasn't allowed to write! I never learnt to be happy, till I got home. But that's life.

Then when I got home and learnt what she did, I thought 'No, no, no ...' I'd have pulled up a long time before she did! And when she heard about how I used to work, she said, 'No way in the world I'd work for a man like that . . .'! But I tried to explain to her, 'No, this was about owning something'. I thought the kids might have wanted the property when we finished up, but she worked just as hard, mentally. 'Cause I just worked with men, she worked with an army! An army!

One of the ways Isabel had survived in the often frustrating conditions at Collarenebri was by keeping her sense of the ridiculous alive. She had a quirky, ribald sense of humour and an unquenchable desire to make fun of the circumstances they all faced as Rose recalled:

Rose: Everyone knew Isabel as a political, powerful woman, but we'd been separated for over 30 years. And when I came home, I got to see this powerful woman, building houses, making things work for her people. But there is another little side of her I liked. We often did things that no one could believe that this powerful woman would be doing.

It started off one night. At two o'clock one morning she beeped the horn at my place in a bus down on her Block. I thought something was wrong, I run out, 'What now? What now?' 'Oh I got a meeting in Bourke tomorrow and I'm worried about these fellas'. This business she was going down to was that Orana Haven was folding in Brewarrina at the time and she had to go down there to try to sort that out. I said, 'Well what's that got to do with me?' 'Come on', she said, 'down there tomorrow I've got to part the waters! But I'll show you what I can do tonight'.

So, I went back in and got my shoes on, and we went downtown. She parked up near the Land Council and she was looking down the street there. And she said, 'I bet I can do something you never thought I could do! I can drive on the footpath of Collarenebri and no one can see me!'

And I said, 'No!!!' 'Way she went on the footpath! She turned around there near the pub and came up again near the bank.

And she says then, 'I'll bet you I can do something you never thought I could do!' 'Ah well, what is it going to cost me?' 'Three fried scones and a dry curry!' This is going on to half-past two, quarter to three by the time she's taken off. So I said, 'What is it you're gonna do?' 'I'm gonna turn my car on a sixpence in the middle of the bridge!' And I said, 'Isabel! Police straight over there!' 'Oh, they're too sleepy to get out of their own way, them fellas!' So then we took off, straight down the street. And she was just like a professional, eh! Braked it and spun the car right around, and I couldn't say nothing! When she faced the car back up towards the Land Council office and she said, 'There! If that's not worth three fried scones and a dry curry I know nothing!'

And I said, 'Don't let people know you done this'. She said, 'Oh no, there's only you but I know you weak; you likely to pot me!' And I said, 'Oh no, you're a powerful woman!' And when we got back to her place she said, 'Now, get into it girl!' So I had to make her these three fried scones and a dry curry!

Rose's presence brought Isabel company, a sounding board and someone to let off steam with. But Rose also brought some much needed administrative back-up to ease the bookwork Isabel still laboriously completed each day. A glimpse of how heavily this weighed on Isabel is in this story Rose tells:

Rose: One day I was sitting down there where I'd come to live, with Ray Hall . . . She come down in the car, four o'clock in the afternoon. She said, 'Mate, get up here, I'm in a mess!' And the look on her face, she was in a mess too! So I grabbed the thongs and went! 'Look', she said, 'I got three weeks missing from the accounts I got to send to the State Land Council. And I said, 'Oh you couldn't have that, you do them every day! And all I do on the following week is check them up'. She said, 'Well, I'm three weeks out!'

So I goes through them. I never went home till one or two o'clock. Isabel come in at one o'clock and said, 'Did you find 'em?' 'Yes', I said. 'You come in the morning, ring up the State Office, and you'll find that those three weeks are sitting in Coonamble, in the regional office. They've already gone!' She said, 'No! They couldn't be, Charlie! I told you I was losing my mind!' Next morning she rings me up, 'What you got to eat down there?' I said 'Nothing, you bring me a loaf of bread and I'll make you a sandwich'. She said, 'No, I want a curry! You make the onion and potato and tomato and I'll bring the cabanna down'. When she brought it down I said, 'Did you ring up?'

She said, 'Yes, those three sitting in Coonamble!' She'd already sent them down, and I only had to put the fourth week for the month in. And look, she was raging, she blamed herself for it, saying, 'I'm too old for this'.

She used to do all those figures herself, and tax! Then when I come there in 1993, I used to do all her monthly reports and that took a bit off her. But she'd do the tax and the super all herself! And all with her limited education, eh? And she did all the bank reconciliations and all the cheque recs. She did all that herself.

Having kept away from organisations in Leeton, Rose was a keen observer of the way the office worked:

Rose: And then on top of that she would handle all the problems of the community. Some would come in: 'Oh somebody went to gaol, he was down there for three days, he's in for 18 months, can I ring . . .' Then there'd be a bit of mix up in gaols, she'd be ringing around trying to find out what gaol these people was in. And then someone'd come in with insurance claims, wouldn't know where to go, and she'd say, 'Look, ring this lawyer, tell him all your problems, make an appointment to see him'. So she set these Murris up with appointments for lawyers. Shearers'd come in, 'What do I do about my group certificates, I lost all my group certificates . . .' 'Oh, this is how you do it, you write to this department . . .' And she'd do that beside the land council!

And bringing people's bodies home! They'd come in there, 'Oh he died in Tamworth or he died in Mildura', or wherever he died, you know, somewhere out of town, and they didn't know how to bring the body home! And she'd say: 'Oh I'll ring so-and-so, they'll know about it, and I'll ring the Land Council down there where you are, and we'll set up a way to bring him home!' And they did that. So you think about that! That wasn't Land Council business, that was *community* business!

Then every meeting up at the hospital now! She'd go up. She didn't have to go up, but she'd go! And meeting with the Shire in Walgett. She didn't have to, but she'd go, because she always said: 'Whatever Collarenebri gets I want to know what they're giving us! They're not gonna push it on us no more!'

The formal parts of community work weren't the only thing that Isabel was involved in:

Rose: Then the football went kaput! They couldn't even get them to train or nothing! So she got onto it, she knew the police and she got onto one of the constables who was willing to start it again. Then she made up raffle books and she said, 'Go on, you go out and sell these'. And they did, and they started to get money in again. She said, 'We having a football knockout this year!' and I thought, 'Oh no, here we go again!'

'Get them Murris together', she told us, 'call a meeting'. She got Brenda's daughter, Bernadette, to print up this notice. They all come to this meeting! So she was elected, her and Pat Mundy, and somebody else. She said, 'You, Charlie, you make sure you count the money when its finished. And get over there, you and your old man, youse do nothing! Get over there and handle the barbeque!' 'Cause Ray had never done nothing like that in his life! And so we into it! Me and him! Gravy and steak! And then she said to somebody else: 'You handle the soft drinks, only the soft drinks!' And 'you', to another one, 'you handle the little bits and pieces'. She had it all set up. 'And you handle the gate, I want the money off the gate, I don't want anybody bullshitting to me', she said. Now she got a bit of money from some funding body or other. And she started it again!

I remember when the knockout was over, she came in and said, 'Here you are, Money Counters! Count this!' and these four people who was involved with the day, we counted the money and we had $7000. And she said, 'Well that's what we made for today. That's not our original outlay. Outlay's in there'. She opened this other bag. And they couldn't believe it that they'd made $7000 for the day! We all sitting round the table, money all rolled up! She had it in a bank bag, with a little rubber band around it. 'That goes to the bank. This goes back to the funding body.' And she said, 'There, youse can do it!' And all these young men saying, 'You neat all right Aunty Is!' And I started to sing . . . 'You're simply the best . . .' and she got up on the chair and was dancin', swingin' her hips! So we called her Tina Turner after that, 'cause she pulled it off! She was 'simply the best'!

Yeah, we had fun! It was a happy time! We had fun. She started that back up from nothing!

And then there was the night the littlies done their Deb. She got the money for the debutantes. And she went up and seen all these little Murri boys in their suits and all the little girls in their prissies . . . And these little kids for 15 minutes. They was little angels. Dancing and walking and posing for photographs.

But the persistent reality of Collarenebri was continuing poverty and a frustrating despair, with all their symptoms of alchohol abuse, violence, community tensions and apathy. Isabel's resilience was all the more extraordinary because she kept bouncing back in the face of inertia, community frustration and disarray—not to mention her own bouts of depression. She had a tough sense of strategy which she applied to all her planning, and she tried to impart some of this to Rose, who had channelled her energies over the years into informally supporting children at risk in one-on-one relationships:

Isabel (left) and Rose (right).

Rose: See, I'm a kid person, and she asked me, 'Do you want to learn about politics with kids?' I said, 'No, no. Politics don't mix with kids, kids is different!' She said, 'You'll find out! You're too headstrong. You think it's all rosie! I want you to learn about politics!'

So she used to take me out on the Mungindi road, and we'd be sitting eating lunch, 'cause she couldn't have peace in town. If she was up at the house, somebody'd be there singing out, 'Aunty Is!' or if she was in the Land Council, somebody'd come and want to ask her something. So she'd say, 'Come on, we'll go up on the Moree road, Sis, park on the river'.

And one day we was sitting there talking about all these little kids, there was about four going through bad times at that time. 'Gee, what we gonna do about them Charlie?' We didn't know what we was gonna do. So she said, 'You got friends in DOCS?[1] Let's try to help these kids'. So we had a few yarns with these people in DOCS. One time they took a child from there, and both of us was involved in it. They took that child illegally! They come along, took the baby off the father. 'Cause the mother had already taken the baby, she was only about 14 or 15. So we were sitting there [in court] and DOCS had all these questions. And then we put *our* argument, that we believed that the child should be with the mother, but the mother was a child herself; whereas the baby, if he lived with his father, the grandmother would be there. So we got away with that one, changed DOCS' mind then.

But our plans on one of these lunch breaks was, one day—probably would have been this year—to try to make some changes through ATSIC.[2] I remember us talking up the road, there in the lunch break, that we was going to go up there and challenge the State Land Council and ATSIC to take kids, every school holidays, get them away from the drugs and the drunks and the abuse, learn them how to shut a gate, open a gate, ride a bike, check the sheep, work with computers ('cause at that time, computers was gonna be the magic thing). And we were looking forward to that strategy, and we was also looking forward to placing kids in year 12 for holidays, in the Legal Services. Not for work experience, but for holidays. She said, 'Kids don't need to be sitting in front of TV all the time', so we was gonna take a year 12 student, take 'em down to the Legal Service, have them hang around there for a week or two. Send them to the Medical Service, have them hang around there for a week or two. Then if Social Security would have them, even [for] $25 a week, or ATSIC or somebody like that . . . trying to make doors open . . .

You know where we drew it all up? On the lunch wrapper of a ham and cheese sandwich. She took the ham and I took the cheese. And she said, 'I don't know why I didn't bring paper'. You know how she'd fuss, but we found this pen . . . and she's writing this up then, see. And I said, 'Do it like a family tree, start from year 12', because this is for 16 and 17 year olds. And we were doing ALSs and AMSs and up like that and when we got to the top, that's when we got to the 13 and 14s. And then she said, 'We can put 12 year olds in too!' It was like a big family tree: these the ones that can go onto properties. And now ATSIC, the ones that I've spoken to, they say, 'Well we have to look at the insurance clauses!' But we're not finished there . . . That was our last plan. We knew that we couldn't beat DOCS with the babies, because there's too much there. Well, we thought we might beat 'em in about five years.

But about the older kids, she said the way to do it was to get an audience; so now I've got to go back and get an audience. I'll do it the way she said!

Each of the Flick sisters knew about difficult marital relationships, with Lubby's tragic death the worst case. The repetitive cycles of beatings and intimidation seemed inescapable at times and all of these women found it was hard to vent the frustration they felt, whether they had escaped violent re-lationships or whether they were still locked into them.

For Rose, her married life had involved violence as well as repressive isolation. For Clara, the violence had been entangled with alcoholism in a series of relationships. When Rose came back home to Collarenebri, she found herself drawn in to Isabel's strategies to protect Clara if possible, or at least to intervene in emergencies:

> *Rose:* Now one time, Isabel comes down about three o'clock in the morning, beeping the horn, 'Come on, come on!' she was saying. 'What's wrong now?' 'Come on, we got to go over to Clare's', she said, 'her and her bloke fighting'. 'Oh gee' I said, 'I wish she'd leave that man!' 'Me too', she said, 'but we can't help it'. So we gets over there and they're sitting there. Isabel says, 'Get in here, go on, get in here'. Clare says, 'Oh I'll go anywhere with you, Sis'. She was half cut anyway, and she's sitting in the back. Isabel turned the corner and she was heading for Moree. Now we're going along, and then she stopped the car in the middle of the road, must have been out about 20 miles. She stopped the car, and here's this massive big kangaroo standing in front of her headlights, eh? And she said to me: 'Get out there. Now, that's Clara's man out there. Get out there and kick shit out of him!' And I said, 'You mean it?' She said, 'Yeah, and I'll help you!' Now Clare's sitting in the back, and I can hear the seatbelts click; she must have moved forward to watch what we was gonna do.
>
> So I go out and I called this kangaroo everything! And I'm pretending to kick my legs in the air, and Isabel's getting out on the other side. And this went on for about five or 10 minutes. We called this kangaroo *everything*! And the kangaroo's just standing there looking at us! And she's poking her head out over the door and she's swearing at him: 'I'll kick your guts out! If I can get you on the ground I'll jump all over you!'
>
> Then all of a sudden, lights went on over on the side of the road. There was a caravan parked in the dark near a tree! Isabel saw it and she called out, 'Oh, quick Charlie! Run!' Well, I had to run about 15 metres, because this kangaroo was up the road, and I run back all right. I can remember Isabel's old legs getting caught in the door when she tried to get her legs back in quick! And the drunken one in the back was laughin'! Just pissing herself! Isabel put her car into gear and took off down the road! And you can imagine when I got back in. My heart was pounding so much, 'cause I was exhausted from kickin' this kangaroo to death, eh? And then to have enough breath to run!
>
> Well, we laughed from there right up to Belalah Hall. Isabel said, 'Oh dear that was fun!' And Clare said, 'Yeah, I'm sober in the back here now!'

There were a lot of phantoms on the Moree road that night getting their just deserts in this pantomime which was the closest to revenge most of the women were ever likely to get.

Having Rose around had lightened Isabel's load, but by the end of 1994 she was tiring. She gave a speech that year to Tranby students on a quick trip to Sydney. Her edginess showed in the words she used to begin her talk: 'We move from one anxious state to another. I would say this state of mind is our inheritance'.

Over the years, Isabel had developed ways to cope with the pressures of small town politics. Rose was seeing some of them, but Isabel had others. She drew strength from the places like the cemetery, which, she explained, had brought her close not only to the people who had died, but to the memories of how they had coped with life:

Isabel: We never feel that the people we've lost are too far away from us. When I was working in the organisations, I used to feel sometimes that the people didn't understand what I was doing, especially when I was involved with Land Councils and the Land Rights Act. One lot tends to think that you're Black Power, that you're really involved in that. Another lot just can't see any sense in having those kind of things. So you become an isolated person. And you have to condition yourself to continue to work along to try and achieve what you wanna do.

And I felt a lot of times that when I came up here to the cemetery I was able to relax. I could think about some situations that we faced with Dad. And different other people that might not be of my family, but who had a lot of really coping qualities. You look back and you can think, 'Oh dear, I don't know how so-and-so coped with that kind of situation when that happened in their family'. And I used to go away from here feeling so inspired by coming up here and spending time. I'd go back and think, 'Well I can handle that'. Whereas when I came up at first, I'd think, 'Well I can't handle anymore'.

And I'd gone through a period when the people see you as an official. Like when I was involved in Mangankali, the housing company. You had to make decisions according to constitutions and whatever. And when your people don't understand anything about policies or constitutions, you become just an official. And then you know that you're dealing with tough blokes and tough systems. And I used to feel very isolated.

But there was always people I could turn to. I suppose over the years I've become a very rich woman, because I could ring someone up in Sydney and say, 'Oh look, I need to go down to Sydney, I haven't got any money. I think I have to get away from this'. And they'd say, 'Oh, no worries', you know. And you get away and relax a bit and come back. Or it might be someone down at Bourke I'd ring up, somewhere, living on a reserve; you still had that kind of support of special people, you know. Just a few days away to relax a bit, I reckon. I always said to my friends, 'I'm a very rich woman in one way, because I've got a terrible lotta friends in all kind of circles, you know?'

Isabel had continued to try to recruit younger people for the administrative roles in the Council, but there were few in the town who already had the skills or who wanted to stay long enough build them up. She was often left with little clerical assistance. Bernadette, Isabel's granddaughter, was employed as secretary at one point, and received some computer training. As Isabel feared, this led to mutterings about nepotism and her computer training was refused by the Local Land Council chairperson. Isabel repeatedly offered to stand Bernadette down if the Council directed her to do so, but she was frustrated by the Council members' reluctance to take on an active role in the management of the Local. Her attempts to pass her own hard-won knowledge about bookkeeping across to the Council members had not borne fruit:

> *Isabel:* Mangankali and the Land Council were both about the same to work in. You never got a lot of people that learnt a lot—that was my disappointment, because I really tried. Before every meeting at the Land Council I would say: 'Look, I'd like to just put out all the books for you to have a look at, they're your books. In the end, you're responsible. And I want you to have a look at your books to see what kind of cheques have been paid out, what kind of income we've had so you all know what your Council is doing'. And you know, people used to say: 'No, we know it's right'. And then I'd say: 'But that's not the issue. You might trust me so much, but you should look at them and learn for yourselves'. But not a lot of people wanted to do that . . .

But the problems ran more deeply than a lack of confidence on the part of the Council members. There continued to be severe problems with misappropriation of funds in the Wollai rents, an issue raised by the auditor in 1993 when he noted that a sum of over $34 000 for that year alone was in question. Land Council members still would not move against their openly dishonest relations. Tensions were rising between Isabel and several office bearers of the Council who wanted to direct funds to non-Land Council matters. Isabel was unhappy in the unpredictable situation. 'One minute you're working with butterflies and the next minute they're hornets . . .'

She decided to take six weeks' long service leave early in 1995 and went on a trip along the river, staying with old friends until she could come back refreshed. On her return in June, there was good news. A submission she had put in for funds to return the carved trees to Collarenebri from Adelaide and Brisbane had been granted and a cheque for $25 000 was waiting to be used. But the tension within the Local Land Council had become even more pronounced. Isabel was confronted with a demand to approve an expenditure of $500 from Land Council funds which already had been used to pay for a bus and other expenses for the football club. She refused to do so. In retaliation, the Chairman and Treasurer of the Council refused to sign her pay forms, leaving her without an income. Then they refused her the use of the Land Council car when she needed to travel to Moree for medical tests. Isabel appealed to the State Land Council, but they offered little immediate assistance other than to suggest that an independent audit needed to be carried out, in addition to the annual one which all Locals were required to undertake.

Isabel wrote an impassioned letter to all the Local Land Council members, expressing her distress as well as her firm resolve not to concede to the demands to endorse the misappropriations.[3] She told them in her letter that she had no alternative but resignation. It began: 'The past seven months have been most stressful for me, I have never suffered such rudeness and disrespect in my 40 years of involvement in "Aboriginal affairs". As I worked for the better of our people I have travelled Australia-wide and have felt nothing but respect. These past seven months have pushed me to the point of resignation . . .'

Isabel detailed her concerns about misappropriation and thefts of various types, intimidation and abuse of staff, cancellation of meetings and the serious irregularities now existing in the housing priority list. She finished: 'Nothing will change until members play the major role in decision making. This can only happen if meetings are held on a regular basis. Until proposed policies are introduced and the "rule by fear system" is stamped out and members have more support from the State Land Council, I am afraid that all our previous efforts are in vain.'

The Local Land Council members were shocked at the conflict but, intimidated by the tactics being employed from the Wollai and by the office bearers of the Land Council, were unable to respond effectively. In the confusion, one of the office bearers took the $25 000 cheque for the Collymongle trees and cashed it at the local RSL club![4] The club soon realised it wasn't legally allowed to cash a cheque of that size, and had to apply to the police to ensure that the money was forcibly repaid. But that was little satisfaction to a miserable community.

But Isabel was now facing another crisis. Her medical results had shown alarming signs and it appeared she would be facing major surgery. She altered her resignation letter to the Local and State Land Councils to make it an application for medical leave and began the sombre task of packing for a hospital stay in Sydney.

It was becoming chillingly clear to Isabel that she was now leaving not just a job but Collarenebri itself. And that she was going to have to do so alone. After all these years of their close relationship, Ted Thorne had found the abuse and threats towards Isabel to be more than he could stand. He lashed out verbally at the office bearer who had been the most aggressive in attacking Isabel and promptly found himself hauled before the police to answer an apprehended violence restraining order. Angry and frustrated, Ted felt he had to leave town and perhaps even the relationship, because he couldn't trust himself any longer not to retaliate further against her attackers.

Isabel reached Sydney but the first thing she did was to write this letter to Ted:

> Sydney, Sunday
> My Dear Edward,
> I'm still hoping that you will think about what I said to you. If you hurt those blokes we will all suffer the rest of our lives. I beg you to think about our lives, you and me!
> You are the main part of my life, and I know I mean a lot to you. Only you can give up the Anger and the Grog.
> I'm sorry I messed up both of our lives. I'll always blame myself.
> I'm going to the doctors tomorrow.
> I will keep in touch. So all I can say is help me save the rest of our time. Forget about the 'boys'. Think about the wonderful love we have together. Which is most important?
> My love always,
> Bell.

The news in Sydney was bad: Isabel had bowel cancer. But although she would need surgery, the doctors told her it was likely to be successful and that she would make a full recovery. As she prepared herself, Isabel remembered how frightened she had been when she had her hysterectomy in 1975. This time it was hard, but at least Isabel had beaten the smokes at last.

She was being warmly looked after by Kevin Cook and Judy Chester, who gave up her bed for Isabel and nursed her day and night. And Ted had answered her letter by heading for Sydney straight away and he was soon beside her. Her family were all either in Sydney or in close touch. Among the cards and notes she kept from this time, Isabel treasured a letter from Larry's daughter, young Lubby:

December 1995

To my dearest Grandmother,

Life seems to be getting harder and harder every day for everyone. But as you always said 'everything has to get worse before it can get better'. All I can say is that I'm hoping and praying that you get better, not only for your sake but for ours too. You are the core of this family, even though you sometimes disbelieve it. Nan I love you, you are a fighter and you always come out winning. See you when you get home. Love you Nan, always will,

Lubby

11
A Wider Focus, 1995–2000

Isabel began to regain her strength soon after her operation in December 1995, although it took her longer to recover from the distress of the Land Council conflict. Eventually it became clear that however painful it had been, the conflict had actually released her from the frustrations of local politics. Isabel could now look more widely across the broader expanses of her country and of her life. Even straight after the operation, she knew she needed to remake her life again, and she began by looking for constructive things to do.

Tranby offered what she needed for a while. She could mentor students and contribute where she could as a community board member. Her old friend Kevin Cook was unwell himself now, his working days shortened with severe emphysema, and he was often at home with Judy. He encouraged Isabel to use his office in the quiet old Tranby building at Glebe to organise her letters and keep in touch with her interests. Isabel had conducted her own vast correspondence over the years with her many handwritten letters and cards. But here at last, with Tranby staff like Chris Kerr, Isabel found the resources she needed to research and to keep track of her correspondence so that she could contribute to campaigns no matter where she was. She started out straight away by writing to the Royal Prince Alfred Hospital in February 1996, thanking the staff for their care during her surgery and taking the opportunity to remind the Director and the Chairman of the Board about the need for more hospital accommodation for the visiting families of rural patients.

Isabel Flick

Collarenebri was never too far away from her thoughts. Rose had been going through eerily parallel health worries, also safely resolved. Characteristically, they began planning how they could turn what they were learning to some advantage for Collarenebri girls and their families:

> *Rose:* When we were both diagnosed with cancer, Isabel rang me up and said, 'You know what I got? I got that big *yanggal*.[1] Cancer!' She had bowel cancer and I had ovarian cancer. That was a bad time for both of us; but afterwards, Isabel started thinking about it: 'We got to get these girls in there, get them checked'. We wanted to get them into the breast screening, and have them tested for ovarian cancer, 'cause they was all having sex early and some of them were being raped. And all this was worrying us! But the breast screening, they only take them when they're over 40. Our argument then was, nine out of 10 grandmothers or aunties are looking after those kids' kids. And those mothers and grandmothers have got to keep fit. They can't come down with breast cancer, or ovarian cancer. But it's up to them girls to go back up to their mothers and grandmothers and say, 'Hey, you got to go up and have a breast screen. I've been in there!' . . . And they'll be more influence, then, to make their parents and grandparents go up there and have a screening.
>
> And I just got a letter back this year, to say when the van comes back next year, they will let in young girls to look at radiology, to look at how that screening's done, and educate them. And I gave that letter to the teacher last week. Now we planned that. We're talking about in 1996 and it's only just starting to happen now in 2002. The other two she and I planned, I'm having trouble with. Getting the kids off the streets. I don't know why that should be so hard. But the breast screening, that's one come out of it, see!

Isabel didn't want to live in Collarenebri, but she didn't want to be too far away. Looking around, she thought Gunnedah was promising, nestled in among hills, very different from the level floodplain of the Barwon. Close enough to Collarenebri, it was a fair-sized town offering more resources and relief from the pressure cooker of small town politics.

Isabel needed a town where she was known well enough to feel comfortable, but not so well known that she would be called on to take a major role in organisations. Her children would not be too far away. Tony was working in a cotton gin at nearby Caroll. Although many Murris had gained little but heartache from the cotton industry, Tony was one whose knowledge of machines and talent for level-headed management thrived in the heavy industrial conditions of the cotton gins. Isabel went to stay with Tony in his flat at Gunnedah for a week and liked the feel of the town. Tony's real estate agent had played football with Ben and so, as Tony remembered, the agent had 'forgotten all that racial discrimination stuff' and found him a good-sized semi-detached flat when he first moved to town. The agent was pleased to meet Isabel, too, and when the front flat on Tony's block became vacant, he offered it first to her.

Isabel was eager to get started, but wherever she was, she knew she wanted to be living with Ted. She wrote:

> 26th February 1996
> My dear Edward,
> Just a few lines to let you know that by the time you receive this letter I will have a flat in Gunnedah. The people are going to help me with furniture and all.
> So come on up if you want to have a go at living in Gunnedah with me.
> I miss you very much. Love you very much,
> Bell

Soon they were back together again, settling in to the comfortable ground-level flat on a gentle hillside in Gunnedah. Since the start of her job at the Land Council, Isabel had kept an appointments diary, which she used to record meetings and sometimes to rough out plans for her various activities.

Isabel and Ted outside their flat in Gunnedah.

She continued the diary at Gunnedah and it shows how her life had changed. From the Collarenebri pages crowded with terse notes of meetings, deputations and disputes, the days at Gunnedah stretched out quietly and serenely, the pages only sparsely marked. There might be notes about a diet she was trying or records of her exercise, with some motivational notes to herself here and there. Isabel wanted to try to tackle her health problems now that there was some support. Rose remembers her buying bike shorts and joining the swimming club, good resolutions but harder to keep! There are occasional meetings in Gunnedah in the early part of the year, and Isabel and Ted travelled by train to Sydney for a meeting about rural people's tenancy conditions.

But sometimes the emptiness of these pages suggests that things might have been too quiet, as if there was a sense of loneliness around the edges. With her health returning, it is not hard to imagine that Isabel was becoming eager for some community work she could get her teeth into. So she volunteered to help organise a festival in Gunnedah and this began to fill the days. On 24 September 1996, Isabel's diary notes sketch out the quickening tempo of her life: 'I had a wonderful conversation with Marion Punch who said the Arts Council is holding a meeting tomorrow at four-thirty and that I should contact Michelle Thomas from the Dorothea MacKellar Foundation. I did and had a long talk re the festival for Gunnedah. She mentioned a few people and I'm hoping to meet them tomorrow. I invited June Cox in for afternoon tea. Lent her my copy of Heather's book. She asked me if I'd like to stand for Chairperson of the "Red Chief" Land Council . . .' But then at the end of the entry: 'I was glad I got busy today because we got word this morning that we'd lost Roy'.

Isabel and Ted went back to Colle for Roy Thorne's funeral, Ted grieving for his brother and Isabel for a good friend. Isabel said in her eulogy:

> *Isabel:* The highs and lows of Roy Thorne were many and varied, spreading across the times of Aboriginal Protection to the present system, ATSIC. We went to school together, which was correspondence classes at the 'Manse' in Collarenebri. Roy always had a desire to see changes for our people, especially young people, as I did. So we spent most of our lives advocating changes, together. Sometimes I think I spent more time with Roy than Josie, his wife, because we hitchhiked everywhere attending meetings. I'm honoured to have shared some of Roy's dreams.

This was a difficult time for both Isabel and Ted, because they each lost people they were close to in quick succession. There was Rene Mills, a good friend and sister-in-law to Isabel because she was the sister of Aub Weatherall, Doreen Hynch and Rosie Flick. And then there was Ted's sister Jessie Hall, who had been one of Isabel's greatest mates. Isabel remembered travelling to see each of them. They were all now living outside Collarenebri, but their friendships had endured:

> *Isabel:* We lost a couple of my real dear friends, first there was Aub's sister Rene, and then there was Ted's sister, Jessie. They sent for me to go there for Aub's sister. She was in Tamworth. I did want to go and I didn't want to go, and in the end I just packed my swag and away I went. And as soon as I walked in she said: 'Oh, my sister's come to see me'. And she was just *done*, she had lung cancer. And she said: 'Oh I was silly I wouldn't take notice of you'. Because I used to be riding her about smoking and I said: 'Oh, we did it different. I used to smoke too, you know'. And she said: 'Yes, but you tried to get me off them. And I couldn't take any notice. But I just want to tell you I love you. You were always like a sister to me'. Oh God! I don't know what I said. When you're feeling so much emotionally . . . there's nothing else you can say except to just hold their hand and things like that. And everybody trying to be cheerful and everything around her, you know. And old Aub was there and Doreen and you know, it was a real sad time.
>
> And then we just get over that . . . and then this other one sends for me. The same thing. I went back a couple of times to visit her. She'd say: 'Oh, my old mate's coming to see me. But, she's not a mate, she's my sister. She was my sister long before she got to Ted, you know'. I can still hear her saying: 'Oh, we was always sisters, we did everything when we was kids'. We *did* do everything together too, even smoked bloomin' roots in the gully—our first cigarette.
>
> It was hard to go through all that again. I realised I had to get going quick. It was a time when I knew I couldn't sit down and grieve. And I'd think . . . I've got to get up and stop feeling bad about that, because I'm wasting time. And oh, I just didn't want to be in the one place. And I don't think I've stopped since then.

During that sadness, the relationships which were building in Gunnedah gave Isabel some comfort. When she finally did get to her first meeting about the festival, she wrote: 'Attended the Gunnedah Festival Committee and joined that committee of 10. I was made to feel very welcome.'

Isabel's trips back to Colle, although they were times of grief, also allowed her to spend time with her family and her old friends there, like Doreen Hynch and Josie Thorne. Funerals, with their familiar rituals and time for reflection, gave Isabel a chance to renew her deepest and easiest relationships with the place and the people. It was a relief to return to her home without the baggage of a role in any organisation.

The enduring value of her Land Council work was becoming clear. The land claim over the cemetery finally came through in June 1996, so at long last this important place was officially back in the hands of its owners. By this time, the independent auditor's report into the Local Land Council had vindicated Isabel completely, endorsing her concerns and supporting her recommendations. The Local itself had been brought under the control of an administrator, an outside accountant whose sole job was to get the organisation back into an orderly financial state. The auditor's report was satisfying for Isabel, but in fact she had moved on. She had a new sense of urgency, but also a wider vision of the things she wanted to accomplish.

A compelling desire was to draw together the threads of her mother's family. In many ways much of the work Isabel had done in Collarenebri was because she had accepted her father's sense of responsibility for his country, his history. On Mick's death, Isabel and her brother Joe, perhaps more than any of the other family members at that time, had taken on Mick's role as advocate for the people and the places of Collarenebri. But over the years Isabel had come to recognise the interference in family life which the old 'Protection' system had caused.

As she nursed her mother before her death, Isabel had become more aware of how deeply Celia had been disturbed by the severance from her family and how effectively it had cut Isabel and her brothers and sisters off from their

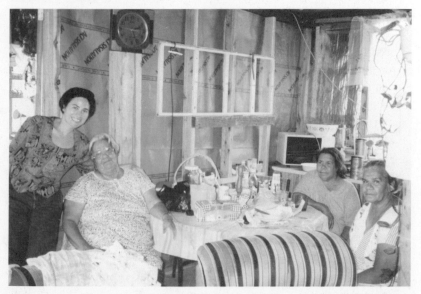

Isabel, Clare and Rose around the time they were planning their trip to Queensland. They are having lunch with Rose's daughter, Marjorie (on left), where Rose was staying while her house in Collarenebri was being built.

relations on the Queensland side of the border. Since Rose's return after the long years away at Leeton, the reunited sisters all felt the need to reconnect with the family they had lost. Isabel's diary in 1996 mentions the letters she was writing and then the phone calls to cousins and aunties in Cherbourg and Townsville, kin she had been dimly aware of but had never really followed up. She began to learn about the struggles they had had under the notorious Queensland Act from which her parents had escaped. Isabel began planning a trip for herself, Rose and Clara, by bus to Cherbourg to meet their Aunty Marge, their mother's remaining sister, for the first time since Isabel's childhood.

> *Rose:* Well, Isabel wanted to go and see Aunty Margie. She said 'Okay, we off!' It was five o'clock in the morning we had to leave. She was all spiffy and bubbly. So we'd made the plan that I would handle the meals, Clara would handle the luggage and Isabel would handle the bookings. See . . . co-operation! So I packed all the meals, eh? Clara draggin' all these cases over. Nine out of 10 times somebody else'd help her 'cause they'd see this old woman draggin' the cases over. We gets to this place then and it's lunchtime. Made Isabel have her little salad sandwich, great. Get to another place for tea time.
>
> I spread the meals out again. Old Sister was missin'. So we go in there to the shop and she's sittin' in there, big plate of veges and chips and chops. She said, 'There's yours there, Charlie, you're a vegetarian!' Chips and gravy! 'See how you eatin' bad again', I said to her. But that's what she'd do to us.
>
> But when we got to old Aunty's, eh? Isabel had all the accommodation all organised. When we got to Brisbane, the bus come and picked us up, took us down to the hostel. Everything was just neat. Clara draggin' the luggage along, and I'm carrying the food bin along, 'cause Isabel wouldn't eat the good food I'd brought! She wanted to have her cabanossi and cabanna! Well then, when we seen Aunty then, we couldn't believe it, 'cause Aunty looked like Clara!'

The trip was important to Isabel, as well as being good fun to be on the road with her sisters, and she wanted to do it again. This time, a strong support for her was her youngest daughter. After her tearaway youth, Amy had developed a mature confidence as she reared up her own children, and she was eager now to find her own place in the wider family. So they began to organise again, as Rose remembers:

> *Rose:* Then Isabel rings up and says she wants to go back. I said, 'Well, make it a pension week!' So we off again! I drove my car this time, and

we had me and her, Amy come with us that time, and Clara. And we drove all the way. And Isabel laughed and giggled all the way up . . . The first time we went there, when we went away old Aunty stood there and laughed. She thought to herself that she'd never see us again.

And then this time, when we're driving away, Aunty stood at the gate and she just cried. She was hooked up to oxygen, but she cried. And then Clara started crying, then Isabel cried, and so I had to pull the car over on the side of the road and the three of us cryin' on the Murgon road then . . . Yeah! But it was great fun!

For Isabel there was a painful gap in her mother's story and this was the baby sister they had lost when Celia was visiting Isabel and Joe at Toomelah during the early 1940s. Isabel had never seen the baby's grave, and only knew that she had been buried in Goondawindi, the Queensland town just across the border, on the northern side of the Macintyre River to Boggabilla and Toomelah. Now, as she travelled around, she was often in Toomelah, so she started to make inquiries from the Goondawindi authorities to try to find that grave. She believed it was in the Anglican section, as that was the nominal religion her mother would have put down on the forms, but although the family searched, they couldn't find the grave.

Isabel's trips to Toomelah had borne fruit in another way. She had been talking with old friends there like Julie Whitton and Ada Jarrett about a way to record their early memories of the community. This was a time of cultural renaissance in Toomelah. Work was being done by community members like Autrey Dennison, Les and Ursula McGrady and others in tracing their histories and considering how they could restore confidence in speaking their language to the younger members of the community. They had been supported by friends like Dick Buchhorn and Peter Thompson to help with research and submissions for funding. The upshot was a series of community-controlled projects which linked memories, places and language into educational programs in the local schools.

This was work which Rose had plunged into when she came back from Leeton, and she was eager to work on Gamilaraay language with the Toomelah community too. Isabel, Rose and their friends developed the idea of a record of their generation of women's memories of life and language at Toomelah in the 1930s and 1940s. Their submission was welcomed by the National Parks and Wildlife Service, which was interested in the documenting of women's heritage at that time. So with Carol Kendall's support in NPWS, and with filmmaker Kate Richards, Isabel joined with the women with whom she shared her youth in Toomelah and made the film, *Inard Oongalli: Women's Journey*.

The filming was done in sessions over 1998, with final sections still being shot early in 1999. Isabel was tired by then, busy with many other projects, and it was a great effort for her to get to that last filming session. But she was determined to be there, so Carol and Kate picked her up with Rose from Collarenebri where Isabel was working with me on the documention of the Collarenebri cemetery. They spent two hectic days shooting interviews. Isabel's presence on film is vivid and evocative, showing her tiredness, but often catching her relaxing into warm anecdotes and laughter.

While they were there, Isabel and Rose decided to have one more determined look for Ceatrice's grave:

> *Rose:* So we went across to Goondawindi and looked through *all* the records. It was as if she had it pre-planned . . . 'We'll go here, then we'll go to the Shire . . .' And we went from the Shire down to another place . . . everything . . . but all the doors were sort of blocked, you know. She wouldn't have it. She said, 'I'll go and have a rest and I'll come back this afternoon and I'll up this bloke. There's something this *wanda's*[2] not telling me! 'Cause they only showed her one book, see, one register. So she come back in the afternoon, and she up him again, about two-thirty, and then they brought this other book out then, that was it! She was buried in the 'paupers' graves!
>
> And we went out to the cemetery, but there was nothing there in the paupers graves, nothing there where the Heathens and the Chinamens was, nothing there. Then we were just turning around and we looked and there was Granny Jane just behind us. We'd never found her grave before. And then Isabel said, 'Well, we'll stay here tonight and we'll come back in the morning'.
>
> And in the morning she went back, and she up'd them again. Next minute he went in and came back with another record. Then he went out over to the graves and he put a peg there. 'That's where she is there', he said. And that's through her persistence. A lot of people like me, I would have just drove off and left it, but not her.

For Isabel, this lonely grave on the border kept returning to her thoughts, reminding her of the damage done to their family by the removal policies of two governments and by the destructive border itself. She was hurt by the baby's location in the 'paupers and Chinamens' section. The many babies' graves in the Collarenebri Aboriginal cemetery were always dug close to those of grandparents or aunties, bringing some comfort to the grieving family who felt that the older relations would look after their recently dead children. Isabel felt deeply that Ceatrice should be resting close to her parents, where her grave could be cared for by her living relations at Collarenebri. As Isabel and her family talked it over, the idea slowly formed that they would try to have their sister's remains reburied at Collarenebri. Knowing this would be a long process, Isabel called on her old friend Peter Thompson, whose archaeological training would allow him to carry out an exhumation once the Council had approved the process. Isabel trusted him to look after Ceatrice's remains and bring them home for her family.

Isabel had been thinking about the cemetery since she left Collarenebri, working out how to consolidate the research she had commissioned previously, and to do it in such a way that it could be updated whenever new burials took place. She was interested in how computers could help the community do this, both by drawing maps which could be updated easily and by developing databases which could become a family history resource in the hands of the community. She called on the computing teachers at Tranby to give her some advice, and drew me in too because I was using digital media to portray Aboriginal history with her niece, Karen. Isabel wasn't interested in computers for their own sake; she wanted to use them to put resources into the hands of people in Collarenebri, so they wouldn't need any particular individuals, including herself, to be there in order to sustain their control over their own culture and history.

We travelled up to Colle for field trips in 1997 and 1998, talking to everyone in the community about how they would like a database to work. We spent days in the cemetery, walking slowly around with different groups of people, comparing memories about who was buried in each of the unmarked graves. Some of the graves had been identified with help from Harry Denyer, Henry's son—who was now the town's undertaker—during the painstaking reviews of death registers and undertakers' records done by the Ward, Egloff and Goddard group in 1988. But still many remained unidentified and there were clearly stories yet to be told about why each grave had been positioned in particular relationships to others. We talked with members of all of the family groups who remained living in the town. Where Isabel felt people wouldn't be comfortable talking with her around, she quietly drifted off somewhere else while I talked with them. Where a grave's identity was still not clear, we worked out who would have dug the grave, and visited or phoned them, talking over the location and the circumstances of the burial until we were confident we knew who was buried where.

As we went about identifying more and more of the burials, the patterns in the cemetery became clearer. As Isabel's brother Joe had pointed out, the main principle was that you would be 'buried with your mob'. So the relationship of graves told not simply about the immediate family relationships of parents and children and grandparents, which would be apparent to western families, but about second cousins, and even more widely extended family, and finally about the bonds of a traditional kinship which still ties people to each other in this community. The desire to bury babies close to protective grandparents or older family members is clear in the cemetery, showing in the small knots of tragedy and hope as tiny graves are clustered around an adult grave here and there.

There have been troublesome confusions about the identities of people buried in some graves, and these have tended to be those of people with few family in the town, perhaps a woman who married in from another community, but who left no children in the town to mark and remember her gravesite. Confident memories about grave identities depend on continuing strong and attentive families, who could look after the sites, but also keep their memory alive among the broader community. The graves of people who had only been in the town a short time, travellers or occasionally single men who had settled in the town later in life, tended to be clustered towards the north-eastern corner of the cemetery, just above the more easterly section where the Flick family had buried their dead.

As we worked, it became clear that Isabel had been thinking about these patterns for a long time. She had spent a great deal of her life protecting the cemetery and she had a deep respect for the community's continuities, which linked the people with their traditional past as well as more recent histories. She explained that community feeling about the cemetery in this way: 'We're proud of the fact that we continue to bury in a tribal site. And we have a lot of traditional feelings, and it's a strong bond in the community.'

Yet she didn't see tradition as rigid or unchangeable. Isabel had a confidence which allowed her to see tradition in a dynamic relationship with the people of the present and the future. Her decision about where to be buried, in a plot some distance from her own family's graves, showed her thinking:

> *Isabel:* Well, this northern side's not been used much. And I noticed that nearly all the people buried on this north-eastern side are people from other towns and I always feel strongly that there shouldn't be any strangers' portion. Not that people *said* that's a strangers' portion. But that's how it appears to me. And I feel that this position that myself and Ted Thorne's chosen is a special section in this cemetery yard. And I know that some of the older people living today disagree. I wanted to try and clear it up before it happened, so I mentioned it to a couple of the older people. They don't feel that I should be buried over there, so far away from my family portion. However, I think we all have a freedom of choosing these particular sections. And my family know that's where I'll

> be buried. And so that's why it's a special section for me. And I hope it
> overcomes the feeling that the northern side is a strangers' side.

The rich stories of the cemetery unfolded in our peaceful days there. Some of them were about tragic or violent deaths, but many were about the eventful lives of the people buried there. They were stories about relationships, loves and losses, jealousies, separations and reunions, eccentricities and 'characters', about work and travels and adventures along the way. Isabel felt that these stories of life were at the heart of the cemetery's powerful value in the community. Something was needed which would tell those stories of rich and colourful lives, not just the stories about deaths. So she began to plan for a 'heritage walk' along the roadway approaching the cemetery, with perhaps granite stone blocks along the path, engraved with brief biographies, glimpses which would celebrate the lives of the Murris buried in the cemetery.

Isabel's interest in celebrating lives wasn't limited to those of people who had already died. The Toomelah filming was proving to be an enjoyable experience for Isabel and her sister Rose. They were not only remembering their own pasts, but were learning a great deal about how other women had seen the experiences they had shared. On top of that they were contributing to the regeneration of Gamilaraay language as the older people were finding how much more they could remember when they were talking together than

Working day in the Aboriginal cemetery, 1999, Collarenebri. Members of the Weatherall family, standing, and Rose (Flick) Fernando and Doreen (Weatherall) Hynch, seated on right.

when they tried to recall vocabulary on their own. The process of combing over the Collarenebri cemetery to identify the graves had been work largely undertaken by women and as Isabel worked with them the possibilities of having a day to celebrate their lives and the lives of their older surviving mothers and aunties began to take shape.

Isabel particularly wanted to celebrate the work of women like Nanna Pearlie Mason, the midwife who had delivered so many babies for Murri women, including Brenda on the Block in the difficult days of 1956. Women like her sister-in-law Rosie Flick who had been the first and only teacher for many Murri kids when she ran the bough shade school on the Old Camp. And of course women like Bessie Khan, whose red high-heeled shoes had inspired a generation of young girls on the Camp. Isabel and her sister Rose were planning to give those great women a picnic and a day out, perhaps at the Old Camp or at other places they knew from their youth and childhood, to show them how much they were appreciated and to allow them the pleasure of sharing their memories with each other and the younger members of the community.

In all of this, Isabel hadn't forgotten the men of the community either, or the particular piece of unfinished business which concerned them. The Collymongle trees still weighed on her conscience. The $25 000 grant for research and restoration of the trees was still inaccessible, but using her Tranby resources, Isabel began to track down the locations of the Collymongle trees in cities like Adelaide and Brisbane and to trace rumours she had been hearing about a travelling exhibition of the trees which she feared was going to have these objects, which should have been restricted to men's view, shown publicly. Ted Thorne and Isabel's brother, Joe, and his son Joey, joined her in a set of letters to the various museums involved and to the Australia Council, believed to be funding the exhibition, to express their concerns.

The proposed exhibition was indeed in the planning stages, but the representations Isabel, Joe, Ted and Joey made were able to restrain the process until the plans were shelved. Yet this was hardly a satisfactory outcome for the Collarenebri community, who were still hoping, however uneasily, to be able to bring all the trees home. This needed a keeping place, where they could be housed in reasonable atmospheric conditions and safety from vandals, as well as fulfilling community desires about restricted access. So Isabel and Joe reactivated the discussion about keeping places and began exploring the possibilities for funds.

All this travelling often separated Isabel and Ted, but his constant support sustained her. 'A couple of times over the years I've said: "Oh bugger this. I've had enough of the politics and the travelling . . ." Well, two years ago I said I was finished. I had given up. But Ted said, "No, I don't reckon you should give up. I'd be very disappointed if you stopped doing this and you stopped doing that."'

Isabel was working in many ways to heal the tears in her family's fabric in the mid-1990s. Her work in the cemetery and with the Collymongle trees reflected the continuation of her father's commitments, but it was the links with her Queensland family she was renewing by travelling across the border to get to know her mother's relations and by trying to bring her baby sister's body back across that same border to be properly buried with her family in Collarenebri. Isabel was acknowledging and exploring her relationship with the people and lands on the Queensland side of the border in a way that she had seldom done before. So it is ironic that the language and legalities of land rights politics were shifting at just this time in ways which turned her Queensland affiliations into an accusation to challenge her role in community politics in New South Wales.

The Mabo case before the High Court established in 1991 that indigenous people did hold common law property rights before the invasion and that in some circumstances this 'Native Title' might continue after colonisation. In 1993, the Keating Labor Government passed national legislation acknowledging Native Title and allowing Aborigines to claim what remained of their Native Title rights if they could prove their connection to the land and so their status as 'traditional owners'. The nature of this 'connection' was not defined by the legislation, and prior to the invasion, Aboriginal people's ownership of land appears to have been a complex interaction of their biological and cultural inheritance—from both their biological family, their wider kin and from the places where they were born—in combination with the degree to which they actually took up these obligations and responsibilities in later life. So no one could just passively, biologically 'inherit' ownership of places.

But in the ensuing Native Title court cases, the working definition of 'traditional owner' has become ever more narrowly defined as the biological descent from an ancestor who can be demonstrated to have lived on that land at a very early stage of colonial settlement. The evidence for such claims has narrowed, too, until it is really only European documentation, like early ration lists, which will be accepted as 'proving' such descent. So memory and oral tradition—for millenia the central modes of transmission of Aboriginal culture—are now relegated to secondary supporting evidence, and are often dismissed altogether.

It took a few years for this definition of 'traditional owner' to begin circulating in Aboriginal circles, and some time too before claims were lodged in New South Wales, because alienation of land in that state by freehold or lease had been so widespread as to call into question any persistence of Native Title at all. But suddenly in 1997 there were several contentious situations for Collarenebri Murris to face, in which the definition of who was and who was not a 'traditional owner' was crucial. The first one was an extensive Native Title claim, the Euhalayi case, filed on behalf of members of the Dixon family from Angledool, to a wide area north of the Barwon river, from west of Goodooga to east of Collarenebri, including the Aboriginal cemetery.

This claim alarmed many white residents in the area, from the opal miners at Lightning Ridge to graziers, who misunderstood the nature of Native Title and thought they would lose their property. But it also alarmed Aboriginal people, from the State Land Council Aboriginal managers of the grazing properties in the claim area to the Collarenebri community, because it included their cemetery. As the claim was made for one family only, it seemed to be a disrespectful challenge to the wider community's sense of ownership of their family graves, on land only newly won back into community hands. Non-Aboriginal graziers in the area disputed the claim on the basis that western lands leases extinguished all Native Title, and in mid-2002 this was accepted by the High Court, taking most of the power out of the claim.

But in the five or six years after it was first lodged, this claim generated intense feelings on all sides, and set off a flurry of conflicts among Aboriginal people as they tried to determine who had the 'traditional' right to demand to be included in the claimant group. While most Aborigines have been long advocates of recognition of their rights to their land, the original Euhalayi claim was universally criticised by the region's Murris as being a single family's grab for resources which were rightly due to the whole Aboriginal community. But because of the language of the claim and the legal demand that you had to be a 'traditional owner' in order to participate or to challenge it, Murris were forced to define themselves in a way that suited the white courts rather than a way which arose from their long established history and feelings about what was right and true about their communities. And because documents were the only acceptable evidence for 'claimant' status before the court, Murris were being forced to search for scarce birth certificates or school rolls or wages books instead of seeking advice from their old people about who really belonged to which part of the country.

The differences in the way 'Native Title' was defined by the courts and the ways in which community membership and leadership were understood on the ground were deep and often unbridgeable chasms. Isabel, for example, was someone whose whole approach to political organising was inclusive. She had managed each consultative process in which she was involved by ensuring that everyone, even the people she couldn't speak to, would nevertheless by able to have their say. Her interventions in the housing lists had always been to try to achieve a fair distribution to all the members of the community, not just to one family, but including the most disadvantaged and those least likely to have their voices heard. An approach to defining rights in 'Native Title' according to a hierarchy among the longest standing families in the community, by validating those whose ancestry could be confirmed by white documentation and invalidating those who could not, was in direct contradiction to the central principles on which Isabel had always operated.

Not only did this approach conflict with her fundamental commitments, but it challenged her own standing, because there was little documentation about Mick's early life. With Celia's family well known to be from Queensland, and Mick bringing Celia back from over the border when they married, there was a persistent impression that Mick too was from Queensland. Isabel herself had been born in Goondawindi, and only the youngest members of the family could claim Collarenebri as a birthplace. The implication was that Isabel was somehow claiming to be a custodian of a place to which she had no links. She was hurt by the hint of interrogation in the voices of some old friends when they now asked, ' . . . And where were you born Isabel?'

Just as Isabel began to talk with Collarenebri people about how they would respond to the Euhalayai land claim over the cemetery, another even more explicit challenge to her standing arose. The Indigenous Land Corporation (ILC) had been established by the Federal Government in parallel with the Native Title Act to provide funds for purchasing land in recognition of the limited possibilities of succeeding with Native Title claims. The ILC could purchase land on the application of community organisations, and its practice was then to separate the land title holding body—to be made up of the traditional owners—from the management body, which would be made up of different local people, who would manage day-to-day in the interests of the traditional owner title holders. The ideal situation was that the title holding body and the management body would be established before the application for land purchase was made to the ILC, but in many cases this did not happen.

In Collarenebri, a company formed by an individual family—in which the husband was a white man and his wife an Aboriginal woman from Walgett—applied for the ILC to purchase a property called Eurool, just a few kilometres out of Collarenebri. This family's arrival had already stirred alarm because the husband had recently been convicted of a number of very serious offences in Walgett. Their application to the ILC had listed many people as the interested community members and likely traditional owners, but they all came from Walgett. The ILC had agreed to the application and purchased the property without any consultation with any members of the Collarenebri community. The director of the ILC reported that their officer had travelled through Collarenebri, but had not been able to find any Aboriginal people to consult! Almost everything about this situation distressed Collarenebri Murris, but a basic frustration was that, after years of the State Land Council failing to deliver a nearby piece of land which could be used for community, cultural as well as economic purposes, the ILC had now agreed to turn this piece of land just up the road over to a newly arrived family, to the exclusion of any of the people who had actually lived in Collarenebri over many decades and had links to the earliest traditional owners.

This was a period when the ILC was under heavy public criticism for a number of examples of poor judgement and practice, some far worse than the Eurool problem. So, having already purchased the land at Collarenebri, the ILC was eager to try to resolve the dispute. Consultant anthropologists were engaged to clarify just who should be regarded as the traditional owners of Eurool, and how the title holders' body should be constituted.[3] The trouble is that no one knows what the traditional patterns of land holding were like in detail in this area, because of the severe disorganisation caused by the invasion violence and then the waves of epidemic illness which swept across the plains. The families who had been in Collarenebri township for the longest time, like the Mundys and the Murrays, were acknowledged. But others—like the Flicks and the Thornes who had lived on stations when the present eldest generation was young before moving to town in the early 1930s—or like the Weatheralls, who had moved across when Angledool was shifted in 1936, were made to feel insecure and intimidated, not so much by the consultants, as by the process of prying and questioning into births, deaths and parentage. The inquiry severely polarised the Walgett claimant families from the Collarenebri groups who were left feeling marginalised and disrespected. The fact was that first Mick and then Isabel had wrapped their lives around Collarenebri, knowing that of all the places from which their families arose, their link to Collarenebri was the fundamental one for them. But their histories of commitment and sacrifice to speak up for the place and its people seemed irrelevant to the search for a 'pristine' traditional owner!

All of the Flick family were involved in the long meetings and consultations to try and sort out the intractable mess which the ILC purchase had caused. Rose remembers that she and Joe both became less articulate as they became more angry and more offended. But she describes Isabel as becoming cooler and more focused under pressure. At these ILC meetings, Isabel would straighten in her chair, her elbows resting on the table and her long, elegant fingertips meeting in front of her in icy calm as she penetrated to the focal issues and relentlessly drove home her arguments:

Rose: I remember seeing her angry. That was over that Eurool thing. Oh, you've never seen a face like that. I'd seen her face when she was worried. I saw her face when she'd come back from some of them other meetings and threw her papers on the table and she'd say, 'Yes this so-and-so's this and this so-and-so's that!' or, 'This black bastard this and this white bastard that'. I saw that face! But when those people come along a couple of days later and said, 'I'm sorry about what happened down there at that meeting'. She'd say, 'Oh are you? Well come here I want to talk to you about that!' Different look, see. 'So come here . . .' and she'd shut the door and talk it out with them, see?

But when Eurool come up, this was an anger that was different! It showed right through her body. Not a give-up type of anger, but anger that said, 'I'm gonna see this through, you know! I'm determined about this here!' You see every document that come back about Eurool, it had criticism of the Flicks. 'The Flicks are doing all the talking. The Flicks are doing all the bargaining!' And every time Isabel read it she said, 'This is not about Flicks, this is about Mundys, Murrays and Combos getting what they deserved. We always lived on the bank of the river. We're right! But this is about *these* blackfellas'.

At the next meeting, Isabel took her stand.

Rose: The ILC had their lawyer there, and their director was standing there. I remember sitting at this table, Isabel's legs were astride like this and her two hands up like that on the table. And she said: 'This is not about Flicks! This is about Mundys and Murrays and Combos. There they are there, sitting right there and we Flicks are going to shut our mouths and see what you get out of them!' But all those people said, 'No you talk for us Sis, you talk for us Aunt! We got nothing to say, Aunty Is talks for us!'

And that's how it was! They just keep passing it back to Aunty Is, 'Aunty Is will do it!' And she said, 'No, they want you fellas to talk. I'll read you what they say about us!' And she read it to them. And they was saying, 'Well, they can go and get fucked!' They was going on real wild! And they said it again: 'Aunty Is'll talk for us!'

The Eurool problem remains unresolved, but it seems to have become clear to the ILC that the original purchase and management plan was neither meaningful nor principled. The applicant family has since moved away, and the ILC is reconsidering the future of its purchase.

Isabel and Heather at Tranby College during the launch of Isabel's research project to write her life story.

The 'traditional owner research' process was bruising for the Flicks and for the Thornes, and for other families who felt their long histories in the community and their commitment to their country hadn't been well represented. It got Isabel thinking about how much her life *had* been entangled with places—places where she had been taught about her past and her people; some places she loved and other places which had taught her hard lessons; some where she felt close to her people and to the spirit of her country, and many where she had shared the rich events of her life.

At around this time, Kevin Cook was approached by the Union of Australian Women to suggest an Aboriginal woman whom the UAW could support to tell her life story. Isabel had not often paused to think about telling her own story before this, but Kevin raised it with her at just the time she was reflecting on how her life had been shaped by places and people. She was interested in teasing out answers to the questions of her past. So with some amusement she agreed to have a go at telling this life story of hers. She asked me to help, having already recruited me for her continuing work at the cemetery.

So we started out, not really sure how we were going to do it, but thinking that recording her memories was a good beginning. Isabel recorded a series of tapes during 1997 and 1998, when she was making fairly frequent trips to Sydney. These sessions were directed first by the questions I asked her, but increasingly Isabel took over the interviews, directing them towards themes she was composing her memories around, like her continuing experience of

245

confrontation and the lessons she drew from it. She was less interested than I was in her recent accomplishments. Instead she wanted to dredge her memories for her earliest glimpses of her mother's relations and the childhood she remembered in Collarenebri. She wanted to find answers there to her own questions about why her life had taken the course that it had. One thing she was looking for was a model of the community life she remembered to have been so strengthening for her, the warm security which had made her feel that she 'owned the world'. She was looking for a way to convey that feeling and to explain to the Murris of today the way communities in the past had created that sense of security.

Pretty soon, Isabel decided that the way she wanted to tell her story was to be in Collarenebri when she was recording. She wanted to be with the other people with whom she had shared her past so that they could talk over their memories, confirming or comparing. And just as importantly, she wanted to be at the places where the key events of all their lives had taken place as she told the stories about what had happened. The cemetery work was well underway then, so we worked on the two projects together, richly entangled as these stories were. These trips were journeys along the pathways of Isabel's life and, as we went, Isabel anchored each of her stories into the very ground she was talking about.

So we travelled the story of her life, visiting all sorts of places around Collarenebri, making a new geography visible, following the tracks that Isabel had walked as a kid, the places she was allowed into and the places

Isabel in 1999 outside the verandah of the Colle Manse where she had learnt to count in 1938.

Day on the river bank at the Old Camp with Auntie Bessie Khan during Isabel's research, 1999.

where she was not. Isabel wanted to stop at each place and talk it over with her old friends and family, to ask Rosie Weatherall Flick what she remembered about the bough shade school, to talk to Ted Thorne about the days learning to count the pebbles on the Manse verandah, having her sisters Clara and Rose remember the annex school, and to have Doreen talk about the colour bar at the Liberty Picture show, and the 'Seg Ward' at the hospital, and about carrying water up the steep bank to the Old Camp. Some of these places marked out starkly the lines of conflict and confrontation. Others carried the rich detail of long remembered childhoods.

One of the best days was one with lots of people, adults and kids, at the river below the Old Camp. The very elderly and frail Auntie Bessie Khan was able to come down with her carers, and listened while people remembered her when she was a gorgeous young woman there in her elegant flash clothes and her red high-heeled shoes. In breathless, whispered snatches, Bessie began to recall the people and relations of the old days, stories about her younger brothers and sisters, of who was related to whom, about how Mick Flick had been brought up by Granny Fanny, about the layout of the Old Camp, and the trips into town on her horse, Creamy. And she laughed outright as Isabel and Rosie described how the heels on those flash red shoes must have been at least five inches high!

Isabel, Rose, Rosie and Doreen, sharing memories and arguing the point on the riverbank at the Old Camp.

Isabel's book was the reason that these trips got started. They kept on happening because they were rich and enjoyable days, looked forward to by everyone for the bitter-sweet pleasure of sharing memories and for the chance to show the children there the places where their parents and grandparents had grown up. Many of these places were ones which Isabel had mentioned in her earlier recorded interviews in Sydney, but the stories came alive when she told them to and with her old friends and family around. They all contributed, adding, contradicting, correcting until they were happy that the stories reflected some part of the memories they had carried all their lives.

And the memories her sisters and old friends had of Isabel filled out some of the gaps she had left in her own story. As Rose reflected: 'You see, I love all the politics. And I got a deep respect for all the people who give her all the credit for all the things she done, which is true, like those people said, "Aunty Is'll talk for us". But I'm glad I got my pocket, on the side, of funniness, of silliness! Stupidness! I'm glad I got that!'

12
The Dipping Place

There was one place that Isabel had talked about again and again on her tapes, returning to it as she puzzled over its meaning for her then and now. She not only talked about this place, but she began to draw it, sitting in on an art class at Tranby so she could try and paint her vision. This was the dipping place, where the Old Camp families had drawn their drinking water from the Barwon. She wasn't satisfied with her painting, catching the 'knottly' roots, but unsure about the number of trees on the bank. Then as we talked about pictures she might have in her book, one kept coming to her mind, a beautiful portrait of her taken by Penny Tweedie for a story about land rights in the early 1980s. When she found it, it was clear why. On Isabel's suggestion back in 1981, this photo had been taken beside the dipping place itself.

The picture shows Isabel sitting on the bank, the solid rise of it behind her, with her feet immersed in the river and her hand trailing ripples as the Barwon flowed past her. Even at a glimpse, the picture shows the contrasting themes of Isabel's life: the steadfastness and stability of the rocks at the bank and the transience of the continuing flow of the river. The way Isabel, like the bank, had been a steadfast anchor for everyone else in her life, a solid rock for all of us to steady ourselves on and from which to push ourselves off. And the way she had recreated her life so many times, as fresh and mercurial as the river water's flow.

The ironies of the photo are right too. Isabel knew well the way the black soil bank would dissolve in floods until it flowed away itself. And she had seen the flowing river dry into stagnant puddles in drought. Just the same way

Isabel at the Dipping Place, photographed by Penny Tweedie, 1981, and published in the
National Times *(578:20 & 29) 28 February to 6 March 1982. (AIATSIS N3061.10.*
Reproduced with permission from Penny Tweedie and AIATSIS.)

as what was solid and what was transient in her own 'many lives' was always
unpredictable, and never what it seemed to be.

But there was a deeper meaning to the dipping place which was the one
Isabel was searching to express in her tapes and her painting, perhaps in her
decision to be photographed there. Certainly she sought this meaning in the
days sitting by the banks with her mob. It was the dipping place that Isabel
really wanted to talk over with everyone else at the Old Camp site, to see if
their memories coincided with her own, to stand right there beside it again
while she talked about what it meant to her, about what it was she wanted
that place to say to young people. These were her words in 1999 as she looked
across at the dipping place and reflected on what it meant:

> *Isabel:* We had this special place we called our dipping place. It was
> special because it was about the law. We'd all come down here and two
> or three different lots of people would be making the fire and setting
> their boilers up so they can boil the clothes . . . But there was only this
> one place where you could dip for the water that you take home to drink.
> Now, I'll never know how they made sure that the dipping place was not
> to be for just anything. But it was just for taking the water up home, for
> our cooking and drinking. Now you see the place you'll know what

I mean. Just a bit further on, not far, be about 20 steps I suppose, was where we could go and fish. You could chuck your line in and do what you like there, but you wouldn't dare put a line in here. And nobody broke that rule, you know?

Then on the other side of that there was a place where the kids used to be able to swim, and there was a little bit further over, that's where all the grown ups would swim. So there even was two separate swimming places . . . And see, the older ones could swim there, but *we* used to swim in the rocky part. And they couldn't swim *here* see. That was the good part of it, they respected the law. That was a good community time for people there. And that's what I wanted to make sure was recognised as the special place for me.

The dipping place for Isabel had become a symbol of the order and respect at work within a traditional community. Its laws were invisible to outsiders, but she saw them acted out in her memories of all those people living close together in what appeared on the surface to be casual, disorderly lives, but who were in fact interacting, with each other and with their country, in regulated, disciplined ways arising from mutual respect and protective care. This meaning for the place had been growing in Isabel for years, but she wanted to be there and talk it over, especially with older people like Auntie Bessie, to be sure it was a meaning shared by her mob. As she said while we were packing up after the day at the Old Camp:

> So I think we've got to get all that down about how important this here is. Old Auntie Bea remembers the old dipping place. She recognised it. So now I just need to keep confirming things with those older people and I'll be right. Funny how those things become important for what you're on about, eh? I've got some real ties with this place. Being here on the actual spot clarified a lot of stuff for me. And then with Auntie Bea here. She knows what she's on about. She recognised this place. So yeah . . . I'm pleased I've got this clear now.

Isabel's days were very full during 1999, as she drove herself on to fulfil the many ideas and plans she felt she had. The family had been touched by tragedy yet again in February, when Amy's daughter's newborn child, Jackahl, died after only five days. Isabel helped Amy and Georgette to cope with their loss and then as she had learnt to do when she was grieving—she worked all the harder.

Whenever I spoke with her she was planning, delegating, suggesting new ways to work or new people to talk with, encouraging me and everyone else to grasp the hard jobs and get them done for her. She seemed to be everywhere.

Isabel and Ben at the Friends of Tranby dinner, 1997.

When she wasn't at Gunnedah with Ted and contributing to the Land Council there, she might be at Collarenebri at the cemetery or at Toomelah filming at the old mission site or at Walgett or Brewarrina visiting old friends.

Isabel often expressed her sense of inadequacy when she recorded stories of how her father Mick had enriched his grandchildren's lives in his latter years. She felt she had not been able to give her children and grandchildren the time she would have liked to be able to do. But she nevertheless kept in touch with everyone, and one of her great joys was that Ben was around more, visiting her and Ted in Gunnedah and travelling more to see his brothers and sisters than he had been able in earlier years. He was one of the motivating forces for her in recording her memories:

> *Isabel:* I didn't realise that it was important for me to do that until my son Ben came down from Bathurst for a Friends of Tranby dinner. And he said: 'Gee, Mum I didn't know you were doing this or into that ...' I thought: No, I don't think they would know because I don't have time to sit down and tell them. But I think a lot of those things have become so important to me that I must get this down so that at least my grand-kids will know something about me too.

Isabel was in Sydney often, where she could be found in the office at Tranby dictating letters about the Collymongle trees or visiting Yasmah Children's

Detention Centre, trying to work out how to help young girls caught up in the juvenile justice system, or counselling young Murri kids at St Scholastica High in Glebe about how to develop 'reconciliation' activities. She seemed to me at times to be tiring. She had missed one filming session at Toomelah because she simply did not feel well enough to make the trip. So the last shoot was a special one for her as she made that focused effort to be there, and had been rewarded with the welcome finding of her sister's grave. But if she seemed more tired, her planning never stopped and she had half a dozen projects in full flight in November when she received dreadful news.

Ben had had a massive stroke and was being rushed from Bathurst to Sydney with fears for his life. Isabel came to Sydney immediately, with Brenda and Amy, and they haunted Westmead Hospital to spend as much time as they could with Ben. He seemed stronger at first, with periods of consciousness, and they were there in time to talk with him. But his periods of wakefulness became more rare, and it was soon clear that he was slipping away.

Distraught as she was, Isabel suddenly found she could not ignore the fact that she was feeling weak and extremely unwell. Putting it down to a reaction to her fears about Ben, she reluctantly agreed to take time away from him to allow Paulie to examine her. The X-rays showed an ominous shadow on her lungs, and the diagnosis was the grim one of inoperable lung cancer. Isabel was so focused on her eldest son she barely considered what was happening to her, but her family galvanised as they tried to cope with this second shock.

Brenda and Amy cared for her in Sydney as she went through the only form of chemotherapy which offered a possibility of slowing the disease. Tony travelled to be with her and to talk with Paulie about how her illness might develop, and Larry and Aubie were in constant touch. Ben died on Christmas Day, after a long period of unconsciousness. Isabel made an heroic effort to fight her illness so she could be at his funeral, flanked by her children, as Tony gave a eulogy, talking of how Ben had been a role model for his younger brothers and sisters.

Then her children took Isabel back to Gunnedah, hoping she would be restored to a fairly normal life at least for a while, but grief had finally overtaken her. Unable to eat, she clearly needed to come back to Sydney and Tony drove her down non-stop in mid-January. Paul organised a bed for her in the Prince Alfred, so he could supervise every step of her care. Brenda was her constant nurse, joined over the coming weeks by Amy and by their daughters, Bernadette, Isabella and Georgette. Ted Thorne was always there, in the ward or downstairs on a seat under the huge trees in the grounds.

There were bright spots. Larry and Jedda held a formal engagement ceremony at her bedside, promising her that after all these years together they

Doreen Hynch, Linda Hall and Josie Thorne, with Collarenebri children, open the sealed road from Collarenebri to the Aboriginal cemetery, November 2002.

would marry on Isabel's next birthday. One of the nursing sisters joked with Isabel about how boring Paul Torzillo's trademark red ties were, and Isabel staunchly defended her doctor's taste, promptly sending her girls out to buy him a new red tie so she could give it to him herself.

Her daughters cared for her while a constant stream of visitors came, with stories and news, memories and jokes to try to cheer her up, and fruit and ice to coax her to eat. Tony, Larry and Auby were all there, with Isabel in the ward or with Ted out under the trees. Each of us were there to say goodbye, but it was often too hard to put words to it. Barbara, Karen and Joey came with Joe and Isobelle. Clare and Rose each sat with their sister in turn. Doreen and Rosie were in touch by phone. Eventually the visitors were too tiring for her, but Isabel made a point of asking for particular people to whom she wanted to talk, her final handing over. She talked to those close friends, like Judy Chester, and by phone to Cookie. She talked to me about how to finish her book. She talked to Karen and Barbara about the work they had shared and what she wanted them to do next. She talked with each of her children and grandchildren about their tasks for the future and her hopes for them all. Peaceful at last and with Ted and all her family around her, she slipped away on 16 February 2002.

Isabel was buried in the February heat in Collarenebri, in just the place she had chosen, in the shade of two small trees and just a little beyond the strangers' portion. Her sons and Ted managed the ceremony there as she had

'Bell's Way': The sealed road to the cemetary was named after Isabel. Here Larry, Amy, Georgette and her daughter Tjanara stand beneath the sign at the opening in 2002.

wanted them to do and her grave was heaped high with flowers. Isabel had arranged for all her papers and photographs to be carefully kept, but she had left other instructions about her most personal possessions.

In the afternoon of her burial, as she had wanted, her children handed over all her clothes and personal things to her sisters and nieces. Rose, Clara, Barbara and Karen took them up to the Block and prepared a fire. They had asked Paul and I to come too, and we held Karen's baby and helped in turns. One by one, each of Isabel's things was burnt, slowly at first, then faster as the fire blazed more and more fiercely. It was intensely painful to handle each of those things which had been so closely identified with her, but there was also a release as each disappeared into the flames and rising smoke.

Exhausted, but elated too, feeling this had all been done properly, we came back into town. Our family had to leave to fly back to Sydney, but Karen, Barbara, their mother Isobelle and Rose and Clara went back to the cemetery at dusk. They joined Isabel's children in straightening flowers and sweeping the ground around the new grave, spending some time yarning together in the quiet.

The heat had gone out of the day, and it was clear and still. Finally Barbara and her mother began to leave, driving reluctantly away from the cemetery towards the gate. Not far along, they were startled to see a large goanna, walking slowly across the road. Goannas are seldom seen in this country and if they are sighted, they are always gone instantly with a lash of their tail. This one wasn't in a hurry. It continued its stately walk across the road, staring back at them calmly as the twilight gathered around them. Barbara asked her mother what kind of goanna it was. 'That's a Mangankali', Isobelle told her quietly. 'That's from your Auntie Is, telling us that everything is all right'.

Then it slowly climbed a tree beside the gate, hanging suspended half way up the trunk. They edged the car past it, expecting it to disappear, but it stayed, only turning its head to follow them with its eyes. And the Mangankali was still there when they looked back as they rounded the last bend and headed for town.

Notes

Introduction: Making Trouble

1 *Murri*: an Aboriginal person, 'one of our people'. A widely used word in northern New South Wales and Queensland arising from indigenous languages. Plural is '*Murris*'. Gamilaraay was Isabel's father's language, and its people come from the country around Collarenebri and to the east and north. Yuwalaraay is closely related and its people's country is the land just to the west of Collarenebri.

Chapter 1 'Owning the World'

1 'The Rules' is a widely used term in Aboriginal English, referring to the ceremonies to initiate boys into manhood, which is usually carried out in early adolescence.

2 A Queensland Government-run 'station' or settlement, usually called a 'mission', although not under the direct control of the churches. Other missions were church run, but all of the New South Wales missions and some of the Queensland missions were actually government institutions. One in particular—Palm Island—became a notorious prison for people who challenged the repressive conditions of the 'Queensland Act'.

3 Isabel's early memories of her father's attitude reflect the anxiety felt by northwest Murris during the mi le 1930s when, in an effect of the Depression, the NSW Aborigines Protecti Board gained new powers to take more control over Aboriginal people's reside ice and movement. From 1932, a marked increase in Protection Board officers' activity could be felt on the ground. Many communities were forcibly moved in the northwestern areas to be concentrated at Brewarrina and later Toomelah government stations in the northwest and at Menindee in the far west. More aggressive government and police intervention occurred in many areas, and some communities—like those at Moree and Collarenebri—although not eventually moved, were nevertheless threatened with wholesale removal or with the removal of their children.

4 Other families, like the Adams, who were associated with Collarenebri for many

years were often camped on nearby pastoral properties, like Collymongle, while the Kennedy family lived in town.

5   Billy Hardy was brother to Bob Hardy, a family whose traditional country extended from Dungalear to Bangate. Both brothers worked on these and other pastoral properties around the immediate vicinity of Collarenebri.

6   The Weatherall family came from Angledool as a result of the deeply unpopular enforced removal of the Aboriginal population on the government station there to Brewarrina by the Aborigines Protection Board. Ned Weatherall and his wife, Eadie (née Hardy) brought their daughters, Rose and Doreen, and son, Aubrey.

7   *Porcupine*: this American term is widely used by northwestern Aborigines in preference to the Australian term 'echidna'. 'Porcupine' may seem closer to the Gamilaraay name for this animal: *pikipila*.

8   Pearl Parker was aunty to Eadie Weatherall and great aunt to Doreen, Rosie and Aub Weatherall. She was married into the Mason family.

9   This game had many variations and many names, but by one or another it is recalled by Aborigines across the state. It involved flipping stones with wooden pegs.

10   This was recorded down on the river 18 June 1999.

11   Rose Weatherall Flick (born 1924) was recorded as she told this story to Isabel at the Old Camp in 1999, and also in an interview with them both conducted by their niece, Karen Flick, at Thallon in 1995. The following account is an edited transcript drawn from both recordings. Rose is a member of the Weatherall family, daughter to Ned and Eadie, sister to Doreen Hynch and Aubrey Weatherall, and widow of Isabel's oldest brother, Lindsay. She was born in 1924 and arrived at Colle with her family in 1936 from Angledool in their escape from the Aborigines Protection Board move to Brewarrina.

12   *Muni*: headlice.

Chapter 2 Toomelah Mission

1   The Tingha community was one of the victims of the Aborigines Protection Board's forced migration program in the late 1930s, as the Board tried to rationalise infrastructure and reduce its expenditure by 'concentrating' scattered but coherent Aboriginal communities onto centralised missions, forcing them into often uncomfortably close proximity to unfamiliar country and communities. The uneasiness which Isabel remembered was characteristic of the anxieties felt by Angledool and Tibooburra Aboriginal residents when shifted to Brewarrina and the even deeper alarm of the Carowra Tank community dumped at Menindee during the same period. See Goodall, *Invasion to Embassy*, 1996, chapter 15.

2   The Aborigines Protection Board had been forced by parental protests in 1919 to allow apprenticed girls to return to their communities once their indentures were completed. The Aborigines Protection Board managers were instructed in 1920 to ensure that returned apprenticed girls were married respectably. This appears to have been one of the causes, as in the case Isabel remembers, for rushed and collective marriages. Mission residents, however, tend universally to suspect managers, their sons and other white male staff of sexually exploiting young Aboriginal women and needing to arrange hasty marriages with local Aboriginal men to cover up unwanted pregnancies.

3   The conditions of Aborigines Protection Board stations had worsened dramatically in the 1930s. Many Aboriginal workers were thrown out of work, but then

they were refused unemployment relief and forced to move onto Aborigines Protection Board stations to get any relief at all. Numbers of residents on the stations soared and overcrowding led to severe epidemics in the late 1930s of pneumonia, dysentry and eye disease. The children were treated for trachoma (then called sandy blight) with a harsh combination of copper sulphate (blue-stone) and iodine paint (the pink paint) applied directly to the surface of their eyes. A false accusation that Aboriginal people were suffering from some form of gonorrheal eye disease both inflamed racial prejudice and ensured that these painful treatments were carried out aggressively.

4 Mentally ill, unstable.

5 Throwing stick, men's hunting weapon.

6 The Salt Water song is one of the most commonly remembered songs in the area. These are the words as Isabel remembered their pronunciation in 1980. A version very similar to the one Isabel remembered was recalled and recorded in 1999 by Eileen [Wibble] McIntosh and Julie Whitton, who both grew up in the Toomelah community in the 1930s and 1940s. Their performance of it appears in their film about Toomelah, *Inard Oongali: Women's Journey*. Isabel was not present on the camp at which this filming was done. A slightly different version was remembered by Gabriel Wallace at Narrabri and recorded in 1970 (AIATSIS Archive Tape A10610). Wibble McIntosh, like Isabel, remembered that the song told about Aboriginal people watching across the salt water as 'that big ship came' bringing the first British invaders. Ada Jarrett, who was also involved in the filming, recalled that she understood it to tell the story of Aboriginal mothers looking for their children after they had been taken away (by the Protection Board). Their accounts also appear in the film.

7 A reference to the locally composed songs like those of Dougie Young from Wilcannia, usually in country and western style in the 1980s, which reflected western Aboriginal lifestyles and expressed an assertive, contemporary Aboriginality.

8 The architecture and layout of all the Aborigines Protection Board missions maximised the manager's ability to see what was going on all over the mission grounds, into the Aboriginal huts laid out in a grid pattern and to observe movement through the gate. The wide verandahs on the manager's home were a common country style, but also served to allow ready surveillance. Buildings for the white staff were more substantial than the small huts for Aboriginal residents, and the staff homes and offices were clustered together, presenting an intimidating fortress effect.

9 This would date the meeting in 1940 or 1941. Ferguson and Groves made a series of country trips and held meetings at missions from 1938, discussing the changes they advocated to the Aborigines Protection Board and then attacking the amendments the Government introduced to empower the 'new' Aborigines Welfare Board, established in 1939, which was the body that introduced the 'Dog Licence' or 'Exemption Certificate' in 1941. Isabel left Toomelah some time in 1942.

Chapter 3 Leaving From the Street

1 J.J. Fletcher, 'The NSW Education Department and the Education of Aboriginal Children, 1880–1940', *The Leader*, 5(3) 1973; and J.J. Fletcher, 'Collarenebri—An Attempt to Integrate Aboriginal Children', *The Leader*, 6(2) 1975:30–36.

Marie Rea, 'Colour Prejudice at Collarenebri, NSW', *Aborigines Protector*, 2(3) 1947.

2 There was no imposing architecture in this small town, so the School of Arts hall was often referred to as the 'Town Hall'.

3 *Ngarragaa:* If you feel sorry for someone, they are 'ngarragaa'.

4 *Waajiin:* whitewoman.

5 *Bandu:* untidy, messy.

6 An Aboriginal English term used for traditional kin and affiliation. The two words commonly used in the Collarenebri community were 'meat' and 'skin'. 'Meat' refers to one's 'totem' or affiliation with a particular animal or plant, which is one aspect influencing choice of marriage partner. 'Skin' refers to the four (exogamous) kinship 'sections'—Mari, Gabi, Hibai and Gambo—each of which became transformed into a surname in the various recording processes of colonisation. These surnames are common in the Aboriginal families from the area around Collarenebri, and are usually spelt as Murray, Cubby, Hippai and Combo.

Chapter 4 Building Pressures

1 Many Aboriginal shearers and rouseabouts became deeply involved in this factional conflict within the Australian Workers' Union in this period.

2 *Collarenebri Gazette*, 22/3/1939.

3 *Wanda:* a commonly used word for white person.

4 Granny Ada Woods, Isabelle Walford Flick's grandmother.

5 Lubby, who died in 1973.

Chapter 5 Confrontations

1 Faith Bandler and Len Fox, *The Time was Ripe*, pp. 61–70.

2 *Collarenebri Gazette*, 3 August 1955.

3 Barbara Flick wrote about these events in 'Colonisation and Decolonisation: An Aboriginal Experience' in *Playing the State*, edited by Sophie Watson, Allen & Unwin, Sydney, 1990, p. 63.

4 Interview, 18 March 1999.

5 *Report of the Aborigines Welfare Board*, year ending 30 June 1961, p. 11.

6 Letter from Minister for Education, C.B. Cutler, 30 November 1966, to local Member, G.R. Crawford, responding to the petition from Isabel, Rev. B. Marrett and Mr T. Bayty of Collymongle.

7 Harry Hall has played a major role in Aboriginal politics in Walgett and in the region. An established activist before the Freedom Ride bus came, he introduced the students to the Walgett Aboriginal Community and focused their actions on key local issues.

8 The Foundation for Aboriginal Affairs, a community controlled welfare and social organisation, a branch of the Foundation that had opened in inner-city Sydney in December 1964. It had been set up by white and Aboriginal activists and had Charles Perkins as its first project officer. Ann Curthoys, *Freedom Ride*, 2002, Allen & Unwin, Sydney, p. 21.

9 *Wanda:* white man, white person generally (but *wajiin* is more commonly used for white woman).

10 Peter Tobin, Report to Abschol, 1969: 'Fringe-dwelling Rural Aborigines and the Law', typescript.

11 National Aboriginal Congress, the first attempt under the Federal Labor Government to establish a national forum of Aboriginal leadership.

12 See chapter 7. In 1973, the Aboriginal cotton chippers staged a strike (see *Wee Waa Echo*, 18/1/73; 1/2/73). A report was commissioned by the Federal Minister for Labour, Clyde Cameron, and printed by the Department of Labour, 1973 as *Report on the Grievances of the Seasonal Workers in Wee Waa and Narrabri*. They had had poor assistance from the AWU, to which many belonged as pastoral workers, because unions find organising among seasonal workers difficult and had delayed signing up members in this new industry. The strike drew in AWU organisers, but as Isabel explains, the Social Welfare system which emerged in the 1970s undermined the potential for union membership. Changing technologies in the cotton industry have decreased the need for the large armies of chippers seen in the late 1960s and early 1970s. Although it still provides significant short-term work, chipping is no longer the extensive social event which it was in those years.

Chapter 6 Entangling the City with the Bush

1 P. Pholeros, Rainow, S. and Torzillo, P., *Housing for Health: Towards a Healthy Living Environment for Aboriginal Australia*, HealthHabitat, Sydney, 1993.
2 *Wee Waa Echo*, 30/11/72; 7/12/72; 14/12/72; 21/12/72.
3 *Wee Waa Echo*, 11/1/73.
4 *Wee Waa Echo*, 11/1/73; 18/1/73; 25/1/73; 1/2/73; 8/2/73; 22/2/73.
5 *Wee Waa Echo*, 22/2/73; 8/3/73.

Chapter 8 Changing Collarenebri

1 *Koorier*, newsletter of the NSW Ministry of Aboriginal Affairs, December 1983, p. 4.
2 Paul Pholeros, senior architect, HealthHabitat, Sydney, October 2002, personal communication.
3 Address read on behalf of Isabel Flick at the launch of *Too Much Wrong: Report on the Death of Edward James Murray*, 26 November 1999, Human Rights & Equal Opportunity Commission, Sydney.
4 *Sydney Morning Herald*, 28 December 1981.
5 Audio recording of meeting, Western Women's Council, Winbar, 7 April 1985.

Chapter 9 Land Rights on the Ground

1 This was an important difference between the NSW Land Rights Act and the later Federal Native Title Act. For the NSW Land Rights Act, only the present status of the land is important. Its past as a grazing lease is not relevant as long as it has reverted to vacant Crown land. The Native Title Act, however, has a historical component built in, so that any alienation in the past, such as a lease, could wipe out Native Title once and for all, no matter if the land reverted to Crown land in the future.
2 There is a more detailed account of this important, complex meeting in Goodall, H., '"Speaking What Our Mothers Want us to Say": Aboriginal Women, Land and the Western Women's Council, 1984–1985', in Peggy Brock (ed.), *Words and Silences: Aboriginal Women, Politics and Land*, Allen & Unwin, Sydney, 2001.

3   Walgett Shire Council to Isabel Flick, 20 January 1994.
4   Brian Egloff from the University of Canberra, Graham Ward from the Australian
    Institute for Aboriginal and Torres Strait Islander Studies, and Luke Godwin
    from NPWS. See Ward, G., Egloff, B., Godwin, L., 'Archaeology of an Aborigi-
    nal Historic Site: Recent Research at Collarenebri Aboriginal Cemetery',
    Australian Aboriginal Studies, 1989 (2), pp. 62–7.

Chapter 10 Sisters
1   NSW Department of Community Services.
2   Aboriginal and Torres Strait Islander Commission, the Federally established and
    Aboriginal-managed body overseeing a range of administrative and funding
    processes in relation to indigenous communities around the country.
3   21 November 1995.
4   These events were documented by the auditor's report in 1996, which confirmed
    the substance of Isabel's accusations and fully corroborated her concerns.

Chapter 11 A Wider Focus
1   *Yanggal*: vagina, often used as a convenient alternative to the English swearword
    'cunt'. Isabel was also using it as a pun on the English phrase 'the big "c"'—
    a colloquial euphemism for cancer.
2   *Wanda*: white man.
3   The report was formally released November 1999, but drafts had been circulat-
    ing over many months before. Memmott, P., Stacey, R. and Chambers, C. 'A
    Study of the Traditional Ownership of Eurool', for the Indigenous Land Corpo-
    ration, 4 November 1999.

Index